KV-172-540

THE CAVENDISH Q & A SERIES

EUROPEAN COMMUNITY LAW

TITLES IN THE Q&A SERIES

THE CAVENDISH Q & A SERIES

EUROPEAN COMMUNITY LAW

Mike Cuthbert
LLM, LLB, BSc(Econ), BA(Law)
Head of School of Law and
International Business
Nene College

Cavendish
Publishing
Limited

First published in Great Britain 1993 by Cavendish Publishing Limited,
The Glass House, Wharton Street, London WC1X 9PX.
Telephone: 0171-278 8000 Facsimile: 0171-278 8080

First edition   1993
Second edition 1995
  Reprinted   1996, 1997

British Library Cataloguing in Publication Data

Cuthbert, M
European Community Law – (Q & A Series)
I Title II Series
341.2422

ISBN 1-85941-264-5

Printed and bound in Great Britain

Contents

Introduction

European Community law is unlike any area of law that you may have encountered in your other legal studies. It does not follow the traditions and principles you have encountered in your previous studies. It is different and that fact, perhaps with the added importance given to it by the legal profession and business in general, is why it is increasingly attractive to students. However, although it may have different sources, traditions and terminology, it still requires the student to approach examinations with the same preparation as any other examination.

Wide reading and a detailed review of both the syllabus and past examination papers is important for European Community law, just as it is for contract, tort, etc. Many topics in European law are inter-related, as you will see from the questions in this book. Some students have difficulties because being so different from the common law tradition they are unsure what is important. They 'cannot see the wood for the trees', in that they study particular topics but find it hard to see the connections. Then it suddenly clicks! Hopefully this happens before they enter the examination hall! It will happen sooner if you read one of the basic textbooks on European law, making sure that it is the latest edition you can find.

The answers to the questions in this book are not the only possible answers. They have been written at a particular time. If I had to write them again I would probably change some of the contents, perhaps bringing in different cases or changing the emphasis. However, the main points would remain the same. By reading these answers I hope that you will obtain a clearer view of European Community law and the relationship between different topics.

As you will see there are some basic cases which are authority for a number of principles of Community law. They appear in answers to many questions. You should ensure that you are familiar with these and gradually build up your confidence with the topics. Start with the definitions and basic principles, looking for an authority either through a case or article of the treaty, etc.

This approach will help you when you come to the examination hall and read the questions for the first time. Don't panic! You should have grasped the essentials of European Community law from your studies. In your preparation you should consider the following suggestions:

- Read the question paper carefully. Underline what appear to you to be the key points. This is especially important for problem questions which may be quite long.

- Write on the question paper or one of the pages of the answer book any ideas you have when you first read the question. This might be definitions, cases, treaty articles, quotations or other references. This is good practice because it may help you decide the best questions to tackle, but more importantly when you return to answer that particular question these notes will help you to concentrate on the new topic. As you are writing other answers, ideas and cases may suddenly come into your mind. Write them down before you forget them! You can always put a line through these notes at the end of the examination so that the examiner will not bother to regard them as part of your answer.

- When you start to answer a particular question, plan your answer carefully. This will help you adjust to the topic, but it will also help you recover from those moments when your concentration lapses through some distraction. It may also help you find your next point in your answer when you ask yourself 'what should I write next?' Remember that you will get little credit for rambling or writing all you know about a particular topic, so planning and following your plan is very important.

- Make sure that you deal with all the parts of the question. This applies to all questions and not just those which have separate (a) and (b) parts. If you do not answer the question fully you are limiting the range of marks you can obtain for your answer. When you are dealing with problem questions remember that the examiner is not just looking for an answer which shows knowledge of principles. Your answer should show understanding of the principles *and* the ability to apply them to the facts in the question.

Lastly make sure that the examiner can read what you have written. This may seem a very simple point but examiners like to follow the logical thread of your answer. If a long time has to be taken to decipher what you have written it does not help the examiner fully appreciate your answer. In this context I would like to thank Christine Blundell who through much practice is able to decipher my handwriting and thus helped in the production of this book. You will not be so fortunate, as it is not common practice to have a secretary in the examination hall. However, like you, what I have written remains my own responsibility!

Mike Cuthbert
January 1995

Table of Cases

Table of UK Legislation

Statutes

Rules of the Supreme Court

Chapter 1

Community Institutions

Introduction

It is very important to obtain a good understanding of the functions, powers and relationships between the main institutions of the European Community. This requires an understanding of four key institutions, which have their origin in the first Community, the European Coal and Steel Community established in 1952. Although there have been some changes since then, the basic principles have remained the same.

It is important to obtain a feel for the need for such institutions. It is sometimes forgotten that the European Community was an innovative idea in the sense that a *supra* national body was being created by the transfer of sovereignty from Member States to a Community which was to act on behalf of all of its Members. Therefore it was important to ensure that the institutions established would provide a forum for an input of the Member States, a body to implement and police policies decided by the Community, a court to settle disputes and provide authoritative judgments and finally a body which would allow an input from a wider base of views from the Member States. Hence, they established in the Treaty of Rome the Council of Ministers, the European Commission, the European Court of Justice and the European Assembly, later to be called the European Parliament in the Single European Act.

The starting point for an understanding of the EC institutions is their origin, ie the Treaty Articles. Although they need not be learned by heart, there are key points which must be grasped as you build up an understanding of their functions and relationships. One of the best ways to get an overview of the variety of institutions is to read material which is intended for the non-specialist reader. Some of the publications produced by the European Commission are very good and have the added advantage of being free. Once an overview has been obtained, you should begin to build up a more detailed picture which shows the more complex functions and relationships between the institutions. This can be achieved through some of the reading given at the end of this book. However, you should always be alert to practical examples of the friction or otherwise generated by these institutions and reported in the media. Such examples are invaluable in impressing the examiner but more importantly they should convince you that you are not dealing with a theoretical group of institutions but 'a living community'.

Checklist

You need to have a good understanding of the functions, procedures and membership and the main Community institutions plus an awareness of the less significant. You should also look at Chapter 12 where some of the proposed changes to the institutions are mentioned. In particular you should concentrate on:

- The European Parliament - Articles 137 - 144 EC
- The Council of Ministers - Articles 145 - 154 EC
- The European Commission - Articles 155 - 163 EC
- The European Court of Justice - Articles 164 - 184 EC
- The European Council, the Court of First Instance, ECOSOC, COREPER, the Court of Auditors

Question 1

'Although the European Parliament has limited powers, one cannot claim that the Community legislative process is devoid of democratic participation'.

Discuss.

Answer plan

This type of question has become very popular in recent years.

This is largely due to the discussion and developments which have taken place affecting the Parliament. The main points for the question are:

- powers and composition of the European Parliament
- procedures of the Parliament
- the role of the Parliament in the legislative process

Answer

Since 1979 the Members of the European Parliament have been directly elected by their constituents in the twelve Member States. Before that time when the Members were nominated by their respective governments they had determined as early as 1962 to call themselves a Parliament even though the Treaty of Rome referred to them as an Assembly. Under Article 137 of the EC Treaty the European Parliament consists of 'representatives of the peoples of the States brought together in the Community'. It was not until the Single European Act 1986 that the Member States formally recognised the European Parliament by this name.

The European Parliament has certain characteristics similar to national Parliaments, such as the UK Parliament at Westminster. There are a number of standing committees which mirror the major policy areas of the Community. The committees carry out enquiries, hear evidence from experts and interested parties including the Commission, and issue reports. In addition Parliamentary questions are an important element of control over the Commission. Under Article 140 the Commission must reply orally or in writing to questions put to it by MEPs. In fact the Council and foreign ministers also take part in this process. It is common practice now for the President of the Council of Ministers to make a report to the Parliament at the end of their term as President.

There are two specific powers associated with the European Parliament. The Treaty made the European Commission responsible to the European Parliament. Once appointed by the Member States, the twelve Commissioners can only be removed by the European Parliament passing a censure motion by a two-thirds majority vote and an absolute majority of its Members. Such a motion successfully passed would force the resignation of the Commission. However, this power under Article 144 can only be used against the whole Commission and not against individual Commissioners. This power has never been exercised, although it has been threatened on a number of occasions.

Perhaps the most important input that would be recognised as part of democratic participation is the involvement of the European Parliament in making European laws, principally Regulations and Directives. There are many policy areas of the Treaty which give the Parliament the right to be consulted on proposed legislation. This is illustrated by the phrase which is very familiar to any student of the Treaty, namely that 'the Council, acting on a proposal from the Commission and after consulting the European Parliament shall'. The normal procedure is that the proposal from the Commission is first considered by one of Parliament's committees mentioned above, which will produce a report and a draft resolution. These then go to the full Parliament for debate before its Opinion including any suggested amendments are sent to the Council. As a result of this Opinion the Commission may modify its proposal but there is no obligation on either the Council or the Commission to respond to it. However, whatever weight is given to the European Parliament's view, its right to be consulted must be respected. Failure to follow this procedural requirement may lead to the measure being declared invalid.

This happened in the cases of *Roquette v Council* and *Maizena v Council*, both reported in 1980. An interesting discussion took place in these cases with regard to the extent this requirement gave power to the Parliament to block legislation. Is the requirement that the European Parliament should be asked for its Opinion or must it actually give it? The Council argued that if the latter was true then the Parliament could delay legislation indefinitely by the simple expedient of not giving an Opinion. The ECJ interpreted the requirement under the Treaty to mean that the Parliament has to give its Opinion. However, it left open the question what would happen if the Parliament were to be deliberately obstructive and the Council wished to go ahead with the legislation. Such an i mpasse has not yet occurred.

It is understandable that in these circumstances where their Opinion carried limited importance to the Council, that the European Parliament was often called 'a mere talking shop' by national politicians. With the direct elections of 1979, MEPs saw themselves as the true representatives of their constituents and increasingly called for an active part in the legislative process. This was given by Articles 6 and 7 of the Single European Act 1986, which amended the original Treaty.

This required a co-operation procedure to be operative in some instances, but by no means all, where the Treaty required the Parliament to be consulted. The main difference is that in theory the views of the European Parliament carry more importance, although in practice this change may not be so significant. When the Council receives a proposal from the Commission, it adopts a 'common position', which is sent to the European Parliament. The Parliament now has three months in which to act. If Parliament rejects the common position, the Council can adopt the proposal only by unanimity. If Parliament wishes to amend the proposal, such amendments are sent back to the Commission for consideration. These amendments may be adopted but there is no obligation on the Commission to do so. The proposal is then sent back to the Council along with any Parliamentary amendments it had not accepted and the reasons for this refusal. The Council can accept the amended proposal by a qualified majority or it can amend it by adopting those proposed by the Parliament or its own amendments. This has to be done by a unanimous vote in the Council.

In practice the co-operation procedure appears to grant the European Parliament very little extra power. It provides for a possible alliance between a Member State and the Parliament in the sense that the Council of Ministers would not have the unanimity to overrule amendments. But does this give more authority to the Member State or the European Parliament? Also the requirement on the Commission under the co-operation procedure to consider Parliament's amendments and to give reasons for not adopting them, makes a legal requirement of something which was a matter of practice before. In fact perhaps the most significant increase in Parliament's powers brought about by the Single European Act is the requirement for its approval in relation to the admission of new Members to the Community or the conclusion of association agreements with third countries. Under the Act the European Parliament thus has a veto in such matters.

An aspect of democratic participation which has always been considered important in any Parliament is the involvement of elected representatives in the setting of expenditure and income levels, ie a budget. Although it is the President of the European Parliament alone who has the power to adopt the budget, the procedure for the Community budget is rather complex and has been varied on several occasions. The effect of these changes has been to transfer certain powers from the Council to the Parliament. The European Parliament's right to make changes in the budget depends on the distinction between expenditure which is 'compulsory' and other expenditure which is 'non-compulsory'. Compulsory expenditure covers that expenditure which is committed under Treaty provisions or Community legislation.

The main example is expenditure on the common agricultural policy. Parliament can only propose modifications to this category of expenditure, thus giving the Council the final say in such matters. However, non-compulsory expenditure which includes all expenditure which is not the inevitable consequences of Community legislation, can be amended by the majority of MEPs voting in favour of such proposals. This expenditure includes the Community social policy, regional and industrial policies, and accounts for about 37% of the total Community budget. For this type of expenditure it is the European Parliament which has the final control. Therefore, although the Parliament does have some powers of approval as far as the budget is concerned, these are weak with regard to compulsory expenditure, which is the vast majority of the total budget.

However, in 1975 the European Parliament was given increased powers in relation to the Community budget by a conciliation procedure. The aim of these powers is to give the Parliament more effective participation in the budgetary process, by seeking agreement between the Parliament and the Council of Ministers. If the Parliament refuses to pass the budget as presented to it by the Council, a number of important consequences follow. First the budget cannot be implemented, which has implications for the expenditure level of the Community which is limited to ½ of the previous years budget per month. Secondly a 'conciliation committee', consisting of the Council and representatives of the European Parliament is established to try to resolve the disagreement. The European Commission assists the work of the committee.

Ultimately the Parliament may reject the budget outright under Article 203 of the EC Treaty by a ⅔ vote cast by a majority of its Members. This has now happened on four occasions, in 1980 by the newly directly elected Parliament eager to use its budgetary powers and in 1982, 1986 and 1988. Although it may reject it, the Parliament cannot increase the total amount of the budget beyond the maximum rate of increase set by the Commission, unless the alteration is agreed by the Council.

The disagreement is generally therefore centred on the distribution of the budget. Such disagreements sometimes erupt into public and have been subject to proceedings before the ECJ, as in *EC Council v European Parliament* in 1986. In 1988, in an attempt to improve the budgetary procedure, an Institutional Agreement was entered into by the Council, Commission and the European Parliament. While recognising the varying competencies of the institutions in the budgetary field, it fixed new rules for co-operation between the institutions.

The normal authority of a Parliament is that the national government is dependant upon its confidence and continued support to remain in office. There is no such relationship between the European Parliament and the main political decision making body in the Community, the Council of Ministers. The ministers who form the Council are representing their national governments who in turn must retain the support of their national Parliaments. Therefore any vote cast by a minister at Council meetings must be supported by their national Parliaments. Is this the main democratic control over European legislation? Are the national Members of Parliament, representing the same constituents as the MEPs, exercising democratic control? In theory this could be possible, at least for major issues. However, it has one major drawback in that the national Parliaments rarely have the procedures or time necessary for clear debate of issues before they are discussed and agreed at the Council of Ministers. Although attempts are being made to ensure better information and debate in national Parliaments of European issues this is not happening at the moment. The only really genuine and consistent debate takes place in the European Parliament, but what authority does that have? As indicated above it has some powers, but at present they remain limited.

Question 2

'The European Court of Justice is unlike any English court.'

Discuss.

Answer plan

This question illustrates the type of essay question on the ECJ which is very common. The task is for the examinee to discuss the special features of the court. This has a special impact for the UK because it is very different from the national courts, including the House of Lords.

The main points for this question are:

- function of the ECJ as defined by Article 164 EC
- personnel, term of office, function – judges and advocate-generals
- procedures and languages
- form of judgments
- comparison with English courts

Answer

The European Court of Justice is one of the main institutions of the European Community. It provides the independent judicial function necessary to ensure, as Article 164 of the EC Treaty states, 'that in the interpretation and application of this Treaty the law is observed'. The main influence on the characteristics of the ECJ was the French legal system, notably the highest administrative court in France, the Counseil d'Etat. However, this is not the only reason why the court is different from any English court. Another important factor is that the court was established to work not within a state but within a community which brought together a number of states in a new relationship, which had implications for their own legal systems.

There are thirteen judges on the ECJ with each Member State providing at least one judge. Appointed for a term of six years, the judges elect their own President of the court who serves in that post for three years. Like all posts within the court it is possible for the period in office to be renewed.

Although this fixed but renewable term of office is not found in English courts, the attributes the judges should have are the same. Article 167 specifies that they should be independent and qualified for the highest judicial office within their respective countries. However, an important difference is that whereas English judges are selected from barristers and to a lesser extent solicitors, judges in some Member States are chosen from a much wider field, including academic lawyers. Thus when the judges in the European Court deliberate they are bringing together a variety of legal backgrounds which would not be found in an English court.

Perhaps a striking difference about the ECJ is the role given to Advocate-Generals, a post derived from the French legal system and unknown in English law. There are six Advocate-Generals appointed to the court. They have the same backgrounds as judges, the same term of office and perhaps most importantly the same status. Therefore Advocate-Generals should not be seen as inferior to judges, as the precedent within the court for both depends upon the date of appointment and not the designated office. Advocate-Generals are given a specific role under Article 166 which states that 'it should be the duty of the Advocate-General, acting with complete impartiality and independence, to make, in open court, reasoned submissions on cases brought before the Court of Justice, in order to assist the court in the performance of its tasks. Unlike senior English courts where a full judgment is given, including dissenting views, only one judgment is given by the ECJ. All the judges must agree to the one judgment which is why they appear so terse and lacking in any real discussion of the law. They do not contain the *obiter dicta* as well as the *ratio decidendi* found in the common law tradition. Hence the importance of the Advocate-General is that he hears and reads all the evidence as a judge would do but he gives his Opinion to the court as to what the judgment should be before the judges themselves reach their decision. In his Opinion the Advocate-General can range over the case law of the court or if appropriate the jurisprudence of the Member States. In this way some insight is given as to the direction European Community law may take in the future.

Obviously the judges do not have to follow the Advocate-General's Opinion but if they do not it can be just as illuminating as when they do! The work load of the ECJ has increased tremendously since the court was established in 1957. To help the court deal with cases, the thirteen judges sit in chambers of up to five judges, but always with an odd number so that there can be a clear decision in the case. In 1989 the Court of First Instance was set up to assist the ECJ by taking a specific jurisdiction with the safeguard of appeal to the ECJ itself.

This is not unusual as all Member States have a hierarchy or structure for its courts. The ECJ itself has a general jurisdiction with regard to Community law only fettered by the types of action specified in the Treaty. There are a number of direct actions available which include judicial review (Article 173), actions against a

Member State for failure to fulfil an obligation (Articles 169 and 170) and illegality (Article 184). In addition there is the special procedure for preliminary references under Article 177.

Under this procedure courts in the Member States can ask the ECJ questions regarding the interpretation of the Treaty or validity and interpretation of Community Acts. This does not amount to an appeal relationship but is the recognition of a 'co-operation' between the national courts and the ECJ. The nearest procedure like this in English law is appeal by case stated in criminal cases, but this is insignificant compared to the preliminary reference procedure.

As indicated above the greatest influence on the ECJ has been the French judicial system. Perhaps it is to be expected therefore that although cases may be brought in any of the ten official languages recognised by the court the working language of the court is French. Whenever a case is brought to the ECJ, whether as a direct action which is heard in its entirety only by the court or a request for a preliminary reference from a Member State under Article 177, it is processed by the court Registry to ensure that the progress of the case can be recorded. This is especially important with preliminary references where the whole procedure is dominated by the 'file' of written documentation sent by the national court. The procedure is that on receipt by the Registrar, the President of the court will assign the case to one of the six chambers and nominate one of the judges to act as 'rapporteur'. The First Advocate-General will at the same time designate the Advocate-General for the case. The role of the judge rapporteur is that although all the papers will go to every judge hearing the case, only he will have studied them closely in order to produce a preliminary report. This report, together with any views expressed by the Advocate-General will help the court decide what the relevant issues are. It may be decided that the case should be heard by the full court, as normally happens with cases between the Member States or Community institutions. These early stages covering the written proceedings and the preparatory inquiry are held in private. Where oral proceedings follow, as with direct actions, these are held in open court in Luxembourg. The next stage is for the Advocate-General to deliver his Opinion to the court. Some time after this the court will deliver its judgment. If it is a preliminary reference the answers given by the court to the questions raised by the national court will be sent back to that court so that it can complete its hearing. If it is a direct action the court will deliver its judgment which may take the form of a declaration as with Article 171. However, if the judgment needs to be enforced, for example against a company, the court itself has no mechanism for enforcing its judgments. Any enforcement has to be left to the appropriate judicial machinery of the Member State.

Notes

See Chapter 4 on Direct Actions and Chapter 5 on Indirect Actions before the European Court of Justice.

Question 3

Briefly describe the role of at least two of the following:

(a) the Committee of Permanent Representatives

(b) the Court of First Instance

(c) the Economic & Social Committee

Answer plan

This question follows the tradition mentioned above of essay questions on the institutions. However, instead of asking a narrower question on only one institution this question gives the student the opportunity to exercise some choice. However, it must be remembered that this type of question is not as easy as it looks with regard to obtaining marks!

Answer

(a) *The Committee of Permanent Representatives (COREPER)*

The Council of Ministers is the main political power within the Community, bringing together as it does the government ministers of the twelve Member States. However, such ministers are busy individuals with many demands upon their time. They are Members of their national Parliaments and governments.

They do not have the time to spend in long debate on routine Community matters. To assist them COREPER, an acronym from the name of the Committee in French, was established first under the Council's Rules of Procedure but then formally under the 1965 Merger Treaty. The Committee of Permanent Representatives is composed of individuals of ambassador rank who are accredited to the European Community. Their main task is to carry out work preparatory to Council meetings and other work delegated to them by the Council.

The Committee works very closely with the Commission as it seeks to represent the views of it's government in the discussion of Commission proposals. In order to carry out this task effectively it is very important that there is very good liaison between Members of COREPER and the appropriate national government departments. Thus in discussing draft Community legislation, national viewpoints can be aired. This is not just a one-way transmission of information in that the views of the representatives of other government can be channelled back. In this way, disagreements can usually be ironed out before the proposal comes before the Council to make its decision. When the Council of Ministers meets to discuss Commission proposals there are two agendas, A and B. Items on the A agenda are those upon which provisional agreement has been reached in the course of the preparatory COREPER meetings.

This allows the Council to concentrate on the items on the B agenda where there is still disagreement and where political compromise is needed.

As the activity of the Community has increased, so the workload on COREPER has led to it being divided into two. COREPER 1 is composed of deputy Permanent Representatives who generally discuss matters of a more technical nature, and COREPER 2, composed of the Ambassadors, who discuss politically important matters.

(b) *The Court of First Instance (CFI)*

This court was established under the Single European Act (SEA) and came into operation in 1989. The European Court of Justice, which had been established by the Treaty of Rome, had experienced increasing difficulties in coping with the work load as the number of Member States had increased and the policy area had expanded. The solution finally accepted by the Council of Ministers was to 'attach' the CFI to the ECJ and to give it a limited jurisdiction with a possible appeal to the ECJ itself.

Although it is quite common for judicial structures in the Member States to form a hierarchy of courts, the SEA uses the word 'attach' quite deliberately. The CFI is not a separate institution. It shares not only the building in Luxembourg with the ECJ but other facilities such as the library. It appoints its own Registrar but other administrative services are shared.

The CFI is based on Article 168A of the EC Treaty. There are twelve judges appointed to the court, one from each Member State. Although there are no Advocate-Generals specifically appointed to the CFI, the need for such a role to be fulfilled is recognised.

What is proposed is that where an Advocate-General is required in a particular case, one of the judges will be requested to carry out this role. This will not happen in every case before the CFI. The court may sit in chambers of three or five judges in order to hear cases brought before it.

Like the judges appointed to the ECJ, those appointed to the CFI have a six year term of office, which is renewable. Unlike their colleagues, the criteria for selection as a judge in the CFI is not so high as the ECJ. In the ECJ, prospective judges must possess the ability for appointment to high judicial office. Article 168A(3) states that for the CFI, judges are to be chosen 'from persons whose independence is beyond doubt and who possess the ability required for appointment to judicial office'. As already indicated, the ECJ's workload has increased dramatically in the 1980s, and they expressed concern about the affect this was having in the time it was taking them to deal with cases. The resultant jurisdiction of the CFI indicates that one of the problems encountered by the ECJ was those cases which required a long examination of questions of fact. These are very time consuming and involve shifting a great deal of evidence. There are three categories of cases which will come before the CFI. These are staff cases, where employees of the Committee have a dispute with regard to their employment; the second are cases brought under the European Coal and Steel Community Treaty concerned with production and prices; and most importantly, competition cases brought under either

Article 173 or Article 175 of the EC Treaty. If these cases also contain a claim for damages, the CFI can hear that claim as part of the action. However, claims for damages outside these categories of cases must go to the ECJ.

Appeals from the CFI are to the ECJ and have to be brought within two months. The appeal will only be heard on points of law and not of fact. Some writers believe that large companies involved in competition cases will always seek to appeal to the ECJ and therefore the reduction on the ECJ's workload envisaged by establishing the CFI will not materialise. It is something which only experience will tell, but the time consuming factual aspects of the case will not be something which can be raised on appeal and will not therefore take up the time of the ECJ. The three grounds of appeal mirror the grounds of annulment under Article 173, namely lack of competence, breach of procedure or infringement of Community law by the CFI.

(c) *The Economic & Social Committee (ECOSOC)*

The Committee is established under the EC Treaty but it is not an institution of the Community. It is in fact an advisory committee appointed under Articles 193 and 198 of the Treaty. It consists of representatives of the various sections of economic and social life of the Community. It provides a sounding board for informed and general Opinion of matters relating to the policies of the Communities and this helps the Council and Commission as they develop European legislation.

Although the Opinions of the Committee are not binding they do appear to have influence. The Commission has a very good working relationship with the Economic and Council Committee. This is perhaps reflected by the fact that generally the Committee supports the proposals put forward by the Commission. The relationship with the Council has not been so well developed although attempts have been made in recent years to improve this. Since 1987 it has become a regular practice for the person holding the office of President of the Council to address the Committee on matters discussed at the European Council. This has spread to ministers from the Member State holding the Presidency to address meetings of the Committee.

Although advisory, the Commission or Council consult the Committee when it considers it appropriate in addition to those instances where it is obligatory. Some Articles of the Treaty require the Council or the Commission to consult the Committee. An example of this is Article 75 which deals with international transport within the Community and the common rules established to implement the policy.

There is a total of 189 Members of the Economic and Social Committee. These are allocated to the different Member States to reflect their size, with the large countries such as France, Italy, Germany and the UK having 24 each, down to 6 for Luxembourg. The Committee reflects three particular groups of people. The Employers Group which is made up of representatives of employers organisations and chambers of commerce, the Workers Group which represent trade unions and a group of 'Other Interests' which includes small businesses, family, environmental and similar representatives. Within these groups can be found the representatives of the various categories of economic and social activity specified in Article 193. It is impossible within the limited number of Members from each country for all these interest groups within that country to be represented. This is recognised by the obligation placed on the Council to ensure that the total Committee at community level reflects the requirement of Article 193 as stated in the case of *Confederazione Italiana dirigenta diazienda v EC Council* in 1988. In order to achieve this each Member State submits a list of potential Members amounting to twice its actual allotted Members. The Council appoints the Members on the basis of unanimity. Once appointed the Members of the Economic and Social Committee act in their personal capacity and not as representatives following instruction from their Member State or interest group.

Question 4

Critically review the procedures of the Council of Ministers in carrying out its tasks under the Treaty.

Answer plan

This question allows you to draw upon other parts of the syllabus to look critically at the work of the Council of Ministers. The main points to cover are:

- Articles 145 - 154 EC - Treaty source for the Council
- membership and procedure of the Council
- relationship of the Council of Ministers with the European Council
- support given by COREPER
- the voting procedures of the Council
- the co-operation procedure and the European Parliament

Answer

The Council of Ministers is specified in Articles 145 to 154 EC. This is the main political institution of the EC. Its membership is made up of one representative of each Member State, ie twelve. Although the main representative is the foreign minister of each Member, the actual minister varies with the main business of the meeting. Thus if the Common Agricultural Policy is being discussed it will be the agricultural ministers who will attend and so on. The task of the Council is to ensure that the Community's objectives set out in Part 1 of the Treaty are attained. These objectives are generally specified in economic terms with a commitment to improving the standard of living and closer relations between the Member States. In order to achieve this the Council is given authority under the Treaty to play a very important part in the legislative process of the Community.

The Presidency of the Council is held in rotation by each Member State for a period of six months. This means that each Member State will hold the Presidency once every six years. The minister representing the Member State holding the Presidency takes the chair of meetings of the Council and has the important role with regard to setting the agenda and progressing Community business. This causes problems for the small Council secretariat as the focus of the political element of the EC moves around Europe. It has also been criticised on the grounds that the period is too short for individual ministers to acquire expertise in the role. The formal reference to the role of the Presidency in the Treaties and the Council's Rules of Procedure, are extremely brief. The Presidency's basic duty is simply to get results. Each Presidency usually begins with the holder making a statement with regards to what they hope to achieve during their six months period of office. The Presidency of the Council of Ministers coincides with the Presidency of the European Council where the procedural framework is less rigid but the need for good conduct and organisation of business is even more pressing in view of the potential importance of the results.

The sheer burden of business now coming before the Council causes problems. This has been affected by two developments in the 1980s. The Community had basically achieved the objectives it had set itself originally and was operating in a less economically favourable time. This had led to discussions in the Council becoming more narrowly national in character, with the Members of the Council negotiating more strongly within an inter-governmental forum. Secondly, the Council's position as the main seat of political authority has been eroded by the establishment of the European Council. When the European Council, composed of the Heads of Government, was first introduced in 1974 it was to provide political initiatives to deal with policy deadlock. However, it now seems to deal with many of the major decisions facing the Community. It was formally recognised in the Single European Act.

However, is it realistic to expect government ministers to play a significant role in the Council of Ministers to develop policy at Community level as against making decisions to adopt such policies or legislation? For example any British minister who may be involved in a meeting of the Council of Ministers is in charge of a government department, and takes part in debates and answers questions in the House of Commons or in exceptional cases the House of Lords. As an MP there are also constituency problems and interests to deal with. How much time is there for EC matters? Obviously there has to be some time because it is part of his job, but a great deal of the work of the Council of Ministers is undertaken by the Committee of Permanent Representatives or COREPER. This group of diplomats represent the views or interests of their particular government. They liaise with the various government ministries and bring these views to the discussions which take place in Brussels. The idea is that when the Council of Ministers meet much of the preliminary discussion has taken place and the ministers can concentrate on those issues which may require a political compromise or are politically sensitive.

However, the main discussion and action involving the Council of Ministers has centred on its voting procedures. In Article 148 EC it was envisaged that the Council would move, after the transitional period, to majority voting except for those specific matters identified by the Treaty as requiring unanimity. This was not to be a simple majority but generally a qualified one on the basis of Article 148. This Article gives each Member State a number of votes depending roughly upon the size of its population, ranging from ten for the largest Member States to two votes for the smallest country, Luxembourg. On any issue before the Council it requires a combination of the larger and smaller Member States to accumulate the necessary votes to adopt the measure. This seeks to ensure that no interest group in the Council can dominate the voting and encourages a compromise in the sense that the measure must be acceptable to a range of Member States. The necessary voting majority is fifty-four in favour of the measure. The intention of the Treaty was hindered by the events of 1966 which led to the Luxembourg Accord or Compromise, which was instituted to obtain the co-operation of the French government in the working of the EC. This recognition of a 'veto' in the sense that unanimity was required on particular issues not specified as requiring them under the Treaty, slowed down the actions of the Council in that it could not proceed faster than its slowest participating government. Governments who joined in the 1970s and 1980s assumed that they did so with a power of veto on issues they considered important to them, although they were politically shocked on occasions when they tried to exercise it. It was not until the Single European Act that attempts were made to speed up the decision making process of the Council of Ministers to meet the target of completing the Internal Market by 1 January 1993. Although academic debate still continues on whether the veto still exists, it is important to recognise the political nature of the Council. If the President of the Council is aware of the political implications of calling for a vote where a minority of the Council have strong objections, it is likely that such a vote will be postponed for further discussion.

The Treaty recognises the final say which the Council of Ministers has on legislation and concluding treaties or agreements with third countries. However, the Council can only act on the basis of a proposal from the European Commission and after consulting the European Parliament and on some issues the Economic and

Social Committee. Article 7 of the Single European Act (SEA) replaced Article 149 EC and introduced the co-operation procedure which gives the European Parliament greater involvement in the legislative process on certain issues. If the Council wishes to ignore Parliament's amendments to its common position it must do so by unanimity. Likewise if it wishes to amend the proposals from the Commission it must do so unanimously. As the European Parliament, as indicated above, exercises more authority in the legislative process it has to be at a reduction of that held by the Council. However, the Council of Ministers remains the main political power within the Community institutions.

Notes

See Chapter 12 on the possible impact of the Maastricht Treaty on the relationship between the Council and the European Parliament.

Question 5

Critically assess the powers and functions of the European Commission.

Answer plan

This question allows you to draw upon the other areas of the European law syllabus to illustrate the powers and functions of the European Commission. The main points to cover are:

- Article 155 EC and the general duties of the Commission
- the appointment and organisation of the European Commission
- the role of the Commission and Community legislation
- the Commission's role in external relations
- the enforcement powers of the Commission under Article 169 EC
- the powers of the Commission with regard to competition policy

Answer

The European Commission is sometimes thought of as a kind of European civil service, which it is not. Civil servants are merely expected to carry out the wishes of their political masters. It will be obvious from the work of the Commission that their role goes much further than this. There are seventeen Commissioners, with two each from the big four Member States plus Spain and one each from the remaining Member States. Articles 155 to 163 EC deal with the European Commission. Generally Commissioners have held political office in their Member State, but once appointed they are to act completely independently as required by Article 10 of the Merger Treaty. They are not to be 'mandated' by their Member State or to be seen favouring one Member State or organisation. This may not be welcomed by the government of the Member State which nominated them, as Mrs Thatcher's accusation that Lord Cockfield had 'gone native' illustrates. They are sometimes referred to as the 'true Europeans' in that they are to act in the best interests of the Community as a whole. They are appointed by common accord by the governments of the Member States for a term of four years, which is renewable. They can only be removed as a group by the European Parliament. One Commissioner is appointed to head the Commission as its President. This office is held for two years and is renewable. Each Commissioner is allocated a portfolio or area of responsibility from the twenty Directorates-General covering all Community policy.

The functions of the European Commission are found in Article 155 EC, and indicate the key role envisaged for it by the Treaty. The important functions of initiator of Community policy and executive arm of the Community are clearly stated. Although the main political power of the Community rests with the Council of Ministers, the Council are dependant upon receiving a proposal from the Commission before it can act. These proposals cover the full range of Community policy specified in the Treaty and the general power under Article 235 EC. In exceptional cases the Council can request proposals under Article 152 EC, but even here a proposal must come from the Commission. The introduction of the co-operation procedure by the Single European Act whereby the European Parliament's legislative role in certain policy areas has been increased, requires the involvement of the Commission. If the European Parliament wishes to amend the Council's common position, such amendments are first considered by the European Commission which can either adopt them or give reasons for their refusal to the Council.

Once the Community Act has been passed, such as those mentioned in Article 189 EC, it is for the Commission to ensure that they are applied. Some observers refer to this as the policing role of the Commission but it goes further than this. The Commission is acting in an executive role, implementing the agreed policy of the Community. In order to ensure that Member States implement the Community act and generally fulfil their obligations under the Treaty, the Commission is granted a power under Article 169 EC. This Article gives authority to the Commission to deliver a reasoned Opinion to those Member States which it feels are failing to fulfil an obligation. If the Member State is unable to satisfy the Commission that it is not failing to do so, the Commission can bring the matter before the European Court of Justice. If the court agrees with the Commission's view it can make a declaration under Article 171 EC requiring the Member State to comply with its judgment. This is a very powerful weapon given to the Commission, which has led to it being called 'the guardian of the Treaties'. The Commission has complete discretion as to whether to bring an action under Article 169, but this has to be seen within the context of its overall duty under Article 155 to ensure that the Treaty and the associated measures taken are applied.

As the Commission is seen as the body representing the Community interest it perhaps follows that it should be given a special role in the Community's external relations. The Community is a large economic trading area and as such belongs to a number of international organisations, such as GATT. In addition the Community is party to bi-lateral and multi-lateral agreements with countries or trading blocs. Under Article 228 EC such international agreements are to be negotiated by the Commission, although they are concluded by the Council of Ministers after consulting the European Parliament.

It is perhaps in the important area of competition policy where the wide powers of the Commission can be observed. The competition policy of the Community is founded upon Articles 85, 86 and 90 EC covering both the private sector and the activities of governments of Member States. The authority of the Commission with regard to the private sector is not restricted to those undertakings which are based in the European Community but includes all those who are involved in an economic activity within the Community. This was a lesson learnt by ICI before the UK became a Member of the Community in the *Dyestuffs Case* in 1972. As indicated above the Commission is involved in the Community acts specified in Article 189 EC. In the specific area of competition policy this results in decisions being taken which are binding upon those to whom they are addressed. Thus the Commission exercising its powers under Regulation 17/62 can investigate restrictive practices or abuses of a dominant position affecting the Community and if the competition policy has been breached they can impose very large fines. Many of the undertakings involved in such cases complain that the Commission's powers are excessive in that they are 'prosecutor, judge and jury'. However, there is the possibility of appeal to the Court of First Instance. The Commission's role with regard to mergers was also increased by the Merger Regulation 4064/89. Under this Regulation the Commission must approve such mergers between undertakings with a worldwide turnover of more than 5,000 million ECUs, where at least two of the firms have a combined turnover of more than 250 million ECUs in the European Community. Actions by governments of Member States which may affect undertakings by providing subsidies or other unfair treatment are also within the powers of enforcement by the Commission.

It can be seen that the powers and functions of the European Commission are very wide. Without the European Commission the European Community could never have been constructed and developed to the extent it has. The Commission has also taken a very pro-Community stance, supported by the European Court of Justice. As the influence of the European Parliament has increased so the Commission has worked closely with it in recognition of its democratic role within the Community. With the introduction of the European Council, the role of the Commission was recognised with an invitation to the President of the Commission to join their meetings. However, there have been calls for reform of the Commission. Although it should operate on a collegiate basis the increased number of Commissioners and the policies of the Community make this difficult. It has been suggested that the number of Commissioners should be reduced to twelve, with only one from each Member State. This smaller body should be able to work more efficiently and provide meaningful portfolios to all Commissioners. However, this suggestion has not been accepted. The policy areas of the Community have not been reduced but it has been accepted that the principle of subsidiarity should apply. Under this principle decisions should be taken at the lowest level which is effectively possible. Thus more decisions would be taken at national or local level. This should reduce some of the workload of the Commission.

Notes

You should look at Chapter 4 on Direct Actions where Article 169 EC actions are dealt with in more detail and Chapter 7 on Competition Policy.

Chapter 2

Sources of Law

Introduction

As you are no doubt aware by now, the European Community is based upon treaties which under international law have a special significance. They form the basis not only of the Community institutions but the powers which can be exercised by those institutions and the procedures under which they must operate. Therefore it is no wonder that the starting point for any discussion of the legal basis of the EC are the treaties upon which it is founded. The treaties are considered to be the primary source of Community law.

Although it is perhaps an over simplification to use this analogy, if you think of the Treaty as an enabling Act then what is required is the equivalent of delegated legislation to provide the structure and detail necessary to produce an effective measure upon which individuals can base their actions and the legal system can enforce. Hence we come to what are generally called secondary sources of Community law. These are listed in Article 189 EC as Regulations, Directives and Decisions. Although Recommendations and Opinions are mentioned these are not legally binding. This Article provides the key definitions of these Community administrative acts which are so important to a study of European law.

As every student of a common law system is aware, the judiciary in their deliberation and judgments on the law create rules or principles which are followed in subsequent cases. Although the European legal system does not have such a rigid adherence to precedent as found in the common law, the judges in the European Court of Justice have provided an additional secondary source of law to add to the administrative acts found in Article 189. Examples of this will be found in specific questions throughout the later chapters of this book, but a few points are made in this chapter to show the impact of this source of law. As will be discussed in the next chapter there is a clear acceptance within the Community that the ECJ provides definitive and authoritative judgments on points of European Community law which are followed by the courts of the Member States.

Checklist

You need to have a good understanding of the role of the EC Treaty as an authority for Community acts or judgments of the European Court of Justice. This is not necessarily easy for the student of English law who then has to develop the skills associated with Community law. When you are tracing the authority of a particular Community act you will generally go back to a treaty Article. In addition you should cover the following points:

• Primary and secondary sources of Community law

• Administrative acts defined in Article 189 EC

• General principles of Community law

• Methods of interpretation used in Community law

Question 6

Critically review the development of general principles of law as part of the law of the European Community.

Answer plan

Generally questions covering only general principles of Community law are essay questions, similar to this one. However, you must be prepared to deal with this topic within problem questions where a particular general principle may be the ground which will allow a remedy to be granted to one of the parties. The most common question where these occur is in dealing with an action for judicial review under Article 173 of the EC Treaty. You should look at that chapter to see how the topic of general principles can be integrated into a problem question drawing upon a number of topics in the syllabus.

With regard to this question the main points for discussion are:

• role of general principles within a legal system

• authority for the development of general principles within the EC legal system

• specific examples of Community general principles, including the most important ones

Answer

General principles of law are found in all legal systems, including the common law system. Within the common law system of England they are seen as a device to hide judge-made law, whereby a judge would seek to show that his ruling was derived from a principle of sufficient generality so as to command common assent. In this way a firm legal base could be provided for the judgment. Within the legal systems of the Member States, the development of general principles have taken place over a number of years and have been cloaked in historical respectability or authority. However, the European Community was facing the possible development of general principles in a modern era and therefore had to be more conscious of what it was undertaking. The ECJ has developed a doctrine that rules of Community law may be derived from general principles of law in addition to treaties and Community legislation. What is the authority for the development of general principles within the EC legal system? The ECJ has pointed to three Articles of the EC Treaty to provide some justification for general principles as a source of law. These are:

(1) Article 164 which states that 'The Court of Justice shall ensure that in the interpretation of the Treaty the law is observed'. In view of the word 'law' being used, it is considered that it must refer to something over and above the Treaty itself and is not unreasonable for this Article to oblige the judges of the court to take general principles into account.

(2) Article 173 deals with judicial review and specifies the grounds upon which an annulment can be based. The first paragraph of the Article includes the words '... infringement of this Treaty, or of any rule of law relating to its application ...'. The phrase 'any rule of law' must refer to something other than the Treaty itself. This has been used by the ECJ as a basis for the principle that a Community act may be quashed for the infringement of a general principle of law.

(3) Article 215 (2) is concerned with non-contractual liability (tort), and expressly provides that the liability of the Community is based on the 'general principles common to the laws of the Member States'.

Given this authority from the Treaty three points should be noted before going on to specific general principles:

(a) The court is prepared to apply principles of law even if they are not found in the legal system of every Member State;

(b) Whatever the factual origin of the principle, it is applied by the ECJ as a principle of Community law and not of national law. This is very important as can be noted by the development of the general principle of protection of fundamental rights given below;

(c) There is little doubt that the ECJ would have applied general principles of law even if none of these Treaty provisions existed because of the function of such general principles.

Proportionality

This principle is derived from German law where it underlies certain provisions of the German Constitution. 'A public authority may not impose obligations on a citizen except to the extent to which they are strictly necessary in the public interest to attain the purpose of the measure' (*Internationale Handelsgesellschaft*).

Thus if the burdens imposed are clearly out of proportion to the object in view, the measure will be annulled. Proportionality is important in economic law and therefore has a wide application within the EC. It frequently involves imposing taxes, levies, duties etc in the hope of achieving economic advantages. The ECJ will not interfere unless there is a very clear and obvious infringement of the principle.

An example is the *Skimmed-Milk Powder* case (Case 114/76 *Bela-Muhle Josef Bergman v Grows-Farm* [1977]), where the Council had sought to reduce a surplus of skimmed-milk powder in the Community by forcing animal feed producers to incorporate it in their product in place of Soya, which was the normal protein element used. The drawback to the producers was that the skimmed-milk was three times more expensive than the Soya.

The ECJ held that the Regulation embodying the scheme was invalid partly because it was discriminatory and partly because it offended against the principle of proportionality. The effect of making animal feed producers use skimmed-milk was to increase the price of animal feed and thus harm all livestock breeders. The imposition of the obligation to purchase skimmed-milk powder was not necessary in order to diminish the surplus. On the other hand, the benefits of the policy were felt only by dairy farmers. Therefore, the policy worked in a discriminatory fashion between different categories of farmers.

Non-Discrimination or Equality

Specific reference to this principle can be found in the Treaty, notably in Article 7 which deals with discrimination on the grounds of nationality and Article 119 with equal pay. However, the ECJ has gone beyond these provisions in holding that there is a general principle of non-discrimination in Community law. This does not mean that Community institutions must treat everybody alike, but that there must be no arbitrary distinctions between different groups within the Community. (Example concerning a business see *Skimmed-Milk Powder* case above.) The case of *Sabbatini v European Parliament* (Case 20/71 [1972]) illustrates how the principle applies to discrimination between the sexes. The court has gone further in the case of *Prais v Council* (Case 130/75 [1976]), where it held that the principle also covered discrimination on the basis of religion.

Protection of Legitimate Expectations

According to this principle derived from German law, Community measures must not, in the absence of an overriding matter of public interest, violate the legitimate expectations of those concerned. Thus a business holding a reasonable expectation which it has acted upon in the normal cause of business and suffered a loss, may seek to have the Community measure annulled. The ECJ sometimes seeks to avoid annulment by adopting a strained interpretation of the measure concerned.

In *Deuka v EVGF* (Case 78/74 [1975]), the German intervention Agency (EVGF) was the national authority concerned with the payment of premiums to processors who made wheat unfit for human consumption and only suitable for animal feed. In order to qualify for a premium Deuka had to obtain the prior agreement of EVGF and to carry out the process under their supervision. A European Commission Regulation increased the premium payable as from 1 June 1970, ie during a crop year. Deuka processed a quantity of wheat which had been purchased before 1 June and thus claimed they were entitled to the increased premium. This was refused. Following legal proceedings in the German courts a reference was made to the ECJ. The Regulation was not declared invalid but the court stated that in view of the principle of legal certainty, it should be interpreted so that the increase was payable even if processing took place after 1 June provided that the wheat was purchased and the relevant authority had made an approval before 1 June. Therefore this interpretation gave full protection to the legitimate expectations of the processors. (See also the case of *Commission v Council* (1973) which is concerned with salary payments to Community staff.)

Fundamental Rights

It was not until the case of *Stauder v Ulm* (1969) concerning a requirement for the applicant of cheap butter to give his name, that the ECJ recognised this general principle. The refusal to do so earlier had created pressure between the court and some of the Member States, notably Germany and Italy where such rights had been enshrined into their respective Constitutions. The matter was resolved when an administrative judge in Stuttgart asked the ECJ whether a particular requirement was compatible with the general principles of Community law. The result was that the ECJ expressly included the protection 'of fundamental human rights enshrined in the general principles of Community law and protected by the court'. In the later case of *Internationale Handelsgesellschaft*, the court stated 'that fundamental rights form an integral part of the general principles of the law, the observance of which it ensures; that in safeguarding those rights, the court is bound to draw inspiration from constitutional traditions common to the Member States ...'.

Procedural Rights

These rights have been developed to fill the gaps where EC legislation does not provide specific safeguards for a person's rights. Examples include:

   The right to a hearing - This is drawn from the traditions of English law and was first used in *Transocean Marine Paint*

Association v Commission where Advocate-General Warner submitted that there was a general rule that a person whose interests are perceptibly affected by a decision taken by a public authority must be given the opportunity to make his views known. As the Commission had failed to do this in this competition case, its decision was annulled.

The right to due process - In the case of *Johnston v Chief Constable of the Royal Ulster Constabulary*, Mrs Johnston claimed that she had been subject to sex discrimination by her employer, contrary to Directive 76/207. A certificate issued by the Secretary of State sought to provide conclusive evidence that the derogation from Community obligations was on the grounds of national security. The court held that such a provision was contrary to the 'requirement of judicial control stipulated by ... [Article 6 which] ... reflects a general principle of law which underlies the constitutional traditions common to the Member States.'

The advantage of general principles are the same for the Community legal system as for Member States. They help to fill the gaps which always arise when it is not possible to have a written text to cover every legal eventuality. They constitute the unwritten law of the Community. Also within the Community the characteristic role of general principles as limiting the power of the administration to take measures affecting the citizen has been continued.

General principles of law are relevant in the context of EC law in a number of ways:

(a) They may be invoked as an aid to interpretation in the sense that 'the measure should not conflict with general principles';

(b) General principles may be invoked by both Member States and individuals in order to challenge Community acts;

(c) General principles may also be invoked as a means of challenging action by a Member State, where the action is performed in the context of a right or obligation arising from Community law;

(d) General principles may be invoked to support claims for damages against the Community (Article 215(2)).

Question 7

Explain the nature and legal effect of Regulations, Directives and Decisions made by the Council of Ministers and the Commission of the European Community.

Answer plan

Most questions on sources of law are essay questions like this one. However, you must remember that a good understanding of these topics can be invaluable when answering problem questions which come up in later chapters. The best example is cases brought under Article 173 of the EC Treaty (2), where the ability to discuss what a is meant by a Regulation is very important.

This question is looking for a clear understanding of the definitions in Article 189 EC and the legal effect of a Regulation, a Directive and a Decision.

Answer

The forms of EC legislation or administrative acts are listed in Article 189 of the EC Treaty. This provides the basic definitions for a Regulation, Directive and Decision. Article 189 does not give the authority to issue such legislative measures, as they have to be authorised by specific Articles of the Treaty. However, where the Council or the Commission in order to carry out their tasks do need to issue a legally binding act it is to Article 189 that attention must be given.

Under Article 189 the definition of a Regulation is that it shall have general application and be binding in its entirety and directly applicable in all Member States. It does not mean that a Regulation necessarily has to apply to all Member States. It could be applicable in only one Member State. However, as long as it retains its character of being applicable to an abstract group of persons it will still be a Regulation. This is important if an individual is seeking to challenge the validity of a Regulation by using the Article 173 procedure, as was discussed in the *Watenstedt* case (*E Zuckerfabrik Watenstedt* Case 6/68 [1968]).

It is a requirement of Article 190 that certain formal requirements are completed in order for a valid Regulation to be made. The reasons upon which the Regulation is based must be given and any proposals or Opinions which were required by the Treaty to be obtained must be referred to. The next Article, 191, requires that Regulations are to be published in the Official Journal of the Community. The Council's Rules of Procedure for Regulations requires them to be numbered, dated and signed. Regulations also carry a formula describing their legal effects, ie 'this Regulation is binding in its entirety and directly applicable in all Member States'.

This formula raises two points about the effects of Regulations. The first is whether national legislation is required by the Member State to implement the Regulation. The view of the ECJ is that Regulations have a mandatory effect and have the force of law in the Member States without the need of transformation or confirmation by their legislatures. The court went further in the 1972 case of *EC Commission v Italy* when it stated that 'all methods of implementation are contrary to the Treaty which would have the result of creating an obstacle to the direct effect of Community Regulation and jeopardising their simultaneous and uniform application in the whole of the Community' *EC Commission v Italy* (Case 39/72 [1973]). Although there are exceptional cases where such national legislation is required, in such cases the national law must not disguise its Community character by altering the wording of the Regulation or its date for coming into force.

The second point concerns the meaning of 'directly applicable in all Member States'. Directly applicable means that the Regulation does not require a national measure to become binding upon the citizens and also that national authorities and national measures cannot prevent its application. There is often confusion between direct applicability and the term direct effect, especially as the ECJ itself seems to use the terms interchangeably. The Treaty and other sources of Community law can have direct effect, but only Regulations are directly applicable. In *Politi v Italian Ministry of Finance* (Case 43/71 [1971]) the ECJ held that under Article 189 'Regulations shall have general application and shall be directly applicable in Member States ... Therefore by reason of their nature and their function in the system of the sources of Community law, Regulations have direct effect and are as such capable of creating individual rights which national courts must protect'. Therefore, not only may individuals rely on specific provisions as against other individuals and Member States, they may invoke the general objective and purpose of Regulations as against national legal provisions. Thus in *Amsterdam Bulb BV v Producktschap voor Siergewassen* (Case 50/76 [1977]) - it was stated that 'the moment that the Community adopts Regulations under Article 40 of the Treaty establishing a common organisation of the market in a specific sector, the Member States are under a duty not to take any measure which might create exemptions from them or affect them adversely.

A Directive as defined by Article 189 EC, is binding upon each Member State as to the results to be achieved, but allows the States discretion as to the form and method of implementation. Where legislation is necessary it can take a variety of forms, as the obligation is only that it becomes legally binding. The wording of the legislation adopted to implement a Directive need not contain the same identical words as the Directive itself. However, it is important that any national rules should give individuals a clear understanding of their rights and obligations so that national courts can ensure that they are observed.

A Decision is an individual act designed to be addressed to a specified person or persons. As a 'binding' act it has the force of law and does not therefore require implementation in order to take effect. Decisions may be addressed to States or individuals. An example of a Decision addressed to a Member State would be an act of the Commission requiring a Member State to abolish or amend measures of aid to national undertakings. In contrast an example of an individual Decision would be a Commission ruling that an undertaking had acted in breach of Community competition policy as specified in Article 85 or 86 EC.

It was initially believed that Directives and Decisions gave rise exclusively to rights and obligations as between their addressees on the one hand and the Community institutions and Member States on the other. However, in the important judgment of *Grad* (1970), the European Court held that both Directives and Decisions might contain directly effective provisions which the courts in the Member States must enforce. However, the test for direct effect must be satisfied, ie that the act must be sufficiently clear and precise, unconditional, leaving no room for discretion in its implementation.

Notes

See questions 10 and 11 below dealing with direct effect, and
question 29 dealing with competition policy.

Question 8

Critically review the methods of interpretation used by the
European Court of Justice.

Answer plan

This question fits the normal type of essay question which is
seeking an answer which shows knowledge and understanding of
how the European Court of Justice goes about the process of
interpretation of Community law.

The main points raised by this question are:

• purpose of methods of interpretation

• influences on the ECJ

• methods used by the ECJ - teleological, contextual, literal,
  historical

Answer

With regard to European Community law, the ECJ is the final
arbiter. There are no appeals against such judgments as it may give.
Under the preliminary ruling procedure of Article 177 of the EC
Treaty, the ECJ can be requested to provide a definitive
interpretation of the Treaty or of a Community Act. This can be
extended under other Articles of the Treaty to include other sources
of law which are legally binding in the European Community. In
order to carry out its tasks, the ECJ has developed a number of
tools of interpretation. The European Court 'tool box' is not unlike
the English methods of literal, golden, mischief, etc but with the
very important difference that it has been developed in the context
of influence of domestic law (mainly France and Germany) and
international law. However, like an English judge, the judges of the
ECJ very rarely use one method of interpretation in a particular

case. They use a variety of rules of interpretation and then decide, as part of the judicial art, which is the most appropriate in the circumstance. Given the authority of the ECJ, this gives the judges a great deal of influence on the character and effectiveness of Community law.

Whatever method or approach to interpretation the court may utilise, it must be remembered that they are operating in a legal system which has a strong linguistic dimension. There are nine official languages, so all the Community texts written in the language of the Member States are recognised as having equal validity. The main approaches to interpretation are characterised by the teleological approach which is increasingly favoured by the ECJ. The teleological approach requires the judge to look to the purpose or object of the text before him. As Lord Denning observed in *Bulmer v Bollinger* in 1974, 'the (EC) Treaty is quite unlike any of the enactments to which we have become accustomed. It lays down general principles. It expresses its aims and purposes ... But it lacks precision'. Faced with a body of law couched in such terms, the ECJ uses the teleological approach. In the Article 86 competition case involving Continental Can, the ECJ referred to the 'spirit, general scheme and wording of Article 86, as well as to the system and objectives of the Treaty'. In the *Colditz* case certain social security Regulations were before the court, which declared that 'the solution to this question ... can only emerge from the interpretation of those Regulations in the light of the objectives of Articles 48 to 51 of the Treaty'.

The contextual approach involves the court placing the provision, whether from a treaty or a Community Act, within its context and interpreting it in relation to other provisions of Community law. Given the lack of provision in many Community provisions it is no wonder that frequent reference is made to the 'framework of Community law' as in *Costa v ENEL* or 'one must have regard to the whole scheme of the Treaty no less than to its specific provisions' in the *ERTA* Case. Contextual interpretation is also used for Community legislation.

In the important case of *Defrenne* the ECJ was considering whether the Equal Pay Article (119) had direct effect. It brought together a teleological approach when looking at the socio-economic purpose of the Article but within a particular context (or contextual approach) in that Article 119 has a close relationship with Article 117 which concerned the need to promote improved working conditions and an improved standard of living for workers.

Although not stated in the judgments of the court, writings of past Members of the ECJ indicate that they favour the teleological and context approaches to interpretation because they reflect the way that the Community is changing as it seeks to fulfil its aims and objectives in the future.

The literal interpretation is an approach which every court takes when faced with the question 'what does this mean?' The ECJ is no exception, but whereas the national judge may feel that his task is at an end the ECJ may decide that the plain meaning of the words should not be followed but preference should be given to allow for the aims and objectives of the Treaties to be achieved. In other words the teleological or contextual approaches are given priority. In the *ERTA* case the Commission sought to have the Council decision to co-ordinate the Member States' negotiations under the European Road Transport Agreement annulled. The Council argued that the action under Article 173 was not valid in that the Community Acts mentioned were those found in Article 189, namely Regulations, Directives or Decisions. Despite the clear wording of Article 189, the ECJ held that the purpose of Article 173 was to subject to judicial review all those measures which had legal effect. They declared 'It would be inconsistent with this objective to interpret the conditions under which the action is admissible so restrictively as to limit the availability of this procedure merely to the categories of measures referred to by Article 189'. In *Stauder v Ulm* the ECJ had to consider the different wording of a Commission Decision permitting the sale of cheap butter to those in receipt of welfare benefits. Stauder was a German national who under German law implementing the decision was required to give his name when purchasing the butter, something which he claimed was contrary to his fundamental rights. The Dutch text followed that of the German but the court referred to the French and Italian texts which only stipulated that a coupon referring to the person concerned needed to be presented. The court adopted this more liberal version of the decision which would enable its objectives without any breach of fundamental rights.

Historical interpretation is associated with the attempt to ascertain the subjective intention of the author of the text before the court. It is not used very often because of the lack of documentation available to help the court. The negotiations surrounding the original treaties are shrouded by secrecy and thus the *travaux preparatoires* are not available. However, the Official Journal publishes all legislative proposals by the Commission as well as formal Opinions of the European Parliament. In addition the legislative acts of the Community are required under Article 190 to state in their preamble the reasons on which they are based and to refer to any proposals or Opinions which were required by the act. These preambles give some assistance to the court, as they did in *Markus v Hauptzollamt Hamburg-Jonas* (1969).

EC Law and National Law

Introduction

One of the central principles established by the European Court of Justice is that of the supremacy of Community law over national law. Having gained acceptance for this the court went on to establish the principle or doctrine of direct effect, which gives rights to individuals which can be enforced in the courts of the Member States. Both of these developments were signalled in the early cases of *Van Gend en Loos* and *Costa v ENEL*.

However, it is also important to note that the court has built upon these principles in other topics, such as preliminary references which are dealt with in Chapter 5. Generally the specific questions on this topic are essay-types, but aspects of the principles associated with the relationship of Community law and national law also arise in questions on other topics. These can be of both essay and problem format.

Checklist

Students should understand the principle of supremacy of Community law and direct effect developed in the following cases: *Van Gend en Loos*, *Costa*, *Simmenthal SpA (No 2)* and *Internationale*. In addition the following specific points should be covered:

- The principle of direct effect in relation to direct applicability
- The direct effect of Treaty provisions, Regulations, Directives and Decisions
- The test for direct effect
- Vertical and horizontal direct effect

Question 9

'If the supremacy within the European Community over the national law of the Member States was not always inherent in the EC Treaty it was certainly well established in the jurisprudence of the Court of Justice ...' Lord Bridge in *Factortame Ltd v Secretary of State for Transport (No 2)*.

Discuss.

Answer plan

This essay question requires a discussion of the supremacy of Community law over national law and how it has come about. All the cases which track this development are important and can be used as authority for many of the important topics on Community law. The main points for this question are:

- the Treaty basis used to justify Supremacy of Community law, notably Article 5 EC

- the foundations of the Community referred to in *Van Gend en Loos, Costa, Internationale* and *Simmenthal* cases

- how Community law is incorporated into national law

- the reaction of the Member States to this development

Answer

The establishment of the EC required a transfer of sovereignty for certain specific areas of policy from the Member State to the Community. This meant that some legal matters which had been the sole prerogative of a Member State were no longer within its control. This inevitably led to a situation of conflict between national and EC law. Yet if the Community was to fulfil its aims it was necessary that such conflicts were speedily resolved, with a minimum of uncertainty. However, this question raised Constitutional problems of varying magnitude for all Member States.

As far as the Treaty itself is concerned, there is no specific mention of any priorities in the relationship between national and EC law. However, in the view of the European Court of Justice, the legal basis on which the Community rests necessarily presupposes the supremacy or primacy of Community law. Under international law the question is resolved by the Constitutional rules of the State concerned. Principally it will depend on the means by which international law is incorporated into domestic law of that Member State. There are two approaches to this incorporation in that the legal systems of States are either monist or dualist in their approach to international law. In monist States, such as France, all law is treated equally in the sense that national courts can apply international treaties, as long as the appropriate Constitutional procedures have been followed. In cases of conflict with national law, monist countries usually recognise the supremacy of treaty provisions. Whereas in dualist States, such as the UK, international law and national law are considered to be fundamentally different. International treaties as such can never be applied by national courts, but only domestic legislation brought about by the international treaty. Thus the EC Treaty has to be specifically incorporated into domestic law. In the UK this was achieved by the European Communities Act 1972 and specifically ss 2 and 3. However, whatever the method of incorporation used by the Member State this does not settle the question of priorities.

Given the importance that the ECJ has placed upon the uniformity of application of Community law in the Member States, and the desire to see that the Community was not weakened by diversity, it is understandable that the court would develop its own Constitutional rules to ensure that where there was a conflict between EC and national law, it would be EC law which prevailed. It was in the case of *Van Gend en Loos* where the ECJ took its first tentative steps in this process. The case was an Article 177 EC preliminary reference from the Dutch courts on whether Article 12 EC of the Treaty had direct effect. The court took the opportunity of declaring that 'the Community constitutes a new legal order in international law, for whose benefit the States have limited their sovereign rights, albeit within limited fields'. In *Costa v ENEL* the court went further when asked a specific question by the Italian court on the priority of EC law and national law. The transfer of sovereignty mentioned in *Van Gend* 'comes with it a clear limitation of their sovereign rights upon which a subsequent unilateral law, incompatible with the aims of the Community, cannot prevail.' Thus by establishing a European Community with real powers, the Member States created a body of law which applies to their nationals as well as to themselves.

Subsequently in *Internationale Handelsgesellschaft mbH*, the court was concerned with a conflict between an EC Regulation and provisions of the German Constitution protecting fundamental rights. Under German law the Constitution was superior to a statute. As a country with a monist legal system it was necessary for the EC Treaty to be incorporated into the national legal system and the vehicle used to do this was a statute. Thus given that there was no provision in the Constitution to allow it to be overridden by European Community law, the plaintiff claimed that the Regulation should be nullified. Which should prevail the Regulation or the Constitution? The European Court of Justice took a very strong view and insisted that the legality of a Community act cannot be nullified by national law. The German Constitutional court was concerned about the lack of protection for fundamental rights within the Community. Until this changed the fundamental rights provision of the German Constitution would take priority. This would not mean that they would rule on the validity of a Community act but rather they would conclude that such a measure could not be applied in Germany. This did not happen in the *Internationale* case or in any subsequent German case, but it does indicate a possible conflict in particular circumstances. A similar conclusion occurred in the *Frontini* case, only here it was the Italian Constitution's protection of fundamental rights which were involved. The Constitutional courts in both Germany and Italy were not happy with the hard line taken by the ECJ. The important difference is that the Italian Constitutional court has repeated the possibility of declaring that a Community measure may not apply in Italy. This was in the *Fragd* case in 1990.

Thus as far as the European Court of Justice is concerned all EC law, regardless of whether it is a Treaty provision, a Community act or an agreement with a third country, must take priority over all conflicting domestic law. This applies whether the national law is enacted prior or subsequent to Community law. In the absence of any specific Treaty provision how can this be justified? It in fact reflects the approach of the court which is pragmatic and pro-Community based on the purpose, the general aims and the spirit of the Treaty. In its view Member States apply to join the Community and must therefore take the necessary measures to comply with EC law. The Community was established with its own institutions which have powers under Article 189 EC, with no qualification or reservation, to make laws binding upon all Member States. Regulations are specifically said in Article 189 EC to have 'binding force' and to be 'directly applicable in all Member States. To the court this shows a clear indication of the supremacy of the legislative provisions conferred on the Community. If a State could unilaterally nullify its effects by means of domestic legislation overruling Community law, Community legislation would be quite meaningless.

The European Court of Justice has repeatedly used Article 5 EC to emphasize the fundamental obligation upon Member States to implement Community legislation so that it receives uniform application throughout the Community. Under Article 5 Member States are required to abstain from any measure which could jeopardize the attainment of the objectives of the Treaty. Where Member States fail to fulfil their obligations the Treaty, under Article 169 EC gives authority to the Commission to instigate enforcement procedures. The Community would not survive if States were free to act unilaterally in breach of such obligation. If the aims of the Community are to be achieved, there must be uniformity of application of Community law throughout all the Member States. This will not occur unless all States accord priority to EC law.

A final case provides guidance to national judges faced with a case which shows a conflict between a national law and EC law. In *Simmenthal SpA (No 2)* an Italian judge was faced with just such a dilemma. The judge was faced with a conflict between a Council Regulation on the common organisation of the market in beef and veal and the Italian veterinary and public health laws. Under Italian law domestic legislation contrary to EC Regulations may be held unConstitutional, but only by the Constitutional court and not by the ordinary courts. Should the Italian judge of first instance disregard inconsistent national legislation without waiting for its repeal or a declaration from the Constitutional court making it invalid? The instructions given in answer to the 177 reference were that a national court was under a duty to give full effect to Community law even if there was a conflicting provision of national law and without waiting for a higher court to rule on the matter. This is similar to the *Factortame* case in the House of Lords where Lord Bridge made his statement which is the basis of this question. In that case the House of Lords accepted that directly effective Community law must prevail over any inconsistent subsequent domestic legislation. Any incompatible national law is automatically inapplicable because unless Community law is given priority over conflicting national law at once, from the moment of its coming into force, there can be no uniformity of application throughout the Community.

Within a short space of time the courts of the Member States, despite their different Constitutional rules and traditions, have adapted to the principle of supremacy of EC law. This is perhaps due in part to the persuasive judgments of the ECJ and the attitudes of the courts of the Member States. They have accepted that Community law, stemming as it does from the Treaty, has an independent source. It can not be challenged by judicial process on the basis of any national provisions, however framed, without being deprived of its character as Community law and more importantly without the legal basis of the Community itself being called into question. The supremacy of Community law stems from the Treaties and not from the national Constitutions. The special and original nature of Community law requires that its supremacy over national law is acknowledged. The European Court of Justice recognised the importance of this and, as Lord Bridge stated in the *Factortame* case, established the principle as part of its case law at a very early stage in the legal history of the European Community.

Question 10

Critically examine the development of the doctrine of direct effect.

Answer plan

This is an important topic and it is very likely that in any question where advice is required on enforcing a Community right, it will be appropriate to discuss the topic of direct effect. This question is an essay question but it is not uncommon for problem questions to be asked on this topic. The main points that should be discussed in this essay are:

* what is meant by direct effect
* the difference between direct effect and direct applicability; the test for direct effect
* the direct effect of direct effect of Articles of the Treaty, Regulations, Directives and Decisions
* the difference between vertical and horizontal direct effect

Answer

When a State joins the European Community all Community law becomes part of its own legal system or to use the international law phrase 'directly applicable'. However, the ECJ has also developed a principle of direct effect whereby a provision of Community law may confer rights upon an individual which are required to be directly applied by national courts at the suit of individual litigants, without the need for domestic implementing legislation. Not all EC law is directly effective. This will depend upon the construction of a particular provision, its language and purpose. although there is often confusion because of the phrase in Article 189 which describes Regulations as directly applicable. This does not mean that only Regulations are capable of direct effect. Many categories of EC law are capable of direct effect as long as they satisfy the test established by the ECJ. This began with the case of *Van Gend en Loos*, which concerned a preliminary reference made by a Dutch court about Article 12 EC obliging Member States to refrain from setting new customs duties. The view of the Dutch government and other Member States was that this was a matter which did not allow an individual to bring an action enforcing rights, but should rather be left to an enforcement action under Article 169 or Article 170 EC.

The European Court of Justice set out the basic requirements for direct effect to be identified when it said in *Van Gend* that 'Article 12 EC sets out a clear and unconditional prohibition, which is not a duty to act but a duty not to act. This duty is imposed without any power in the Member States to subordinate its application to a positive act of internal law. The prohibition is perfectly suited by its nature to produce direct effects in the legal relations between the Member States and their citizens'. However, the court has not restricted direct effect to prohibitions. In *Alfons Lüttickes* case (1966), which concerned Article 95(1) EC, it was established by the European Court of Justice that a positive obligation to repeal or amend discriminatory provisions was directly effective.

Subsequent to this case many Articles of the Treaty have been declared to have direct effect, thus giving the citizen the ability to claim and enforce a right under the Treaty which the government of the Member State concerned has failed to provide. A good example of this development is *Defrenne v Sabena (No 2)*. This case involved a claim made by Madame Defrenne for equal pay with male stewards. She based her claim upon Article 119 EC. Whereas Van Gend was seeking to enforce a right against the Dutch State, Defrenne was seeking to enforce a right against her employer, Sabena airlines. This was an important point because before it was thought that direct effect was limited to relationships with State bodies, ie vertical effect. The judgment in *Defrenne* said that the direct effect of Article 119 extends to all agreements which are intended to regulate paid labour collectively, as well as to contracts between individuals. Thus many treaty provisions have now been successfully invoked vertically and horizontally. The fact of their being addressed to States has been no bar to their horizontal effect. It was more surprising for Member States when the ECJ took a similar line with Directives. Under Article 189 EC 'a Directive is binding, as to the result to be achieved, upon each Member State to which it is addressed, but shall leave to the national authorities the choice of form and methods'. They are not described as 'directly applicable' as are Regulations. This the Member States argued was an indication that they should not produce direct effects. In addition, they required further action by the Member State and thus could not meet the test for direct effect indicated in *Van Gend*. However, in *Grad* the ECJ ruled that a Directive and a Decision could be directly effective. The Directive, in this case on VAT, specified a limit for its implementation, as is common with all Directives. These Directives, addressed to Member States, impose an obligation to achieve the required result. As the ECJ said in *Becker*, another case involving VAT, 'wherever the provisions of a Directive appear ... to be unconditional and sufficiently precise, those provisions may, in the absence of implementing measures adopted within the prescribed period, be relied upon as against any national provision which is incompatible with the Directive or in so far as the provisions define rights which individuals are able to assert against the State'.

If the time limit given for the implementation of the Directive has not expired it can not have direct effect, as was stated in *Ratti*. In this case Ratti was an Italian who ran a firm selling both solvents and varnishes in Italy. Two Directives had been adopted covering the packaging and labelling of these products. Ratti complied with these Directives but they had not been implemented in Italy, with the result that he was prosecuted for failure to comply with the provisions of the Italian law. At the relevant time, the deadline for the implementation of one of the Directives had expired but that for the second had not. On a 177 reference the European Court of Justice held that the Directive for which the time for implementation had expired was directly effective, but the other was not. This gave Ratti a defence to the charges relating to the packaging and labelling of the solvents but not for those concerning the varnishes. It must be remembered that in all cases when an individual seeking to enforce direct effect, the test must be satisfied.

Even if the Member State has introduced the required legislative act, it may be that what they have done is defective. In this type of situation the Directive may still be directly effective as was held in *Verbond van Nederlandse Ondernemingen (VNO)* case. However, unlike Articles of the Treaty, Directives cannot have vertical effects. They can not have direct effect as against another individual or company. This type of horizontal direct effect is felt to be contrary to the principles of equality. This was stated in *Marshall v Southampton and South West Hampshire Area Health Authority*, where Marshall was said to be employed by a 'public' body in the form of the Health Authority and thus able to enforce the direct effect of the Equal Treatment Directive 76/207. However, the ECJ has put an obligation on the courts of Member States in *von Colson* to 'take all appropriate measures to ensure fulfilment of a Directive'. Under the *von Colson* principle the Court of Member States should interpret national law as to ensure that the objectives of the Directive are achieved. In *Lister v Forth Dry Docks* the House of Lords took this line by interpreting the UK domestic Regulation on safeguarding employees whose employer's business was transferred on the basis that it had been introduced for the purpose of complying with an EC Directive. This has obviously greatly extended the possibility for an individual to obtain the benefits of the direct effect of a Directive even though the State or any emanation of the State are not the defendants to the action. As in other circumstances where the European Court of Justice has developed the scope of its interpretation, there is one important limitation to the *von Colson* principle. This is in relation to criminal proceedings, as in *Kolpinghuis Nijmegen*, where the Dutch authorities sought to prosecute Kolpinghuis for breach of a water purity Directive which had not been implemented in the Netherlands. The European Court of Justice held that when interpreting national law to comply with Community law, regard must be had to the general principles of the Community, notably that of legal certainty and non-retroactivity.

In addition to Regulations and Directives the other source of law specified in Article 189 EC is Decisions which are legally binding on the person to whom they are addressed. The court stated that these can have direct effect in the *Grad* case. With regard to international agreements the ECJ has not taken a consistent approach. Some like the GATT treaty in *International Fruit Co* were held to be not directly effective. Whereas in others such as *Bresciani* the Yaounde Convention under the ACP policy of the EC were. It would appear that each agreement must be considered by the ECJ on its own merits.

The test for direct effect requires three criteria to be passed by the provision concerned. The provision must be sufficiently clear and precise; it must be unconditional and leave no room for the exercise of discretion in implementation by the Member State or Community institution. Each criteria is given a broad interpretation by the ECJ, so that some provisions which are not particularly clear or precise have been found to produce direct effects. The interpretation skills of the ECJ can always be used to clarify the meaning of the provision. It is also important to note that if the provision has not yet been implemented by the Member State it will not have direct effect. Obviously you cannot enforce an obligation until the time has expired for that obligation to have been fulfilled. However, the development of the doctrine of direct effect has been an important one for the Community but more importantly for the individual.

Question 11

'Directives are addressed to the governments of Member States and therefore cannot give rights to individuals of Member States.'

Discuss.

Answer plan

Although there are general question on direct effect, like the previous question, a topic which has dominated in the last few years is that concerning the direct effect of Directives. Although problem questions are not asked specifically on this topic it does lead itself to being included in particular situations. For example where an individual is seeking to enforce a right based upon a Directive which has not been incorporated in national law. However, it is essay questions like this one, which allow for a discussion of the diverse points arising from the development of the principle of direct effect as applied to Directives which are quite common. The specific areas which need to be discussed are:

- the doctrine of direct effect generally based on *Van Gend en Loos*

- the application of direct effect to Directives (*Van Duyn v HO*)

- the response to the direct effect of Directives (*Cohn-Bendit* case)

- the *von Colson* principle

- the recent developments, notably *Francovich v Italian State*

Answer

It is true that Directives are clearly defined in Article 18. EC as being addressed to the governments of Member States but it also adds that they are binding as to the result to be achieved. There is an obligation on the Member State to fulfil this requirement, even though they have discretion as to how this is achieved. Thus Directives are a source of European Community law and are part of the new legal order which developed with the establishment of the Community. As the European Court of Justice stated in the important case of *Van Gend en Loos* this new legal order is for the benefit not only of the Member States themselves but also their nationals or citizens. The court went on to say that in this way obligations and rights would be conferred on individuals. How does this apply to Directives? Presumably there is no problem if the government of the Member State receiving the Directive fulfils it by selecting an appropriate domestic mechanism, such as an Act of Parliament or Statutory Instrument, to implement it. In this way any rights associated with the Directive will become available to the individual and recognised and enforced by the national courts. However, what if the government of the Member State fails to implement the Directive or does so in such a way as to deprive the individual of some of the rights associated with the Directive? It is in this context that this statement in the question has been made and which will now be discussed.

The principle of direct effect was established by the European Court of Justice in the case of *Van Gend en Loos* which concerned Article 12 EC. The judgment stated that if certain criteria were satisfied the provisions in question would give rise to rights or obligations on which individuals may rely before their national courts, ie they would be directly effective. The criteria are that the provision must be clear and unambiguous, it must be unconditional and it must take effect without further action by the EC or Member State. Could this principle apply to Directives? There are obvious questions to be asked because by definition Directives do require further action in that Member States have the choice as to the form and methods to be used to implement the Directive. The court did not find this a hindrance.

In the case of *Van Duyn v Home Office* (1974) the European Court of Justice held that provisions of Directives could be directly effective on their own. Before this case questions about Directives were always linked with Articles of the Treaty or Decisions so no clear principle could be established. In the *Grad* case, involving a Decision and the Directive introducing the VAT system, the court held that although Regulations under Article 189 EC were directly applicable it did not follow that other categories of administrative acts could not have similar effects. They added that this was particularly the case where the Community had imposed an obligation on Member States to act in a certain way, *l'effet utile* of such a measure would be weakened if they did not fulfil that obligation. It would mean that the nationals of that State would not be able to involve it before the courts and the national courts would not be able to consider it as part of Community law.

In *Van Duyn* the court had to consider in a 177 reference whether a private individual could involve an Article of a Council Directive dealing with the personal conduct of an individual and the derogation allowed to in Member State on the grounds of public policy. Specifically whether the UK government could refuse leave to enter the UK to a Dutch Scientologist because of the UK government's policy towards the Church of Scientology. The court repeated its judgment in *Grad* only making the specific reference to Directives instead of a Decision, as it had done in that case. Thus Van Duyn could ask the national courts to enforce the individual rights given to her by the Directive.

This judgment did not go without criticism, notably by the French Conseil d'Etat in the *Cohn-Bendit* case (1979). Cohn-Bendit wished to challenge a Decision taken by the French Minister for the Interior expelling him from French territory on the grounds of Directive 64/221. An Article in this Directive requires the person against whom such measures are ordered to be informed of the reasons, eg public security, public policy, etc. In the *Rutili* case of 1975 this Article had been declared by the European Court of Justice to be directly effective. However, even though the Minister had decided not to oppose Cohn-Bendit's entry into France and thus remove the substance of the case, the Conseil d'Etat went on to give judgment. They had not made a 177 reference but gave their clear view that Directives cannot be invoked by the nationals of Member States, ie they cannot have direct effect when challenging an administrative Decision of the State. This was completely contrary to the case-law of the European Court of Justice.

The judgment on *Cohn-Bendit* prompted the European Court to clarify its ruling on the possibility of individuals invoking the provisions of Directives. It considered that if a Member State had not adopted the implementing measures required by a Directive in the prescribed periods, that State should not be able to rely upon its own failure to deprive individuals of seeking to enforce rights before the national courts. This was clearly stated in *Ratti*. However, direct effect as applied to Directives was to have some limitations. Unlike Articles of the Treaty and to a certain extent Regulations, Directives were to be limited to vertical direct effect and not encompass horizontal direct effect. If it was the government which had not fulfilled its obligations arising from the Directive, it should be against the government that rights arising from the Directive should be enforced. In *Becker* (1982) a German credit broker successfully claimed the benefit of a provision of the sixth VAT Directive against the German VAT authorities. However, it was also made clear in this judgment that there was no question of a Directive being invoked to impose obligations on individuals or to have an incidence on mutual relations between individuals, ie horizontal direct effect. The contrast between the UK cases of *Marshall*, who was employed by an area health authority and *Foster* who was employed by a pre-privatised British Gas corporation on one hand with *Duke* employed by GEC Reliance Ltd, a public company clearly show how a right can be enforced by some but not by others under the principle of direct effect of Directives. It would appear, therefore, that unless the individual is able to show that there is some relationship with the State the quotation forming this question is correct.

It is also correct in that every Directive involves a time-scale for implementation. This period, normally two years, is to give the government of the Member State time to formulate and pass the appropriate domestic measure. Until this period has elapsed the Directive cannot, as was confirmed in *Ratti*, have direct effect.

In *Emmott v Minister for Social Welfare*, Mrs Emmott brought an action against the Irish Minister for Social Welfare on the basis that she received less benefit than a man would have done in equivalent circumstances. Under a Directive issued in 1979 all discrimination on the grounds of sex in matters of social security are prohibited. The Directive should have been implemented by 1984 but was not implemented in Ireland until 1988. Mrs Emmott brought her action in 1987 when another case before the European Court of Justice had led to it declaring that the Directive had direct effect. The verticle relationship between herself and the Irish government satisfied the case law of the court. The Irish government, however, claimed that her action was statute barred because it had not been brought within the three months required by Irish law for judicial review.

Could this national procedural requirement be used to deny Mrs Emmott a remedy? The court held that Directives had a particular nature, imposing an obligation on Member States to adopt within the framework of their national legal systems, all the measures necessary to ensure that the Directive is fully effective. Thus Community law precludes the competent national authorities from relying on national procedural rules relating to time limits to stop an action by one of its citizens seeking to enforce a right that that Member State has failed to transpose into its domestic legal system. The time limit does not run until the date when the national implementing legislation is correctly adopted.

In *Francovich v Italian State* the European Court of Justice extended the impact of the law regarding Directives by stating that 'Community law lays down a principle according to which a Member State is liable to make good damage to individuals caused by a breach of Community law for which it is responsible'. Mr Francovich was owed 6 million lira by his insolvent employers. However, because he was unable to enforce a judgment against them, he brought an action against the Italian government for compensation. Under a Council Directive aimed at protecting employees in the event of the insolvency of their employers, Member States were required to ensure that payment of employees' outstanding claims arising from the employment relationship and relating to pay was guaranteed. Unfortunately the Italian government had not set up any Italian system to act as a guarantor in these circumstances, hence his claim against them. The European Court of Justice held that subject to three conditions, damages are available against the State for failure to implement EC Directives. The conditions specified are that the result required by the Directive includes the conferring of rights for the benefit of individuals; the content of those rights is identifiable by reference to the Directive and lastly there exists a causal link between the breach of the State's obligations and the damage suffered by the person affected.

However, the European Court of Justice has continued to evolve its principles with regard to providing the individual with the possibility of enforcing a right derived from a Directive. In the *von Colson* and *Harz* cases in 1984, the court developed an approach to interpretation based on Article 5 EC which requires Member States to take all appropriate measures to ensure fulfilment of their Community obligation. Under this principle the national courts should interpret national legislation as to ensure that the objectives of the Directive are achieved. This assists those litigants who are unable to satisfy the test for direct effect or who are bringing an action against a private employer rather than the State or an emanation of the State. This method of interpretation has maximised the impact of Directives for individuals. As a further development of the von Colson principle, the court held in the *Marleasing* case (1990), that the principle could be applied even if the necessary national legislation had not been introduced to comply with the Directive. The development of the European Court of Justice approach to Directives conferring rights upon individuals has continued throughout the last twenty years. It has been a true reflection of the comments made by the court in *Van Gend en Loos* and subsequent cases that when establishing the European Community the Member States were creating a new legal order which has given rights to the citizens of the Member States and which must be recognised by their courts. In some circumstances the court has applied the principle of direct effect to achieve this and in others it has extended its approach to interpretation. It is clear that although Directives are addressed to the governments of Member States they do confer rights on those who live within the Community.

Question 12

Do the recent decisions of the English courts assist an individual seeking to enforce a Community right?

Answer plan

This essay question provides an opportunity to trace through recent English judgments the approach taken to direct effect of directives and the interpretation of domestic legislation. You should cover the following points:

• direct effect of directives (*Marshall* case (1986))
• vertical and horizontal effect of directives
• European Communities Act 1972
• *von Colson* case (1984)
• *Marleasing* case (1990)
• *Pickstone v Freemans plc* (1989)
• *Lister v Forth Dry Dock & Engineering Co Ltd* (1990)
• *R v British Coal Corporation (ex p Vardy)* (1993)

Answer

When a Member State joins the Community it undertakes to fulfil all the obligations arising from the treaties and other binding sources of community law. This is achieved by accepting that Community law overrides any conflicting national law (*Simmenthal* (1978)). However, there were problems for the individual who tried to enforce a right arising from Community law not recognised in the national courts. For example, if the conditions associated with identifying direct effect, such as the measure being precise and unconditional, were not satisfied. More importantly she may not be able to use direct effect to enforce the right against another private individual (*Marshall* (1986)). In the circumstances where the government was at fault the European Commission could bring an action before the European Court of Justice under Article 169 EC for failing to fulfil a Community obligation. It would also be open to the government of another Member State to use Article 170 EC. However, both articles lead to the same remedy under Article 171 EC. This is mainly declaratory, although under the Treaty on European Union (TEU) the court can impose a fine but this provides no redress for the individuals affected by the Member States' action.

Articles of the Treaty and regulations have been held by the ECJ to have direct effect in both vertical and horizontal terms (see *Defrenne No 2* (1976)). Thus, in such circumstances the individual can enforce the right against the government or another individual. However, the other main source of Community law, directives, were in a much weaker position, even though such measures are important in creating rights under Community law. The European Court of Justice has sought to redress this imbalance by making directives come within the principle of direct effect. In the *Van Duyn* case (1975) the European Court of Justice relied on the binding effect attributed to a directive under Article 189 EC coupled with the civil law doctrine that a legal measure must be presumed to have an *effet utile* or useful effect. Furthermore, the court thought it was inequitable to allow a Member State to rely on its own failure to implement a directive as a defence (*Ratti* (1979)). This view was strengthened by Article 5 EC which requires a Member State to take all appropriate measures to ensure fulfilment of the obligations arising out of the Treaty or resulting from action taken by the institutions of the Community. In this way it became impossible for the Member State to evade an obligation imposed by a directive.

However, the court limited the impact of this extension of the principle of direct effect to directives by limiting it to vertical relationships. Thus, the individual who was employed by the State or an emanation of the State (see *Marshall* (1986) and *Foster v British Gas* (1990)) could enforce a right arising from Community law in a national court and obtain the appropriate remedy. Those who could not prove such a relationship with the government were unable to do either. *Duke v GEC Reliance* (1988) provides a good example of the division the application of direct effect of directives between vertical and horizontal brought about. Unlike Mrs Marshall or Mrs Foster, Mrs Duke was unable to enforce her rights under the equality directives.

There is a potential conflict between the doctrine of parliamentary sovereignty in UK law and the principle that Community law takes priority over inconsistent national laws. The European Communities Act 1972 attempts to deal with this problem by making all provisions of Community law which are directly effective part of English law. Lord Denning in *Macarthys Ltd v Smith* (1980) suggested that English courts would give effect to a directly effective provision of Community law, notwithstanding any subsequent enactment by Parliament unless Parliament had made it clear that it intended to override any inconsistent provisions of Community law. Lord Diplock in *Garland v BREL* (1982) stated that the words of a statute passed after the adoption of a Community measure dealing with the same subject were to be interpreted, if they were reasonably capable of bearing such a meaning, as being intended to carry out the UK's obligations under the Community measure and not as being inconsistent with it.

Mrs Duke (1988) maintained that the Equal Treatment Directive, as interpreted in *Marshall*, required Member States to prohibit discrimination in relation to retirement ages and that s 6(4) of the Sex Discrimination Act had to be interpreted in a way consistent with that requirement. Lord Templeman, giving the main judgment in the House of Lords, rejected this argument. He held that although the Equal treatment Directive had been adopted subsequent to the 1975 Act, s 2(4) of the European Communities Act did not require the courts to give it priority over the 1975 Act in Mrs Duke's case because the Directive was not directly effective as between her and her former employers. Section 2(4) only required the court to construe an Act of Parliament in accordance with directly effective provisions of Community law. This judgment has been criticised as taking too narrow a view of the European Communities Act. However, in *Pickstone* (1989) Lord Templeman made the point in his judgment that the Sex Discrimination Act had not been passed to give effect to the directive. But in *Pickstone* the 1983 Regulations had been introduced to meet the obligations of the directive and the rulings of the court against the UK government.

The division between vertical and horizontal direct effect of directives was circumvented to a certain extent by the judgment in the *von Colson* case (1984). This required national courts to construe national law to give effect to the provisions of a directive. In this way the provisions entered into domestic law and could be relied upon before national courts. The provisions of the directive become an aid to construction of the national law and in this way are enforced by the national court. The *Marleasing* judgment (1992) extended this principle by requiring a national court to construe national law in the light of the wording and purpose of any relevant Community directive, whether the national law originated before or after the adoption of the directive.

This approach has been taken up by the UK courts. In *Pickstone v Freemans plc* (1989) the House of Lords said that English courts must adopt this interpretation even if to do so would involve departing from the normal canons of construction. This could amount to reading certain words into the relevant national legislation in order to achieve a result compatible with Community law. The Court of Appeal encountered difficulties in the appeal by Mrs Webb against her dismissal by her employer when she became pregnant (*Webb v EMO Air Cargo (UK) Ltd* (1992)). The national legislation the Court of Appeal had to interpret was the Sex Discrimination Act 1975. Judgments of the European Court of Justice on the Equal Treatment Directive appeared to indicate that dismissal on the grounds of pregnancy was automatically contrary to the Directive. However, the Court of Appeal held that the Sex Discrimination Act did not automatically forbid the dismissal of a woman on the grounds of pregnancy and to give it that meaning would be to distort rather than construe English law. On the subsequent appeal to the House of Lords it was indicated that national law had to be open to an interpretation consistent with the Directive if the duty of construction were to apply. Following a further reference to the European Court of Justice, it was stated that Mrs Webb's dismissal could not be justified on the grounds of pregnancy (1994).

The House of Lords cited Pickstone with approval in *Lister v Forth Dry Dock & Engineering Co Ltd* (1990) where a claim had been made against a private party. The judgment suggests that where legislation has been introduced specifically in order to complement an EC Directive, UK courts must interpret domestic law to comply with the Directive. In some circumstances this may require supplying the necessary words by implication in order to achieve a result compatible with EC law. In the *Lister* case, no reference was made to the fact that the Directive in question was not directly effective.

However, there is some inconsistency in approach. The judgment in *R v British Coal Corporation (ex p Vardy)* (1993) indicated a reluctance to apply the *Marleasing* principle. In this case Glidewell J found it impossible to follow the House of Lords' approach in *Lister* since the wording of the statute, the Trade Union and Labour Relations Act 1992, was clearly at odds with the Directive. In such circumstances the wording of the statute approved by Parliament was to be followed. In these circumstances an action by the European Commission under Article 169 EC would seem to be the only possibility.

Chapter 4

Judicial Remedies and Review (1): Direct Actions

Introduction

As part of its jurisdiction the European Court of Justice can hear cases brought before it by individuals, Community institutions or governments of Member States. These actions must be brought under specific Articles of the Treaty and are heard solely by the court, hence the term direct actions as compared with indirect actions or preliminary references made under Article 177 EC. These are covered in the next chapter. This area of Community law lends itself to both problem and essay-type questions, as the 'popular' areas are suitable for both question formats.

Checklist

Students should have a general knowledge of how the European Court operates and in particular should be familiar with the following areas:

- Enforcement actions brought by the European Commission under Article 169 EC, including both the formal and informal stages of the procedure

- Enforcement actions brought by Member States under Article 170 EC

- The Remedy available by Article 171 EC to actions under Articles 169 and 170 EC

- The action for annulment under Article 173 EC, especially the question of *locus standi* and grounds for annulment

- The possible action under Article 175 EC and its relationship with Article 173 EC

- The remedies provided for Articles 173 and 175 EC

- The plea of illegality – Article 184 EC

Question 13

What enforcement actions are available against a Member State in breach of its obligations? Are such actions effective?

Answer plan

This question typifies those set on this topic. It should be noted that it is in two parts, both of which must be answered in the essay that follows if good marks are to be gained. It is not sufficient to merely describe the possible actions, as some evaluation must also be included. The main points to be raised are:

- direct actions under Articles 169 and 170 EC
- the remedies available under Article 171 EC
- the role of the Commission under Article 169 EC
- the possible action available in a Member State

Answer

The EC Treaty allows two types of direct enforcement actions under Articles 169 and 170. The most usual action taken against a Member State is by the European Commission under Article 169 EC. Although Member States have a possible action under Article 170 EC, which allows them to take another Member State before the ECJ, as in *France v UK (Re Fishing Net Mesh Sizes)* (1978), this is rarely used. It is therefore Article 169 which is the predominant enforcement action used against Member States who are in breach of their obligations, although it is possible for action to be taken in the national courts of the Member State in certain circumstances.

It is appropriate that Article 169 EC should give the Commission power to bring an action against a Member State in breach of its obligations as they have a duty to make sure that Community law is applied. This duty is found in Article 155 EC which lays down the general duties of the Commission. The instigation of the Article 169 procedure may be due to an act or omission, such as national legislation contrary to Community law or a failure to implement Community law. Therefore a Member

States failure under the Treaty can be sufficient grounds, just as an action contrary to Community law. However, the procedure under Article 169 is lengthy and does not provide a speedy process for getting the breach rectified. Whether it is a failure of a positive or negative act, the consequence of a successful action under 169 is for a declaration by the court under Article 171 EC requiring the Member State to take action to fulfil its obligations.

The first stage of the 169 procedure is often described as the administrative stage. The European Court of Justice has stated that the purpose of this stage is to allow the Member State either to comply with its obligations under Community law or to put forward an effective defence to the complaints made by the Commission. Initially acting on a complaint, perhaps from a trade association, MEP or another government, the Director-General responsible for that sector of Community policy will write to the Member State concerned. These informal communications with Member State will attempt to ascertain the facts and if possible reach a settlement.

They are conducted with discretion so as to avoid any embarrassment that might result for the Member State. The Commission, having fully investigated the possible breach, will consider whether there is sufficient evidence to justify the commencement of formal proceedings. If the Commission has taken the view that a Member State is in breach of its obligations the Commission will write to the Member State under its powers in Article 169, indicating the breach and inviting the Member State's observations. The Member State then responds to this letter with its own view, which is generally that they are not in breach of this particular obligation. If a settlement acceptable to the Commission is not possible, this administrative stage of Article 169 will end with the Commission issuing a reasoned Opinion. This Opinion is very important as it provides the Member State with a final opportunity to remedy its failure and to this end informs them of what, in the Commission's view, needs to be done to accomplish this. If the Commission decides to go on to the judicial stage of the 169 procedure, the Opinion defines the matters which the court will be requested to adjudicate on.

It could be argued that the matter could end before the judicial stage, especially as the number of contraventions of Community law is large. To take all the matters further under the procedure would require a large staff. There is also the fact that many Member State governments resent the initiation of the formal enforcement procedure. Does the Commission have to take the matter further? Some writers argue that the Commission has a discretion as to whether it takes further action. However, this ignores the duty given to the Commission under Article 155 to ensure that Community law is applied. This duty requires the Commission to take the most appropriate action in the circumstances to ensure compliance with Community law. In the Euratom case of *Commission v France* (1971), Advocate-General Roemer indicated that in some circumstances the Commission might be justified in not initiating the enforcement procedure. These included where an amicable settlement may be achieved if formal proceedings were delayed or where a major domestic political crisis could be aggravated of proceedings were commenced concerning matters of secondary importance.

An attempt is made to reach a satisfactory settlement without resorting to litigation and in the great majority of cases this has proved possible. If this is not possible, an action by the Commission can be brought before the European Court. The aim of the action is to obtain a declaration that the Member State has failed to fulfil its obligation. The Member State will be bound under Article 171 to take the necessary measures to comply with the judgment. At present the only sanction available is for the Commission to institute a further 169 action against the Member State if it does not comply. A common form of infringement by Member States has been the adoption of measures that restrict the free movement of goods within the Community, contrary to Article 30 EC. Such measures are against one of the fundamental principles of the Community and are often disguised under legitimate derogations allowed by Article 36 EC. Action taken by the Commission in these circumstances is seeking effective rather than purely formal compliance with the Treaty obligations, ie with the spirit rather than just with the letter. For example in the *Turkey* case (1982) the UK government had imposed a ban on the importation of poultry not vaccinated against Newcastle disease. Although ostensibly to protect animal health, which is possible under Article 36, its affect was to protect the British poultry industry against imports, notably from France. Although the court held that such restrictions were contrary to the UK's obligations under the Treaty, the measure did give the British poultry industry some limited protection before the UK government complied with the Article 171 order. There are many such examples involving all Member States where, perhaps for domestic political reasons, national measures have been adopted only to be repealed when judgment has been given by the court against them. In this sense the 169 action is ultimately effective but its does take time. The Maastricht Treaty makes a number of important proposed amendments to the Treaty of Rome, including one to Article 171 in relation to an action brought under 169. This would allow the court to impose a lump sum or penalty payment on any Member State failing to fulfil its obligations, based upon a sum specified by the Commission when it brings the matter before the court.

The action available to a Member State under Article 170 is very similar to that used by the Commission under 169. However, the Member State must inform the Commission, who are given three months to investigate the matter and deliver a reasoned Opinion. Here the Commission are acting more as an umpire and conciliator than an accuser. After the reasoned Opinion has been given by the Commission or if three months has elapsed without them doing so, the complainant Member State can bring the matter before the court. The burden of proof is on the complainant Member State, with the Commission intervening in support of one side or the other. This procedure is very unpopular with the Member States who generally leave such enforcement actions to the Commission, unless there is a strong political or other reasons for them to do so.

In the early years the Commission did not pursue defaulting Member States with vigour. However, in 1977 the Jenkins Commission decided that in future more rigorous use would be made of the 169 procedure. Nevertheless the volume of work places a heavy burden upon the staff of the Commission, which now encourages complainants to seek remedies in the national courts where appropriate. In the landmark case of *Van Gend en Loos* (1963), the court had recognised that individuals should be able to protect their rights themselves in addition to relying on the Commission. This has become much easier with the development of the principle of direct effect. For example in *Schoenenberg* (1978) and *Meijer* (1979), individuals were able to claim that national legislation was contrary to obligations imposed by the Treaty in the Member State concerned. This was achieved by the courts concerned using the preliminary reference procedure provided by Article 177 EC. This happened at the same time as the Commission was taking action against the Member State under the 169 procedure. However, while the 169 procedure has its value in bringing the Member State into line for the future, action in the national courts coupled with a 177 reference does concentrate the mind of the Member State involved! The developments of the law relating to the award of damages has given new emphasis to the possibility of using the national courts for enforcement purposes. In *Francovich v Italian State* the European Court stated that 'Community law lays down a principle according to which a Member State is liable to make good damage to individuals caused by a breach of Community law for which it is responsible'.

It can be seen that although the Treaty only specifies enforcement action under Articles 169 and 170 these are not the only possibilities. Action under 169 by the Commission does achieve the desired result, but its main draw back is the time it takes to achieve this. Although it is possible to obtain interim measures under Article 186 where proceedings are being taken under 169 against a Member State. For example both the UK government in relation to a temporary subsidy to pig farmers and the Irish government over its fisheries conservation measures, were brought before the court in 1977 and appropriate orders made to stop their infringements immediately. However, the most effective actions are those indirect actions brought in the courts of the Member State concerned.

Question 14

NOALC plc is one of six manufacturers in the EC of a new type of wine substitute made from parsnips. Doddy Drinks was so impressed with the product that it installed new machinery at a cost of £1.2m into its factory to handle the product range it intended to introduce under license from NOALC plc.

Last month the Council was concerned that there would be adverse effects on the Communities grape industry and associated wine producers. A Regulation was therefore adopted imposing a limit on the production of the wine from parsnips. An appendix to the Regulation mentions the six manufacturers by name and fixed their output quota at low levels.

The result is that NOALC can not supply Doddy Drinks in the quantities required to make their planned range economically viable. Given that a great deal of money will be lost if this Regulation is applied, NOALC seeks your advice.

Answer plan

This problem question is the kind of practical scenario question often set on this topic. It requires you to advise NOALC, not merely describe all you know about the topic! This topic is often found difficult by students, but one way of solving this is to break the topic down into a number of small questions, pose them and then answer them as if you were advising someone in front of you. The main points to be raised for NOALC are:

- the procedure under Article 173 (2), including the time-limit
- is the measure a 'true' Regulation - what is a 'true' Regulation?
- the court's interpretation of 'direct and individual concern'
- possible action in the national courts if *locus standi* for Article 173(2) is not accepted by the European Court
- possible action for damages under Articles 178 and 215(2) EC

Answer

If the Regulation is applied NOALC will make a substantial loss on its investment. NOALC should therefore consider the possibility of challenging the Regulation under Article 173 EC. If the challenge is successful the remedy provided by this action will be annulment of the Regulation, thus allowing NOALC to proceed with its business plan. There may also be the possibility of a claim for damages against the Council under Articles 178 and 215 (2) EC. However, it is very rare that a successful action can be brought under 173 by non-privileged applicants like NOALC. Careful consideration must be given, therefore, to the wording of Article 173 and the interpretation given by the ECJ.

Under Article 173(2) any legal person may bring an action against a Decisions addressed to that person or against a Decisions which, although in the form of a Regulation or a Decisions addressed to another person, is of direct and individual concern to the former. Thus, although NOALC wishes to challenge a Regulation they are not barred from doing so provided they can show that it is not a true Regulation but a 'bundle of Decisions'. When approaching this question the ECJ is not restricted by the title of the Community measure. Merely because it is called a Regulation is not conclusive. In *Calpak* (1980) it was pointed out that this is to prevent Community institutions choosing to issue a Decisions in the form of a Regulation so as to deny the opportunity to an individual to challenge the measure. In *Scholten Honig v Council & Commission* the ECJ said: 'in examining this question (re Regulation) the court cannot restrict itself to considering the official title of the measure, but must first take into account its object and context'.

A starting point is the definitions given to various Community measures in Article 189 EC, where Regulations are described as the main legislative instrument of the Community. A Regulation under Article 189 should apply to objectively determined situations and produce legal effects with regard to categories of persons regarded generally and in the abstract. It should have a 'normative' character. As long as the Regulation maintains these objective characteristics, it will still be considered a Regulation even though the number or even identity of the persons to whom it applies can be ascertained. The court insisted in *Scholten-Honig* that an individual cannot challenge a true Regulation.

It is not always easy to clearly state that a particular Community measure is a true Regulation, but in the *Fruit & Vegetable* case (1962) the court said '... a measure which is applicable to objectively determined situations and which involves immediate legal consequences in all Member States for persons viewed in a general and abstract manner cannot be considered as constituting a Decisions, unless it can be proved that it is of individual concern to certain persons within the meaning of 173(2). There have been relatively few cases where the applicants have satisfied the court on this point. One which may support NOALC is *CAM SA v Commission* (1975) where a fixed number of traders were held to be individually concerned because of a factual situation which differentiated them from all other persons and distinguished them individually. Here there was a fixed and known number of cereal traders because the Regulation affected those who had already applied for export licences. This factual situation differentiated them from all other persons and distinguished them individually from others affected by the Regulation. Thus the action was admissible since he was individually concerned because the applicant was one of a fixed and identifiable category.

NOALC may only challenge a Regulation if the 'Regulation' is really a Decisions. Decisions are characterised by the limited number of persons to whom they are addressed. In order to determine whether or not a measure constitutes a Decisions one must enquire whether that measure concerns specific persons. In the NOALC case the number of producers are limited and in fact named in an appendix to the Regulation. They can be said to be directly concerned in that the Regulation leaves the Member State no discretion in implementation, but are they individually concerned as is required by 173(2)? A person can only claim to be individually concerned if the Decisions being challenged affects them by reason of certain attributes which are peculiar to them or by reason of circumstances in which they are differentiated from all other persons and by virtue of these factors distinguishes them individually just as in the case of the person addressed. It will not be sufficient for NOALC to prove that its business interest will be adversely affected. In the cases where it has been successfully pleaded, such as the *Töpfer* case 1965, the Decisions being challenged referred to a fixed list of importers which could not be amended. In NOALC's case there is not this fixed list, although the companies are named in the Regulation. Could it be argued that anyone could enter this business activity, as it was with *Plaumann* clementines? In *Zuckerfabrik Watenstedt* (1980) a producer of raw beet sugar asked for an Article of a Regulation to be declared void with no success. The court said that a Regulation does not lose its characteristics as a Regulation simply because it may be possible to identify the persons to which it applies, as long as it fulfils the objectivity of a Regulation mentioned above.

However, in the *Japanese Ball-Bearing* cases four major Japanese producers of ball-bearings were held entitled to challenge a Regulation. Although the measure was of general application some of the Articles specifically referred to the applicants. Even a 'true' Regulation can be of individual concern to some individuals if it is referable expressly to their particular situation, either alone or as a member of a known or closed class, for example the Japanese manufacturers. The fact that NOALC are listed makes them arguably directly and individually concerned, as there is a close and specific relationship between NOALC and the measure being challenged. However, the European Court of Justice has not always been consistent on this point. The court has laid more emphasis on the requirement of individual concern. If the court can be satisfied on this, the requirement of direct concern is often assumed.

Despite statements by the court in *Plaumann* that the provision of 173 should not be interpreted strictly, it has adopted a very restrictive approach towards individuals seeking to challenge acts other than Decisions addressed to them. NOALC must fulfil all the criteria if the action is to be admissible. As they cannot challenge a Regulation they must prove that it is a Decisions which is of direct and individual concern to them.

All this advice has centred on the question of *locus standi* as this is the major hurdle for any applicant in NOALC's situation. It must be remembered that the proceedings under Article 173 must be instituted within two months from the date of publication of the Regulation. Having obtained the court's agreement that the action is admissible, NOALC has to prove one of the grounds for annulment specified in Article 173(1). There are four such grounds covering lack of competence, infringement of an essential procedural requirement, infringement of the Treaties or of any rule of law relating to their application and finally misuse of powers. It is not clear from the problem the particular grounds that NOALC may plead but the most general one is infringement of the Treaties or of any rule of law relating to their application. If successful the remedy under Article 174 is for the Regulation to be declared void or *erga omnes*. It is possible to challenge the validity of a Regulation in the national courts of a Member State. This would mean that NOALC would have to be a party to an action and the court hearing the case would have to make a reference under Article 177 (1)(b) concerning the validity of the Regulation. As NOALC are likely to suffer financially because of the Regulation, they may bring an action for damages for 'normative injustice' where the Regulation constitutes a sufficiently flagrant breach of a superior rule of law protecting individuals under Article 215(2). In the *Schoppenstedt* case (1971) the court held that the plaintiff company could sue the Council for damages on the basis of an allegedly illegal Regulation even though as a 'natural or legal person' they would have no *locus standi* to seek its annulment under Article 173 (2). The advantage of an action under Article 215 (2) is that it is not restricted to the short time-limit which applies to challenges under Article 173. The disadvantage is that the court has adopted a very restrictive approach towards the Community liability in tort.

Question 15

What is meant by the 'unity principle'? Has its development made it easier to obtain a remedy for failure to act in breach of EC law?

Answer plan

This is an essay question associated with judicial review under Article 175 EC. This generally referred to as 'failure to act'. It is possible to have problem questions arising from this topic or in some complex problems it is associated with Article 173 EC. The reason for this is that in many ways, notably with regard to *locus standi*, the court treats them in the same way, as a kind of mirror image. In this question it is important to deal with:

- possible action associated with Article 175 EC
- the requirements of the Article
- the remedies available under Article 175 EC
- the approach of the court to the Unity principle itself and why it was instituted

Answer

In certain circumstances it is possible to seek judicial review of acts of the Council or the Commission before the European Court of Justice. The action may be brought under Article 173 EC if the remedy sought is a declaration that the act of the Council or Commission is void. If, however, it is a failure to act that is requested to be reviewed the action is brought under Article 175 EC. In either case the appropriate remedy is provided by Article 176 EC. Both Articles 173 EC and 175 EC make special provision for 'privileged applicants', namely the Member States, the Council or Commission, although Article 175 EC is wider in that it merely refers to 'other institutions' of the Community in this context. This category would include the European Parliament which because it is not specifically mentioned in Article 173 has been given only limited *locus standi* by the European Court. This will be changed by the Maastricht Treaty which amends Article 173 to reflect the growing importance of democratic control within the Community and includes the Parliament as a privileged applicant. There is generally no problem for those within this category bringing an action. However, both Article also make provision for natural or legal persons or non-privileged applicants under Articles 173(2) and 175(3). The main stumbling block to such actions is the need to satisfy the court with regard to the *locus standi* of the applicant. It is here that the 'unity principle' has been developed.

There are obvious similarities between these two Articles not only with regard to the types of applicant but also the time period of two months which is used in both. These similarities between Articles 173 and 175 indicate that the original authors of the Treaty saw the relationship between proceedings to quash a legal act and proceedings to require action to be taken by the Council or Commission to be two aspects of the same legal remedy. This was reinforced by the European Court of Justice's judgment in *Chevalley v Commission* (1970). Chevalley was the owner of agricultural land in Italy. In December 1969 the Italian Senate approved a draft law on the rents for agricultural lands which would lead to discrepancies between the Member States. Chevalley was of the opinion that the European Commission should act under its powers in the Treaty to organise consultations with the Member States. He officially requested the Commission to do this in a letter in December 1969. In February 1970 the President of the Commission informed Chevalley's lawyer that the Commission was not obliged in this case to adopt any measure whatsoever with regard to his request. In April 1970 Chevalley made an application to the court under Article 175 EC. However, he also made an application under Article 173 EC in June 1970 with regard to the Commission's letter in February. This reflected the uncertainty he said he had in deciding which was the more appropriate action. There were clearly problems with both these actions in that the Commission had 'defined its position', as required by 175, in February and the letter was not a Decisions within Article 173. However, the point made by the court, before declaring both actions inadmissible, was that 'the concept of a measure capable of giving rise to an action' is identical in Articles 173 and 175, as both provisions merely prescribe one and the same method of recourse'. It is this principle, that the two Articles are concerned with essentially the same remedy, which is referred to as the unity principle. It has important practical consequences as it implies that the conditions and limitations applicable to the remedy should be the same under the two procedures. There is the obvious distinction that one is concerned with a Commission (173) and the other with an Omission (175). However, one would expect under this principle that the applicant would have the same rights in Article 175 proceedings as in those brought under Article 173. Has this principle worked in the favour of the applicant who is seeking a remedy for failure to act in breach of EC law?

Whereas Article 173 clearly identifies the acts which can be challenged, Article 175 offers a potentially wider scope, at least for privileged applicants. Under Article 173 the legality of acts other than recommendations and Opinions can be challenged by privileged applicants.

This has been widely interpreted by the court, beyond those categories in Article 189, to include all measures taken by the Council or Commission which have legal effect. For non-privileged applicants wishing to bring an action under Article 173 EC they must show that the act they are challenging is either a Decisions addressed to them or a Decisions addressed to another person or a Decisions which although in the form of a Regulation is of direct and individual concern to them. This has been very restrictively interpreted by the court to the extent that it is very difficult for an applicant to show *locus standi* under 173(2) unless the act is a Decisions addressed to them. Article 175(1) EC refers simply to 'act'. Given a wide interpretation this could mean that a privileged applicant could challenge a failure to adopt any 'act' in 175 proceedings. Even for non-privileged applicants, Article 175(3) refers to any act other than in recommendation or Opinion. This would merely exclude those types of legislative act under Article 189 EC which was not legally binding. This would appear to be much wider for non-privileged applicants under 175 than is available under 173. Why is it necessary to insert this limitation for non-privileged applicants except to show that no limitation exists for privileged applicants? This wider interpretation has not been accepted by the European Court of Justice. On the basis of the unity principle only an omission to adopt a reviewable act, ie an act having legal effects, can be challenged. This is a very narrow view and has operated against would be applicants. If the Council or Commission have been called upon to act it may, as the Commission did in *Chevalley*, refuse in clear and unequivocal terms the request. Having done this, the Council or the Commission would have 'defined its position' thus barring any proceedings under Article 175 EC. This refusal would not constitute a reviewable act in itself since such a negative act is reviewable only if the act which the defendant refuses to adopt would itself be reviewable. Consequently an express refusal would always constitute a bar to proceedings for a remedy for failure to adopt a non-reviewable act. This happened in the first *Lütticke* case (1966).

However, if Article 175(3) is interpreted literally on the basis of Article 189 all that would be available for non-privileged applicants would be Regulations, Directives and Decisions. However, Regulations are normative in character and affect categories of persons viewed abstractly and in their entirety. They are not addressed to individuals unless it could be argued that they are not true Regulations but bundles of Decisions as can be argued under Article 173. Unfortunately here the argument would be in the abstract because the measure would not exist, hence the Article 175 action. Therefore an individual cannot claim that the Council or the Commission should have addressed to them a Regulation. In *Nordgetreide v Commission* (1972), the applicant had requested that the Commission amend a Regulation dealing with monetary compensatory amounts. the court held that since the measure to be amended was a Regulation, the amending measure would also be a legislative or normative act. Private individuals, such as Nordgetreide do not have the capacity under Article 173 to challenge such normative acts and he would not be able to show that the amending act would be of direct and individual concern as required by Article 173(2). As he would not have the *locus standi* to challenge the act requested, he likewise had no *locus standi* to challenge the negative Decisions refusing it. His action was therefore inadmissible for both 173 and 175. In a more recent case brought by Lord Bethel in 1982, where he was calling upon the Commission to take action against airlines operating against the interests of passengers, the court came to a similar conclusion.

A similar argument would be raised about Directives, which are addressed to Member States and not individuals. All that is left are Decisions. It may be that an individual is bringing the action under Article 175 because the Council or Commission has failed to address to that individual a Decisions. In this case there should not be a problem with *locus standi*. However, if the action is based upon the failure to address the Decisions to another individual, it will be necessary under the unity principle to satisfy the requirement of direct and individual concern to the applicant specified in Article 173. In the *Eridania* case, the applicant wanted the annulment of certain Decisions addressed to other sugar refineries, but was unsuccessful because they were not 'directly and individually concerned' by these. When the Commission failed to rescind the Decisions an action was brought under Article 175. The court declared this action inadmissible because they were concerned than an unsuccessful applicant under Article 173 would seek to use Article 175 to achieve the same remedy.

By applying the tight requirements of Article 173(2) to actions brought under 175(3), the European Court of Justice has not made it easier for non-privileged applicants to obtain a remedy for failure to act. This is perhaps reflected in the almost non-existent case law for Article 175.

However, although the unity principle has had this effect, there are alternatives for individuals to use but these do not offer the potential Article 175 had before this unity principle was evolved. As far as privileged applicants are concerned it has had no impact on them seeking a remedy under Article 175.

Question 16

Critically discuss the development of State liability in damages in the national court for violation of Community law.

Answer plan

This essay question is looking at the availability of damages in actions before a national court. This is in contrast to Article 215(2) EC which is more restricted. The main thrust of any answer is the

Francovich case (1992) and the implications of the case in future proceedings before national courts. At present these are unclear but a discussion of the development of State liability is required.

Answer

The European Court of Justice has now recognised in the *Francovich* case (1992) that individuals may have a right to damages in the national court against the national authorities where they have suffered loss as a result of a non-implementation by a Member State of a directive. The *Francovich* case involved Directive 80/987 which provided for the approximation of the laws of the Member States relating to the protection of employees in the event of the insolvency of their employer. The Italian government had not implemented the Directive with the result that when Francovich's employer became insolvent the employees had substantial arrears of salary.

Consequently, the parties brought an action against the Italian State for failing to fulfil the obligations incumbent on it under Directive 80/987. The European Court, responding to an Article 177 EC reference, developed its analysis of direct effect of directives from *Costa v ENEL* (1964) to deal with the question of damages. It identified three criteria which would have to be satisfied. The court began by restating the criteria for the application of direct effect. These are that the provision must be clear and unambiguous, it must be unconditional and finally its operation must not be dependent on further action being taken by Community or national institutions. In applying these criteria to the facts of the *Francovich* case, the provisions of the directive were insufficiently precise and were not unconditional and so did not have direct effect. Thus Francovich and the other employees involved could not rely on the directive as against the Italian government in order to recover their lost wages.

In the *Francovich* case the ECJ considered the question of the circumstances in which a Member State could be held liable in damages for its violation of Community law. Until this case the approach taken by the court had been to state that it was national law to determine in which courts an action could be brought and what procedural rules should govern the action. On this basis the general rule was that Community rights were to be treated no less favourably than analogous domestic law rights. In this way it was assumed that domestic law would fully protect Community rights by providing a remedy obtainable in national courts. The court stated that the effectiveness of Community law could be called into question and the protection of rights would be weakened if individuals could not obtain compensation when Community rights were undermined by violation of Community law.

The court emphasised the principle that national courts are obliged to give full effect to Community law to protect rights which individuals derive from Community law (*Simmenthal* (1978); *Factortame* (1991)). It also referred to the obligation imposed on a Member State by Article 5 EC to take all appropriate measures to ensure fulfilment of Community law. Arising from these considerations, the court stated that as a general principle, Member States are obliged to make good damage caused to individuals by a violation of Community law for which they are responsible. In those cases where there has been a failure to implement a directive, three conditions are required to be satisfied. These are that the contents of the directive were intended to confer rights on individuals, that the contents of the rights can be identified from the provisions of the directive and lastly that there was a causal link between the damage suffered by the individual and the State's breach of its obligations. It was for national law to determine the courts dealing with such claims and the procedures to apply.

In his opinion, Advocate General Mischo had given weight to the fact that the European Commission had already taken action against the Italian State under Article 169 EC for its failure to implement the directive. This had resulted in a declaration by the court against Italy under Article 171 EC. However, the court did not make this point in its judgment. The ECJ held that all the conditions necessary to give a right of action in damages for non-implementation of the directive were present and therefore Francovich and the other applicants had a right to compensation from the Italian State.

Directives only have vertical direct effect and can be enforced only against the State. In the *Francovich* case the applicants could not rely upon the principle of direct effect as against the State as the State was not the body responsible for protecting the substantive right to payment of unpaid wages. However, if the directive had been implemented the Member State would have designated a body responsible for respecting the substantive right. Italy had failed to implement the directive and the court recognised a right of action based on the responsibility of the Member State for damage caused by its failure to give effect to substantive Community rights in its legislative capacity.

Although *Francovich* involved the non-implementation of a Directive, a broad interpretation of the court's judgment could be that there is a general right to compensation where an individual has suffered loss as a result of a breach of Community law. Thus the right to damages in the future might be understood as extending more broadly than the facts of *Francovich* would suggest. For example, in *Kirklees MBC v Wickes Building Supplies Ltd* (1992), the House of Lords held on the basis of *Francovich* that if the ECJ considered s 47 of the Shops Act 1950 to be invalid as being in conflict with Article 30 EC, the UK might be obliged to make good the loss caused to the individuals by the breach.

In *Bourgoin SA v Minister of Agriculture, Fisheries and Food* (1985), the Court of Appeal were dealing with a situation where a public authority had exercised its public law powers in a way that contravened Community law. The minister had imposed a ban on the import of turkeys contrary to Article 30 EC, which was directly effective. The Court of Appeal had held that the appropriate remedy was a public law remedy, obtainable by way of judicial review. Only if the public body had been guilty of misfeasance in a public office would the public body be liable in damages. This is difficult to prove and would result in damages not being available. In *Kirklees*, the House of Lords doubted whether in the light of *Francovich* the *Bourgoin* case was correctly decided and considered that the UK might be potentially liable in damages for a breach of Article 30 EC.

Francovich clearly represents a further development in Community law on remedies. Further references have been made to the European Court of Justice under Article 177 EC in order to obtain clarification of the implications for individuals who have suffered loss as a breach of Community law.

Question 17

Analyse TWO of the following cases which came before the European Court of Justice and explain their importance in the development of Community law:

(a) *Plaumann* - Case 25/62

(b) *Schoppenstedt* - Case 5/71

(c) *Roquette Frères v Council* - Case 138/79

Answer plan

When approaching a question like this the temptation is to produce too descriptive an answer. The facts are important but are only one element of the answer. You should seek to deal with:

a   the facts, the legal points raised and the Decisions of the court

b   what kind of case was it? A preliminary reference or a direct action? What Article of the Treaty was it based upon?

c   the cases chosen for this type of question have usually played their part in developing or reinforcing European Court judgments - what part has this case played?

Answer

(a) *Plaumann v Commission* Case 25/62

This was an action by one of thirty German importers of clementines against a refusal by the Commission to grant a request by the Federal Republic of Germany permission to suspend the customs duties on the import of fresh clementines from non EC countries. The refusal by the Commission had been made in a Decisions under Article 25(3) EC. The implication for Plaumann was that it had to pay a customs duty of 13% whereas the German government had asked the Commission to reduce it to a 10% duty.

The main importance of this case concerned whether Plaumann could challenge this Decisions by the Commission. It was open to the German government to challenge the Decisions because it was addressed to them. But could Plaumann as a 'private individual' bring the matter before the European Court of Justice. An action for annulment can be brought under Article 173 EC but as far as individuals are concerned Article 173(2) has been restrictively interpreted by the court. It is possible to challenge a Decisions addressed to oneself but if it is addressed to another the applicant must show that it is of direct and individual concern to them.

The Commission contested the case by claiming that it was inadmissible under Article 173(2) because the Decisions addressed to the government of a Member State was of a special nature and therefore not susceptible to challenge by private persons. They also said that Plaumann was not directly and individually concerned. Thus the argument before the court concentrated on this issue of inadmissibility.

The court accepted that Article 173(2) does allow an individual to bring an action against Decisions addressed to another person if they are of direct and individual concern but the Article neither defines nor limits the scope of these words. The words should be given their natural meaning and the broadest interpretation. As the provision provides a right for interested parties to bring an action it must not be interpreted restrictively. Therefore the Commission's argument was not considered to be well founded.

On the question of 'direct and individual' concern the court decided to look at whether the applicant was individually concerned because if the answer is negative it will be unnecessary to enquire whether he is directly concerned. On this question of 'individually concerned' the Decisions must affect them by reason of certain attributes which are peculiar to them. Or there must be certain circumstances which differentiate them from all other persons. As a result of these factors the applicant is distinguished individually, just as if they were the person to whom the Decisions was addressed.

In the Plaumann case the Decisions affects Plaumann as an importer of clementines, a commercial activity which may be practised by any person. Thus he is not distinguished sufficiently to show individual concern. Therefore the court declared the action for annulment to be inadmissible on the second point put forward by the Commission. This case was followed by a number decided on a similar basis, to the detriment of the applicants.

(b) *Roquette Frères v Council* - Case 138/79

This case arose in the wake of a successful challenge to Regulation 1111/77 in the *Isoglucose* case of *Royal Scholten-Honig* in 1978. The result was that the Regulation was declared to be invalid on the ground of discrimination. The Regulation had sought to control the sugar market. Isoglucose is a direct substitute for liquid sugar, of which there was a surplus. As this surplus had to be exported at a loss, it was felt that the isoglucose manufacturers should contribute to export costs by paying a levy. As the Regulation imposing the levy was invalid no such levy was being collected. Therefore a new Regulation was needed which imposed a levy but did not discriminate between the producers. Under the Common

Agricultural Policy such a Regulation required that the Parliament should be consulted before being adopted by the Council.

The problem was a matter of time. The new Regulation was needed to come into force at the same time as the sugar scheme, namely July 1979. By March 1979 the Commission had drafted the Regulation which was based on the one which applied to sugar. Therefore the new Regulation did not discriminate between the two products. However, the Regulation contained an annex which gave precise methods of calculation.

The draft Regulation came before the Parliament in April but no final Decisions was made. June 1979 was the first time that direct elections were to be made to the European Parliament. The old Parliament 'died' before it could give its Opinion, although the specialist Agricultural Committee was in the process of reconsidering the Regulation. The Regulation was urgently needed but there was no Parliament. In the recitals to any Regulation it is normally stated that 'having regard to the Opinion of the European Parliament'. This Regulation said that the Parliament had been consulted but had not delivered its Opinion! The Council believed that the judgment of the court in the *Isoglucose* case had to be implemented before too long and that the Regulation be adopted before the beginning of the sugar year on 1 July 1979.

Who could challenge the Regulation? At that time the Parliament was considered not to have *locus standi* under Article 173, although following *Les Verts v Parliament* (1989) this would not be the situation today. Therefore the only possibility was for an individual to bring an action for annulment under Article 173(2). However, no individual can challenge a true Regulation. There was something special about this Regulation in that it contained the annex which applied the scheme set-up by the Regulation to particular firms. Therefore as far as these firms were concerned the measure affected them 'like a Decisions'. Such firms could also count on the Parliament intervening in the action on their support, as they are entitled to do under the court statute.

The Council challenged the firms' action under Article 173 but the Commission observed that if the action was declared inadmissible there would surely be a reference on the matter under Article 177(1)(b) from a court of a Member State. The court agreed that the action was admissible. The ground under Article 173(1) which was successfully pleaded was the breach of an essential procedural requirement in that the Parliament had not been consulted. This raised the question as to what amounted to consultation? As the Parliament had received the draft Regulation, was this sufficient? The court found that it was not as Parliament was allowed under the Treaty to play an actual part in the legislative process. This reflects the fundamental democratic principle of the Community.

Having found that the Regulation was faulty, the court had to declare it void under Article 174 EC. This case provides a good example of a Decisions which, although in the form of a Regulation, is of direct and individual concern under Article 173(2). The importance of the case goes further in its effects on the balance of power of the Community institutions. Since the case the Single European Act has introduced the co-operation procedure for certain policy areas, but this case shows that the court recognised the importance of the democratic principle and the role it gives to the European Parliament.

(c) *Schoppenstedt* - Case 5/71

The Aktien-Zuckerfabrik Schoppenstedt brought an action in 1971 on the basis of Article 215(2) claiming damages from the Council caused by Regulation 769/68. This Regulation laid down the measures needed to offset the difference between national sugar prices. The European Court is given jurisdiction in disputes relating to compensation for damage by Article 178 EC. However, this jurisdiction is linked to Article 215(2) which states that in the case of non-contractual liability, the Community shall make good any damage caused by its institutions. The case is to be judged in accordance with the general principles common to the laws of the Member States.

The Council contested the admissibility of the application on the grounds that the applicant was claiming compensation for the removal of the legal effects arising from the contested Regulation and not for any wrongful act or omission. Secondly if the action was recognised as admissible it would undermine Article 173 under which individuals are not entitled to bring applications for the annulment of Regulations.

On the substance of the case the court said that the non-contractual liability of the Community pre-supposes at the very least the unlawful nature of the act alleged to be the cause of the damage. No non-contractual liability will arise involving measures of economic policy unless a sufficiently flagrant violation of a superior rule of law for the protection of the individual has occurred. Having set this principle the court had to decide whether such a violation had actually occurred in this case.

Analysing this sentence 'a superior rule of law for the protection of individuals' includes any general principle of Community law. This would include such examples as equality or proportionality. The requirement that there should be a 'sufficiently flagrant' or serious violation has been narrowly construed by the court. In the case of *Bayerische HNL Vermehrungsbetriebe GmbH v Council and Commission* (1978) the court stated that no liability would be incurred by the Community institutions unless the institution concerned had manifestly and gravely disregarded the limits on the exercise of its power. In subsequent cases the court's view has been that the breach must be both serious and inexcusable.

The applicants contended that by adopting different criteria for the right of compensation of sugar producers, the Regulation infringes Article 40(3) EC. However, the court rejected this argument as the prices must be governed by market forces. Therefore the applicants action failed on the substance because the condition mentioned above was not satisfied. The impact of the case has been the test set by the court in actions under Article 215(2) in the field of legislative economic policy. Cases which have followed have been regularly rejected.

Judicial Remedies & Review (2):
Indirect Action - Preliminary References

Introduction

This type of action has proved very important for the development of Community law. It has been used by the European Court of Justice as a vehicle for establishing many of the fundamental principles covered in other chapters of this book. It is very important, therefore, to have a good understanding of this topic which can arise in both problem and essay questions.

Checklist

Students should have a general knowledge of the reasons for such a procedure being incorporated into the Treaty and in particular should be familiar with the following areas:

- The matters for referral under Article 177(1) EC
- The difference between interpretation and validity questions
- What is a court or tribunal within the Article
- The difference between courts which have a discretion and those which have an obligation to refer
- The impact of the *CILFIT* case on Article 177(3) EC
- The guidelines and procedures used in English courts
- The impact of a reference on the parties and subsequent cases

Question 18

What are the objectives of the system of preliminary references?

Has the ECJ extended the use of Article 177 EC beyond these objectives?

Answer plan

This type of essay question allows the student to use their knowledge of areas of Community law to illustrate how the European Court of Justice has extended the role of Article 177 EC within the Community.

The main points which should be covered are:

- objectives of the 177 procedure
- the relationship between the ECJ and national courts under the procedure
- the role of policy in the ECJ
- the extension of the scope of Article 177
- the development of direct effect
- the development of *acte clair* in the context of Article 177(3)

Answer

In the early stages of the European Community, the European Court of Justice made it clear that a new legal order had been established. It was recognised by the author's of the treaties establishing the Community, that a court was necessary to ensure that there was a uniform interpretation and application of Community law throughout the Member States. It would undermine the new Community if the effect of its law varied from one Member State to another, especially in the economically sensitive areas associated with the European Economic Treaty. It was necessary to give ultimate authority to one court whose jurisdiction extended over the whole Community. This was the European Court of Justice. However, the relationship between the ECJ and the national courts was not to be an hierarchical appellate basis associated with national court structures. It was important that the relationship should be seen to be based on a co-operation, with the shared objective that all courts wished to apply the law whether it be of national or Community origin. It was the ECJ which was granted the power to give definitive judgments on the validity and interpretation of Community law.

Thus from the beginning there were seen to be two clear differences between the procedure under Article 177 EC and the action of appellate courts. It is the parties to an action who normally decide whether to appeal or not. Secondly, when a case goes to appeal in a national context, it is normally the appeal court which decides the case and may either uphold, amend or over-turn the Decision of the lower court. Neither of these apply to the 177 procedures. It is the national court which decides whether a reference should be made and only specific issues are referred to the ECJ in the form of questions. Once the ECJ has answered these, they are sent back to the national court for a final Decision. This suggests that national courts are not subordinate to the ECJ but co-equal.

Given this need for uniformity in the Community, Article 177 EC specifies the initial boundaries of the role of preliminary references. Under Article 177(1) EC, the Treaty specifies that references can be made requesting (a) interpretation of the Treaty; (b) the validity and interpretation of acts of the institutions of the Community and (c) in appropriate cases the interpretation of the statutes of bodies established by the act of the European Council. It is (a)and (b) where the important developments have been made in Community law by the use of Article 177 EC references. In the early cases of *Van Gend en Loos* (1963) and *Costa v ENEL* (1964) the ECJ took the opportunity of stressing the relationship between national law and Community law and the legal implications of the transfer of sovereignty when Member States established the Community. Both of these very important cases were brought before the court via 177 references from their national courts. However, perhaps the best example of how the court has used 177 to develop Community law is direct effect. Having established the supremacy of Community law over national law, the ECJ introduced the concept of direct effect.

This was the result of the court's view that a new legal order had been established with the Community and that this gave rights to individuals which their national courts had to uphold. Subject to three requirements being satisfied this meant that an individual could claim a right under the Treaty, administrative act or other act treated as *sui generis* by the court. This very important development was not expressly mentioned in the Treaty, the primary source of Community law. It was implied by the ECJ under its powers of interpretation and within its role in explaining what Community law was. Thus it was possible to identify three issues which could be referred for a ruling under Article 177, namely interpretation, validity and effect.

As a policy Decision the court has developed the principle of direct effect of treaty Articles, Regulations and Directives. However, this is not the only example of how the ECJ has extended the jurisdiction of Article 177 EC. As mentioned above the court has extended 'acts' of the institutions to include not only those specified in Article 189, but also those acts *sui generis*. In the *ERTA* case (1971) the court held that such acts of the Council could be an act for the purposes of judicial review under Article 173 and thus likely to fall within Article 177 procedures. This was taken further in the *Haegeman* case (1974) where the court held that the Association Agreement between the Community and Grece was covered by Article 177(1)(b). As agreements between the Community and non-Member States are normally concluded by the Council, this was sufficient grounds for the court to regard such agreements as Community Acts. It could be argued that as the agreement was concluded by means of a Council Decision this was correct. However, it was not the Decision which was interpreted by the court but the agreement itself. Obviously, the non-Member State was not bound by the court's interpretation, but Member States were. As international agreements between the Community and non-Member States are part of Community law and binding on Member States, it is clearly important that uniform interpretations should be given to the agreement throughout the Community. The agreement had to be brought within Article 177 if it was to be interpreted by the court. Thus the court said that the agreement constituted an act of a Community institution in so far as it concerned the Community. Even if the agreement between the Community and a non-Member State is a mixed agreement in that there is a shared authority between the Community and Member States, this does not seem to have affected the ECJ's view of its jurisdiction to interpret the agreement. This approach is another example of the court's policy orientated interpretation which has extended Article 177.

There are other examples of the impact of Article 177 references on Community law as its scope has been broadened by the ECJ. It is seen by the court as the best way of moving Community law forward within the teleological interpretation of the court. The flow of cases on the direct effect of Directives is perhaps a clear example of this culminating in the *Francovich* judgment (1992). However, the constitutional impact on Member States of references should not be ignored. In the UK the *Factortame* case challenged long standing constitutional principles. However, if the objectives of the preliminary references system is to ensure uniformity and not to allow disparities due to legal traditions, it would appear that the ECJ is seeking to fulfil them. As the scope of Community action has increased it is to be expected that so will the matters coming within

177 references. How else can the ECJ provide the interpretation and validity necessary for uniform application throughout the Community? If the ECJ did not provide these, there would be no focus for the Member States and the danger of various interpretations undermining the Community itself.

Another objective of Article 177 was to distinguish between those courts which had a discretion to refer under Article 177(2) and those which had an obligation to refer under 177(3). courts under Article 177(3) are those against whose Decisions there is no judicial remedy under national law. This does not automatically mean the highest court in the judicial structure of a Member State, but the highest court hearing that particular case (*Costa v ENEL*). In the UK some judges, like Lord Denning consider that only the House of Lords comes within the category of 177(3).

However, whatever the arguments on this point, the ECJ has taken a policy Decision to limit the obligation of such court's to refer. The *CILFIT* case (1982) is the most important development in this respect, where the ECJ held that final courts are in the same position as other national courts in deciding whether they need to refer a question of Community law before giving judgment.

If, for example, the ECJ had already given an authoritative interpretation under Article 177 there is no purpose in a further reference, although it could be made. However, the court went further to say that the correct application of Community law may be so obvious as to leave no scope for any reasonable doubt as to the manner in which the question is raised, thus enabling the 177(3) court to refrain from making a reference. This echoes the principle of *acte clair* so familiar to the French legal system.

The ECJ may have felt that the national legal systems were now so well schooled in the principles of Community law that this development could take place. It may be that they felt that this was a reasonable way of reducing the workload of the court or to further the co-operation on which the relationship with national courts is based. However, to ensure that national courts did not remove this obligation as a matter of course the court indicated the special characteristics of Community law which had to be considered. For example the linguistic nature of the court's jurisdiction, the special terminology and the contextual approach of the ECJ. Only if the national court could satisfy itself on these matters could the obligation to refer be removed.

Given that the preliminary procedure was designed to deal with the danger of divergencies in the interpretation of Community law in Member States, it can be seen that the ECJ has extended the interpretation of Article 177 itself. This is in three respects namely the scope of Community law covered, direct effect and the mandatory nature of Article 177(3). However, there have been limitations on this development as can be seen in the *Foto-Frost* case where the ECJ reiterated that national courts could not declare a Community act invalid but had to make a reference under Article 177.

Question 19

Maureen is a secretary with Harrison's Travel Agents. On a recent visit to Amsterdam Maureen collected a number of packages at the request of her employer, and brought them back with her to England in her car. At Dover she was stopped by customs officials and her car was searched for drugs. Although no drugs were found the packages belonging to her employer were opened and found to contain pornographic films and magazines, much to the embarrassment of Maureen. She was subsequently charged with a criminal offence.

At the Crown court hearing Maureen's counsel stated that the case raised a question of European law and requested that a reference be made to the European Court of Justice. The judge said that he would make no reference as the law was clear in his eyes and he did not wish to delay the case.

Can the judge refuse this request? What guidelines have been developed to assist English judges when deciding whether to make a reference?

Answer plan

This problem question on Article 177 EC requires the application of basic principles including:

* the procedure under Article 177
* the difference between 177(2) and 177(3)
* implications of *acte clair* and *CILFIT*
* English guidelines produced by senior judges
* the *Rheinmühlen* case

Answer

Under Article 177 EC it is possible for any court or tribunal to request a preliminary ruling from the European Court of Justice on a matter of Community law in order for the national court to give a judgment in the case before it. This request can be on a question of interpretation of the Treaty, interpretation or validity of acts of the Community institutions or whether the principle of direct effect applies. The purpose is to provide the means for a definitive statement from the court which will ensure that Community law is applied uniformally across all Member States. Thus the Crown court comes within the category of court which Article 177 EC was designed for. However, within Article 177 EC there are two categories of court. Under 177(2) courts or tribunals have a discretion in that they may make a reference.

Article 177(3) indicates that those courts or tribunals in Member States against whose Decision there is no judicial remedy under national law have an obligation to make a reference. This obligation has been qualified by the case law of the European Court of Justice, such as the *CILFIT* case. As Maureen's case is being heard before the Crown court, Article 177(2) clearly applies. However, in either instance it is the court or tribunal which decides and not the parties to the action. Therefore the judge hearing Maureen's case can refuse the request for a preliminary ruling under Article 177 EC to the court.

Given the importance of the Decision to make a reference to the court, a number of guidelines would appear to be desirable to assist a judge hearing a particular case to decide whether to exercise their discretion to make a reference or not. The European Court itself has refrained from producing guidelines as to the circumstances in which this step should be taken, but it has indicated that it is essential for the national court to 'define the legal context' (*Irish Creamery* case (1981)). However, national judges have attempted to fulfil this need. The first judge to do so in the UK was Lord Denning in the first case to come before the Court of Appeal involving Community law. This case was *Bulmer v Bollinger*, an action over the use of the term champagne when describing an alcoholic drink called BabyCham. In this case Denning indicated what he considered to be important factors. Perhaps the most important was that the point of Community law must be conclusive in the sense that the case must turn on the point of

Community law involved. In other words if Community law was 'x' then the plaintiff would succeed, but if on the contrary it was 'y' then the defendant would defeat the action. It may be that after hearing the evidence the case could be settled on national law, thus making the reference unnecessary. The other factors he specified were associated with the time it took to get a ruling from the European Court, which required a stay of the English proceedings which may have unfortunate results for the parties. Obviously there was the expense of obtaining the ruling and the danger of overloading the European Court with too many references. He also felt that the wishes of the parties should also be taken into account. Clearly Maureen wants a reference made, but this is not conclusive. It may also be that if she is receiving legal aid, the cost associated with making a reference is not important.

These guidelines have been criticised in that they may fetter the English judge, contrary to the principle that national law cannot constrain the judge in the exercise of his discretion. This principle was stated by the European Court of Justice in the German case of *Rheinmuhlen* (1974). In this case the court held that the power of a lower court to make a reference cannot be abrogated by any rule of national law. It also reiterated the importance of the 177 procedure by stating that it is essential for the preservation of the Community character of law and ensuring that the law is the same in all Member States. However, the court did recognise in *Rheinmuhlen* that although there was the widest discretion given to national courts when to refer, Article 177 does not preclude a Decision to refer from remaining subject to the normal national law remedies. Thus it would still be possible to appeal in these circumstances through the national court structure. Although in subsequent English cases judges have been influenced by the words of Denning in *Bulmer v Bollinger*, they have repeated that they are only guidelines and do not fetter the discretion of the judge. However, one important point made by Lord Denning and repeated by subsequent English judges and the European Court itself, is that it is important to ascertain the facts first before the discretion to make a reference is considered. In some civil cases the facts may be agreed by the parties, but in criminal cases such as Maureen's it is normally only after the case has been argued that conclusions can be drawn on the facts of the case. This is apparent in the context of deciding whether the point of Community law is conclusive. It may be that the case can be settled on the basis of national law. However, more importantly it has a crucial role in framing the questions to be put to the Court of Justice in the request for a preliminary ruling. Mr Justice MacPherson in *R v HM Treasury, ex parte Daily Mail & General Trust plc* (1987), provided a useful list of factors which consolidate those of previous English judges. His last point, that he did not find the point raised free from doubt, brings the wording of Article 177 back into focus. The judge hearing Maureen's case has a discretion to make a reference if he considers it necessary to enable him to give judgment. It maybe that although Maureen's counsel has stated that a question of European law has been raised by the case, the judge clearly feels that he has the answer. This may be gleaned from the case law of the court itself on the point raised, which was recognised in the *CILFIT* case (1981). However, English judges have been warned by Lord Diplock in *R v Henn & Darby* (1981) that just because the meaning of the English text seems plain, questions of interpretation may be involved. Where this is necessary the European Court of Justice, as Mr Justice Bingham pointed out in *Commissioners of Customs & Excise v Samex ApS* (1983), are far better equipped than national courts to resolve issues of Community law.

It may be different for Maureen if the hearing was before magistrates and thus without a jury to decide on questions of fact. In such courts, once questions of facts had been decided, it might be appropriate for the magistrates to make a 177 reference if the guilt of the defendant turned on the interpretation or validity of Community law. This was followed in *R v Pieck* (1980) where the incompatibility of English law with Community law led to the defendant having the prosecution against him dropped. However, in *R v Plymouth Justices ex parte Rogers* (1982) the Divisional court dismissed the argument of the prosecution that no court or tribunal could refer questions to the Court of Justice unless all the facts had been admitted or found because this would mean that in criminal cases there would not be an opportunity to request a ruling on the basis of no case to answer unless all the facts had been settled. On the other hand it was better to call all the evidence so that there was no question of the defendant being acquitted on the facts, thus saving the expense and delay of a reference. A case before a judge and jury in a Crown court highlights the problem of delay associated with making a preliminary reference. Lord Diplock stated in *Henn & Darby v DPP* (1981) that it can seldom be a proper exercise of a judge's discretion to hold up the proceedings for over nine months. The delay caused by a reference being made now would probably be at least double this length of time. The better course, he suggested, was to decide the case at first instance and allow appeal against conviction through the hierarchy of national courts.

This approach was subsequently adopted by the judge in *R v Tymen* (1981). It would appear that the judge hearing Maureen's case has complete discretion, but is there any appeal available to her? As mentioned above the European Court recognised in the *Rheinmühlen* case that Article 177 references are subject to the normal appeal processes. If a reference had been made under the Crown court equivalent of the High court procedure in RSC Order 114, there would be a two week period before the reference was sent to the ECJ to allow for an appeal by one of the parties. However, in Maureen's case it is the Decision not to make a reference which she is unhappy with. In these circumstances the judge's refusal is interlocutory and leave to appeal is necessary either from the judge or from the Court of Appeal.

Question 20

Should a national court ever be refused a request for a preliminary ruling by the national law or by the European Court of Justice itself?

Answer plan

The essay question is looking for a well-planned essay which develops the following points:

- purpose of Article 177 EC
- requirements of Article 177(2) and (3), with special reference to the words 'necessary' and 'may'
- RSC Order 114
- *Rheinmühlen* and *Foglia v Novello* (*No 1 & 2*) cases

Answer

Preliminary rulings are a procedure covered by Article 177 EC, whereby a court in a Member State can ask the European Court of Justice specific questions. These may cover such matters as interpretation of the Treaty or questions on the validity and interpretation of acts of the institutions of the Community. The objective of the procedure is to provide uniformity across the whole Community so that Community law is applied in the same way in all Member States. Under Article 177 EC the Court of Justice is under a duty to supply all courts in the Community with the information on the interpretation of Community law which is necessary to enable them to settle genuine disputes which are brought before them (*Foglia v Novello (No 1)* (1980)).

The procedure is available to any court or tribunal of any Member State. What constitutes such a court has been given a wide interpretation by the ECJ. It is not necessary that the body is recognised as a court by national law or what it is called. For the ECJ the important question is whether the body concerned is performing a judicial function. The characteristic of such a function is the power to give binding determinations of the legal rights and obligations of individuals. In the *Vassen* case (1965) an arbitration tribunal which settled disputes regarding a pension fund for the mining industry was recognised by the ECJ as coming within the definition for preliminary rulings. In another Dutch reference case, *Broekmeulen* (1980), the ECJ held that the appeal committee of the Dutch professional medical body came within Article 177(2) EC. In contrast the ECJ refused to give a ruling on a reference from the Paris Chambre des Avocats in the *Borker* case (1980) because it was not exercising a judicial function. Also in *Nordsee Deutsche Hockseefischerei GmbH* a reference was refused because although was arbitration was required under the agreement between the parties, the national courts could review the Decision. It would be possible for these national courts to use the preliminary ruling procedure. In that case, in contrast with *Vassen*, there was no public participation in the form of ministerial recognition of the result of the arbitration.

Article 177 EC actually specifies two possibilities for the national court. If it is a court whose Decision is subject to appeal within the national legal system, that court has a discretion as to whether to make a request for a ruling or not.

The word 'may' in Article 177(2) EC makes this clear. That discretion can not be overruled or stinted by national law. It is for the court itself to decide whether it is necessary for a reference to made in order for it to give a judgment in the case before it. The ECJ made this clear in the *Rheinmühlen* cases (1974), where a German cereal exporter sought to obtain an export rebate under Community law and found himself involved in a clash between federal and local courts. The ECJ was asked by the Federal Tax court whether Article 177 EC gave lower courts an unfettered right to refer, or whether it is subject to national provisions under which lower courts are bound by the judgments of superior courts. The ECJ held that the power of the lower court to make a reference cannot be abrogated by a provision of national law. The lower court must be free to make a reference if it considers that the superior court's ruling could lead it to give a judgment contrary to Community law. The only court able to give definitive judgment on Community law is the ECJ itself.

The attitude of the English superior courts reflect this principle. In *R v Plymouth Justices, ex parte Rogers* (1982) Lord Chief Justice Lane said that the magistrates had the jurisdiction to make a reference, but that certain guidelines should be considered. Lord Denning (*Bulmer v Bollinger*) and MacPherson J (*R v HM Treasury ex parte Daily Mail & General Trust plc* (1987)) provide examples of the type of guidelines which should be considered by the court. These include the time it takes for a reference to be made, the cost and the need to ascertain the facts before making a reference. Where these guidelines have been consciously used by judges, they have made the point that they provide guidance only. In all the cases the discretion of any court falling within Article 177(2) EC is not challenged.

However, it should be remembered that Article 177(2) gives a discretion where the national courts consider it necessary to make a reference in order for it to give judgment.

It maybe that a lower court's order for a reference may be quashed on appeal. This was recognised by the ECJ in the *Simmenthal* case (1978). In these cases the normal national rules of appeal would apply. Under the Rules of the Supreme court RSC Order 144 r 6 an order making a reference is deemed to be a final order, and therefore an appeal lies to the Court of Appeal. In the *Rheinmühlen* case (1974), Advocate-General Warner stated in his opinion that this rule was in conflict with Community law and therefore void. However, the court in its judgment went out of its way to make the point that it was not. In contrast to English law, under Irish law there is an unfettered discretion without any possible appeal to the Irish Supreme court (*Campus Oil Ltd v Ministry for Industry & Energy* (1984)). However, in English law there has been no reported cases of an appellate court reversing the Decision of a lower court to make a reference. This may be due to the fact that under RSC Order 114 the reference is not sent to the European Court until the expiration of the appeal period or, if appeal has been lodged, until it has been heard.

The ECJ recognises the preliminary procedure as having an important contribution towards the co-operation it seeks to develop with the national courts. It does not seek to apply Community law to the facts but to help the national court ascertain what the Community law is. It is very rare, therefore, for the ECJ to refuse a reference if the court or tribunal making it can satisfy it that it is such a body described above. It is after all for the national court to decide whether the reference is necessary. Even if the wording of the reference is not completely appropriate, the court has used its best endeavours to provide the information it feels is necessary for the national court to have. However, there have been cases where a reference was refused.

In the *Foglia v Novello* cases in 1980 and 1982, the court held that the reference was an abuse of Article 177 as the case had been artificially constructed as a vehicle for obtaining clarification of Community law. There was, in the opinion of the court, an absence of any real legal dispute between the parties.

Novello, a French resident had ordered some wine from Foglia, an Italian wine grower. The contract provided that Novello would not be liable for any French or Italian taxes which were contrary to the free movement of goods between the two countries. When a charge was subsequently levied by French customs, Novello claimed it was unlawful under Article 95 EC. The ECJ said that both parties agreed that the French law was incompatible with Community law and the legal action had been a device to obtain a ruling that the French legislation was invalid. The court went on to say that such arrangements obliging such rulings would jeopardise the system of legal remedies available to protect private individuals against tax provisions which were contrary to the Treaty. A subsequent second reference by the Italian judge was an attempt to clarify the role of

Article 177 EC and the relationship between the national courts and the ECJ. However, the ECJ adhered to its earlier Decision not to answer the question arising from the customs duty levied by the French law. It held that the 177 procedure was not to be used to give abstract advisory Opinions, but to contribute to the actual Decisions of the cases. Although these references involving Novello and Foglia have been criticised by academics and jurists, it is accepted that the ECJ does have a right to reject those cases which it feels are an abuse of its process. The European Court of Justice believes that, like any court, it must be in a position to make an assessment to ensure that it has jurisdiction to hear the case. Normally the court will rely on the assessment made by national courts but in exceptional cases they reserve the right to make their own.

Following the judgment in *Foglia v Novello* it was thought that the court would take a restrictive approach to 177 references. However, the subsequent case law of the court does not suggest that it had embarked on a new policy of inquiry into the national court's Decision to make a reference. When invited by the Belgian government in *Walter Rau v de Smedt* (1982) to inquire whether the dispute between the parties was genuine, the court stated that there was nothing in the file on the case to make it doubt that the dispute was genuine. In *Parfumerie-Fabrik v Provide* (1989) the court confirmed that it will not lightly infer an absence of a genuine dispute.

Question 21

Crinkley plc are a large producer of potato crisps in the UK. Like all companies who are involved in manufacturing potato products, Crinkley have to purchase their potatoes from a national marketing organisation as required by EC legislation. Under a recent Community Regulation, all purchasers have to submit a tender together with a deposit of ten per cent of the total value of the tender.

Subsequently, Crinkley failed to take up all the supplies it had tendered for and were informed that they would, under the Regulation, forfeit their deposit. This amounted to a substantial amount to Crinkley and could force them into liquidation. As a result they are seeking to challenge the validity of the Regulation on the basis that it is contrary to the principle of proportionality. They are also suing the national potato marketing organisation to recover their deposit.

Advise Crinkley plc.

Answer plan

This problem question is seeking the application of Articles 173 EC and 177 EC as a means of challenging a Community act.

In particular the following points should be stressed:

*   the requirements under Article 173 EC for *locus standi* and the grounds for annulment
*   the procedures under Article 177 and specifically the power of the Court of Justice under 177(1)(b) on questions of validity
*   remedies

Answer

There are two ways open to Crinkley to challenge the Regulation which has affected them. One possibility is a direct action under Article 173 EC whereby they will bring an action before the European Court of Justice and ask them to annul the Regulation.

If they are successful the court could declare, under Article 174 EC, the Regulation *erga omnes* or if appropriate merely declare void that part of the Regulation which is contrary to Community law and leave the rest of the Regulation as lawful. Such a declaration would have an immediate impact on everyone within the Community. The alternative possibility is for Crinkley to seek to challenge the validity of the Regulation in the English courts, probably in the action against the national potato marketing organisation to recover the deposit. In this situation a successful challenge using the Article 177 preliminary ruling procedure would have an immediate impact on Crinkley.

In order to bring an action under 173 it is necessary to satisfy the Court of Justice with regard to their *locus standi*. Under Article 173(2) it is possible for an individual or company to institute proceedings against a Regulation if it is in fact a Decision and is of direct and individual concern to them. The measure in this problem is titled a Regulation, although the name of the measure is not decisive in the view of the court. A Regulation under Article 189 EC is of general application and has direct applicability throughout the Community. It is thus the main legislative or normative measure of the European Community. The main characteristic of a Regulation is that it applies generally and objectively to categories of persons whereas a Decision binds those named individuals to whom it is addressed.

As far as the court is concerned a true Regulation may not be challenged by an individual, as it stated in *Calpak* (1980). The problem for Crinkley is that the measure they are seeking to challenge does appear to satisfy the requirements of a Regulation. Merely because it has had this financial impact on Crinkley as against its affect on other potato product manufacturers does not stop it being a Regulation. In some cases the court has looked at the other requirements of 173(2), namely that the measure is of 'direct and individual concern' to the applicant, and having concluded that it is they have held that it cannot be legislative in character, ie not a true Regulation (*Sgarlata* 1965). To satisfy the 'direct' requirement it is merely necessary to show that there has been no exercise of discretion on the part of national authorities (*Töpfer v Commission* (1965)). However, 'individual concern' has been restrictively interpreted by the court so as to make it very difficult for an individual to satisfy the court on this matter.

In *Plaumann* (1963), a case involving the importation of clementines, the court gives a good idea of the factors to be taken into account in deciding the criteria of 'individual concern'. If Crinkley could satisfy the requirement of *locus standi* it would still have to satisfy the court as to the ground for annulment specified in Article 173(1). Crinkley has already indicated that they wish to challenge the Regulation on the basis of proportionality. This is one of the general principles of Community law, initially derived from German law but now firmly recognised as being a Community principle. One of the most widely used grounds for annulment is 'infringement of this Treaty or of any rule of law relating to its application', which encompasses the claim that the principle of proportionality has been breached. The principle of proportionality requires that the means used must not be excessive in the context of the aim which it is intended to be achieved. It has been successfully pleaded in a number of cases, including the *Skimmed Milk* case (1977). In this case the Court of Justice had declared invalid an EC Regulation which compelled producers of animal feeding-stuff to add milk powder to their products in place of soya.

As an action under 173 looks unlikely to materialise because of the problem of *locus standi*, it is necessary to look at an alternative possibility before the national courts. In order for Crinkley to use Article 177 a case must be brought before a court. This will be possible if the action is brought against the potato marketing organisation in an English court, probably the High court. The judge hearing the action will have the discretion as to whether or not to make a reference to the Court of Justice. Under Article 177(1)(b) the court can give definitive answers to questions of interpretation and validity of Community acts, which includes Regulations. As the court hearing the case will come within Article 177(2), the judge will have a discretion as indicated above. There are guidelines from previous cases heard in the UK to assist the judge in deciding whether to make a reference or not. The main one which is supported by the European Court is that it is important to ascertain the facts first. The court prefers any reference to be set in the appropriate legal context. With regard to other factors, Lord Denning suggested in *Bulmer v Bollinger* that time, cost, the work-load of the European Court and the wishes of the parties should be taken into account. A number of references have been made by UK courts to the European Court on the validity of Community acts, including Regulations. In *R v Intervention Board for Agricultural Produce, ex parte E D & F Man (Sugar) Ltd* (1985), a large firm of sugar traders brought proceedings for judicial review of a Decision based upon a Commission Regulation. The grounds for the review included that the Regulation was contrary to the principle of proportionality. On a 177 reference the court answered that the Regulation did contravene the principle and to that extent was invalid.

Does it make a difference to Crinkley that they probably do not have *locus standi* under Article 173(2)? In the Berlin Butter case of *Rau v BALM* (1987) the court stated in response to a 177 reference on the validity of a Decision addressed to the German government, that it is irrelevant whether the plaintiff would have *locus standi* under 173(2) or if in fact such an action had been initiated. Thus it should not influence the judge whether to make a reference or not that a 173 action is not possible. Is it possible, therefore, for the judge hearing the case in the national court to declare the Regulation invalid without a 177 reference? In the *Sugar* case (1985) mentioned above, the Divisional court recognised that it could not make an order that the Regulation was invalid. This view was clearly stated by the European Court of Justice case of *Foto-Frost* (1988). In this important case the court held that national courts could reject an argument based on invalidity of a Community measure, but they could not declare a measure invalid. National courts had a discretion whether or not to make a validity reference, but only the ECJ was competent to declare invalid the acts of Community institutions. One of the reasons given by the court for this was that under the rules of procedure of the court, Community institutions whose acts were being challenged were entitled to participate in the reference proceedings before the court. Thus they had the chance to defend their action before the court before the measure was declared invalid.

What if the court considers that Crinkley's view is well founded and agrees that the Regulation is invalid? A special feature of invalidity rulings is the immediate consequence they may have outside the context of the actual case in which the question of validity is raised. In *SpA International Chemical Corporation v Amministrazione delle Finanze dello Stato* (1981), the European Court held that once an act had been declared void a national court could not apply the act without creating serious uncertainty as to the Community law applicable. Therefore, although a judgment of the ECJ under Article 177 declaring a Regulation void is directly addressed only to the national court which referred the question, it is sufficient reason for any other national court to regard that act as void for the purposes of a judgment which it has to give. Thus Crinkley will recover their deposit under national law if the Regulation is declared invalid. However, the court may decide to limit the retrospective effect of its rulings in order to leave previous transactions unaffected. The court claimed jurisdiction to do this in proceedings under Article 177, by analogy with the power conferred upon it by Article 174(2) whereby the court may state which of the effects of the Regulation it has declared void (*Maize & Starch* cases (1980)).

My advice to Crinkley is that there is a presumption under Community law that a Regulation is valid. Therefore in order to defeat this presumption an action must be brought which allows the European Court the opportunity to deliver its view on this matter. As an action under Article 173 is unlikely, given the restrictive nature of Article 173(2), a reference by a national court under 177 seems the best way to challenge the Regulation.

Although the national court under Article 177(2) has a discretion as to whether or not it makes a reference, if a *prima facie* case can be made out by Crinkley it is probable that a reference will be made. In the *Foto-Frost* case the Court of Justice suggested that a national court might grant interim relief even pending a ruling on validity. It has to be remembered that the national court can not declare the Regulation invalid, but merely uphold its validity. If a reference is refused, Crinkley will have to be prepared to appeal in the hope that a court which comes within Article 177(3) will be obliged to make a reference to the European Court.

Question 22

Critically discuss the application of *acte clair* to Community law.

Answer plan

As well as appearing in problem questions concerning cases before courts within the Article 177(3) definition, essay questions like this one can be set. You need to cover the following points:

- role of Article 177 EC
- the specific interpretation of 177(3) EC
- the relationship between 177(2) and 177(3) courts
- the doctrine of *acte clair*
- the impact of the Decision in *CILFIT*
- the approach of UK courts

Answer

The principle of *acte clair* is derived from French law. Its origin lies in the principle that the ordinary courts must seek a ruling from the Ministry of Foreign Affairs where a question of treaty interpretation arises unless the point of treaty interpretation is clear. In such circumstances no question of interpretation arises. It was not surprising, therefore, that the first courts to apply the doctrine to Community law was the French Conseil d'Etat and the Cour de Cassation. In *Re Shell-Berre* (1964) the Conseil d'Etat was concerned with the application by some oil companies for the annulment of a ministerial decree affecting garages selling petrol, contrary to Article 37 EC. The Conseil d'Etat refused to make a reference under Article 177 because that would only happen if there was any doubt as to the meaning or scope of the Treaty as it applies to the facts of the case.

The European Court of Justice has accepted that a national court of last resort is not under a duty to make a reference under Article 177(3) in certain circumstances. These are that the provision in question has already been interpreted by the court or where the correct application of European law is so obvious as to leave no scope for any reasonable doubt. This echoes the principle of *acte clair*. In *Da Costa en Schaake* (1963) the court stated that the same question in this case had been referred in the case of *Van Gend en Loos* (1963) and had been answered to the effect that Article 12 EC had direct effect. Therefore the ECJ merely referred the Dutch administrative court to its previous Decision. It went on to say that if the court had already pronounced on a question of interpretation it may deprive the obligation to refer of its purpose and empty of its substance. Prior to the case of *CILFIT* (1982), the Court of Justice had treated the obligation under Article 177(3) as being a strict one, subject to only these derogations.

However, in this case of *CILFIT SA v Ministry of Health* (1982) the European Court appears to have accepted the principle of *acte clair*. The plaintiffs in this case were Italian companies which imported wool from non-Member countries. Since 1968 they had been paying health inspection charges on those imports under Italian law. They now sought to argue that the Italian law was inapplicable by virtue of an EC Regulation. The defendant, the

Italian Ministry of Health, simply replied that the Regulation did not apply to wool, as wool was not listed in Annex II to the Treaty. In spite of losing at first instance and on appeal, the plaintiffs took the case up to Italy's highest court, 'against whose Decisions there is no judicial remedy under national law'. They claimed that this court was obliged by Article 177(3) to make a reference to the ECJ, although the Ministry of Health resisted the reference. They maintained that the solution was so obvious that it excluded any possibility of doubt as to the interpretation of the Regulation and hence there was no need for a reference. In these circumstances the Italian court did make a reference asking about the obligation to refer under Article 177(3).

The court said that under Article 177(3) the obligation to refer was based on co-operation between the national courts and the ECJ. This had been established with a view to ensuring the proper application and uniform interpretation of Community law in Member States and between national courts, in their capacity as courts responsible for the application of Community law. More particularly it seeks to prevent divergencies in judicial Decisions on questions of Community law. The scope of the obligation to refer must be assessed in view of these obligations.

The court went on to say that it follows from the relationship between 177(2) and (3) that courts and tribunals referred to in 177(3) have the same discretion as any other national court or tribunal, to ascertain whether Decision on a question of Community law is necessary to enable them to give judgment. Accordingly, these courts and tribunals are not obliged to refer to the ECJ a question concerning interpretation of Community law raised before them if that question is not relevant, that is to say, if the answer to that question, regardless of what it may be, can in no way affect the outcome of the case. The same effect, as regards the limits set to the obligation laid down by 177(3) may be produced where previous Decisions of the ECJ have already dealt with the point of law in question, irrespective of the nature of proceedings which led to those Decisions, even though the question at issue is not strictly identical.

Finally, the court dealt with *acte clair*. It stated that the correct application of Community law may be so obvious as to leave no scope for any reasonable doubt as to the manner in which the question raised is to be resolved. However, before a court within Article 177(3) comes to the conclusion that such is the case, the national court or tribunal must be convinced that the matter is equally obvious to the courts and tribunals of other Member States and to the ECJ itself. It is only if these conditions are satisfied, may the national court or tribunal refrain from submitting the question to the ECJ and take it upon itself the responsibility for resolving the point of Community law.

This apparent acceptance of the principle of *acte clair* must be treated with great circumspection. As the court pointed out in its *CILFIT* judgment the matter must be assessed on the basis of the characteristic features of Community law and particular difficulties to which it gives rise. *Firstly*, Community legislation drafted in several languages and that the different language versions are all equally authentic -interpretation therefore involves the comparison of different language versions. *Secondly*, Community law uses terminology which is peculiar to itself - also legal concepts do not necessarily have the same meaning in Community law and in the law of various Member States. *Thirdly*, every provision of Community law must be placed in its context and interpreted in light of provisions of Community law as a whole, regard being had to objectives thereof and to its state of evolution at the date on which the provision in question is to be applied.

In light of all these considerations, the court concluded that the answer to the 177(3) question is that it is to be interpreted as meaning that courts and tribunals against whose Decision there is no judicial remedy under national law is required, where a question of Community law is raised, to comply with its obligations to bring the matter before the ECJ, unless it was established that the question raised is irrelevant or the Community provision in question has already been interpreted or that the correct application of Community law is so obvious as to leave no scope for any reasonable doubt.

In the UK the House of Lords had adopted the approach recommended by the European Court in *CILFIT*. In *Henn and Darby v DPP* (1981) Lord Diplock stated that in the light of the established case law of the European Court, which was so free from any doubt that there was no matter of interpretation of Article 30 EC required. However, because the interpretation of the Court of

Appeal was contrary to this view, a reference was made to the ECJ. The Court of Appeal had held that a total import ban did not constitute a 'quantitative restriction on imports' within Article 30 EC because it did not relate to quantities! In fact it was already well established in the case-law of the Court of Justice that the term 'quantitative restriction' covered not only reductions in permitted levels of imports but also outright bans. In *Garland v BREL* (1983) the House of Lords made a reference not because of any doubt regarding the answer likely to be given by the ECJ but because there was no consistent line of case law on Article 119 which would make the answer too obvious and inevitable.

There are dangers associated with the principle of *acte clair*, as the Court of Appeal aptly demonstrated in *Henn and Darby v DPP*. However, there are other examples where its possible misuse could lead to the misapplication or non-application of Community law by national courts. The case of *Cohn-Bendit* (1980) illustrates this point where the Conseil d'Etat held contrary to the case law of the ECJ that a Directive could not have direct effect. To counter such possibilities happening in Germany, the German Federal Constitutional court has emphasised in *Re Patented Feedingstuffs* (1989) that it will review any arbitrary refusal by a court subject to Article 177(3) to refer to the European Court.

Rasmussen believes that the *CILFIT* judgment means something very different from what it *prima facie* establishes. For him the real strategy of *CILFIT* is not to incorporate an *acte clair* concept into Community law but to call the national judiciaries to circumspection when they are faced with problems of interpretation and application of Community law. 'The reins are not cut loose although that might seem to be what the court ruled in *CILFIT*.' However, it must not be forgotten that in all such circumstances national courts and tribunals, including those in 177(3), remain entirely at liberty to bring the matter before the ECJ if they consider it appropriate to do so. If the principle of *acte clair* is to be invoked in the context of European Community law, it must be on the basis of the criteria supplied by *CILFIT*.

Chapter 6

The Free Movement of Goods

Introduction

This is one of the fundamental freedoms of the European Community and is perhaps the most important one as far as examination questions are concerned.

Examiners set both problem and essay-type questions on this area of Community law and it is one which you are strongly advised to revise thoroughly. The benefit of this hard work is that many important principles have been developed through cases associated with the free movement of goods, that you can use them as examples in answering questions on other topics, such as preliminary references or general principles of Community law.

Checklist

You should have a clear idea of the principles of a customs union (Article 9 EC) and the following specific points:

- Prohibition of import duties on imports and exports within the EC and of all charges of equivalent effect (Articles 12 - 17)
- Prohibition of discriminatory taxation (Article 95 EC)
- Prohibition of quantitative restrictions and measures having equivalent effect on imports (Article 30 EC) and exports (Article 34 EC)
- The *Dassonville* formula and *Cassis de Dijon* principles
- Derogation from Articles 30 to 34 via Article 36 EC

Question 23

Critically review the role played by the European Court of Justice in the removal of non-pecuniary barriers to trade between Member States.

Answer plan

This essay-type of question requires an answer which covers the following points:

* Articles 30 and 34 as they affect barriers to trade
* Directive 70/50 EC
* the *Dassonville* formula
* the first principle from *Cassis de Dijon* and the rule of reason and mandatory requirements
* the second principle of the *Cassis* case on the marketing of goods in Member States

Answer

The European Community is based upon free trade between Member States based upon the abolition of customs duties and charges of equivalent effect.

However, there are other barriers to trade of a non-pecuniary nature which have to be removed. Articles 30 to 34 EC are designed to eliminate these barriers. These Articles are addressed to the Member States but neither the Community institutions nor individuals are free to act in breach of them. Even if the measure concerned is not binding, these Articles will apply. This was provided for by the European Commission in the preamble to Directive 70/50 and confirmed by the European Court of Justice in the case *Commission v Ireland* (1982). The most important one is Article 30 which prohibits quantitative restrictions and all measures having equivalent effect on imports. Quantitative restrictions was interpreted by the Court of Justice in *Riseria Luigi Geddo v Ente Nazionale Rise* (1974) to include any measures which amount to a total or partial restraint on imports, exports or goods in transit.

Measures having equivalent effect to quantitative restrictions is a wider concept than that of quantitative restrictions. More importantly it has been given a very generous interpretation by both the European Commission and the European Court. It has been held to include not just those measures which are overtly protective or applicable to imports or exports, which are referred to as distinctly applicable measures, but measures which are applicable to imports, exports and domestic goods alike. These measures are called indistinctly applicable measures and are often introduced for the most worthy of reasons. They range from regulatory measures designed to enforce a minimum standard such as weight, size, quality, price or content for products to tests and inspections or certification requirements to ensure goods conform to the set standard. They also include activity capable of influencing the behaviour of traders such as promoting goods by reason of their national origin. This occurred in the *Commission v Ireland* (1987) where an agency of the Irish government promoted a 'buy Irish' campaign to promote Irish goods within the Irish Republic, which was held to be contrary to Article 30.

To assist Member States in the identification of measures having equivalent effect to quantitative restrictions, the Commission passed Directive 70/50.

Although this Directive was aimed at the transitional period during which time such measures were to be abolished, the Directive has been seen as providing some non-binding guidelines to the interpretation of Article 30. The Directive was not intended to provide an exhaustive list of measures capable of having equivalent effect to quantitative restrictions. The Directive used the terminology indicated above by dividing such measures into two categories. The first was distinctly applicable measures which hinder imports which could otherwise take place, including measures which make importation more difficult or expensive than domestic production (Article 2(1)). The other category covers indistinctly applicable measures (Article 3) which are only contrary to Article 30 EC 'where the restrictive effect of such measures on the free movement of goods exceeds the effects intrinsic to trade rules', or where 'the same objective cannot be attained by other measures which are less of a hindrance to trade'. Thus such measures appear to be acceptable if they comply with the Community general principle of proportionality.

The European Court of Justice has developed its own definition of measure having equivalent effect to quantitative restrictions. This was first achieved in the case of *Procureur du Roi v Dassonville* (1974) and applied consistently by the court. The *Dassonville* 'formula' is that all trading rules enacted by Member States which are capable of hindering, directly or indirectly, actually or potentially, intra-Community trade are to be considered as measures having an effect equivalent to quantitative restrictions. From this formula it can be seen that it is not necessary to show that the measure is an actual hindrance to trade between Member States, as long as it is capable of such effects. It is necessary however to show some proof of a hindrance to trade because a measure which is not capable of hindering trade between Member States will not breach Article 30. For example where the measure merely affects the flow of trade, as in the *Oebel* Belgian bakery case (1981).

The measure in *Dassonville* was a requirement under Belgian law that imported goods should carry a certificate of origin issued by the State in which the goods were manufactured. Dassonville imported a quantity of Scotch whisky from France. Unfortunately the seller did not have the required certificate so he produced a 'home made one' and was subsequently charged with forgery. In his defence he claimed that the Belgian law was contrary to Community law. The national court made a reference under Article 177 EC to the Court of Justice, which applied the *Dassonville* formula and found that the Belgian measure was capable of breaching Article 30 EC.

The *Dassonville* formula was developed further in the *Cassis de Dijon* case, which identified two principles. Having applied the *Dassonville* formula to the facts of the case, the court stated that obstacles resulting from disparities between the national laws relating to the marketing of products must be accepted in so far as they may be recognised as being necessary in order to satisfy mandatory requirements. Such requirements were listed as those relating to the effectiveness of fiscal supervision, the protection of public health, the fairness of commercial transactions and the defence of the consumer. This is known as the first *Cassis de Dijon* principle. Thus certain measures may be within the *Dassonville* formula but will not breach Article 30 if they are necessary to satisfy such mandatory requirements. This principle has come to be know as the 'rule of reasons'. Before the *Cassis* case it was assumed that any measure which fell within the *Dassonville* formula was a breach of Article 30 and could only be saved by the permitted derogation under Article 36. Since *Cassis*, as far as indistinctly applicable measures are concerned, the rule of reason may apply and save them from Article 30. If the measure is necessary in order to protect mandatory requirements, it will not be breach of Article 30. This is significant since the mandatory requirements permitted under the

Cassis principle are wider than the grounds provided under Article 36. For example in *Commission v Denmark* (1986) regarding disposable beer cans, the protection of the environment was held to constitute a mandatory requirement. However, where the mandatory requirement falls under one of the specific heads of derogation provided by Article 36, the court may prefer to rely on the express provision of that Article. This happened in the *Commission v Germany Re German Sausage* case (1988) where the derogation was on health grounds. In the *Cassis* case itself it was felt that the derogation was not necessary.

The word 'necessary' has been interpreted to mean no more than is necessary and is subject to the principle of proportionality. Other measures could have been used to protect the consumer regarding the alcoholic content of Cassis, such as labelling, which would have been less of a hindrance to trade. It would also have been fair to the domestic producer. The second principle from the *Cassis* case has far reaching implications. It suggested that there is no valid reason why, 'provided that goods have been lawfully produced and marketed in one of the Member States', they should not be introduced into any other Member State. This principle gives rise to the presumption that goods which have been lawfully marketed in another Member State will comply with the 'mandatory requirement' of the importing State.

This can be rebutted by evidence that further measures are necessary to protect the interest concerned. It is hard to rebut this presumption. The burden of proving that the measure is necessary is a heavy one, particularly when, although justifiable in principle, it clearly operates as a hindrance to intra-Community trade. Any evidence submitted in support of the measure will be closely scrutinised by the court. In the case concerning additives in beer (*Commission v Germany* (1985)) evidence was taken concerning the medical effect of such additives from the World Health Organisation and the Food and Agriculture Organisation.

The European Court of Justice has played an important part in removing the barriers to trade associated with measures having an equivalent effect to quantitative restrictions. By the introduction to the 'rule of reasons' to such measures and the extension of the two principles stated in the *Cassis de Dijon* case, the court has tried to balance the need of applying Article 30 EC with the need to respect the mandatory requirements justified under Article 36. Instead of the slow process of seeking Community wide standards under the harmonisation procedures, where the interests of Member States could delay progress, the case law of the court moved the Community forward in the direction of achieving its goal of a common market.

Question 24

James is an English farmer living 10 miles from the Channel Tunnel. He breeds special varieties of pigs and sheep for slaughter and sale to butchers. As a marketing advantage he sells pre-packed joints of meat and special sausages to butchers for re-sale.

With the opening of the Tunnel James has decided to develop links with butchers in northern France. However, he has received a letter containing the following points from French officials:

- as his packs of meat are not labelled in French they cannot be sold in France;
- the pre-packed joints of meat have the weight given in pounds and not kilos and therefore do not comply with French standards of consumer protection;
- the price he is selling his packs at is below the minimum price set in France; and
- the sausages contain additives which, although permitted under English law are not allowed by French legislation.

James seeks your advice as to his position under EC law.

Answer plan

This question represents the typical problem associated with the free movement of goods. The approach you should take is to state the principles and then apply them to the individual aspects of the problem.

You should deal with the following points:
- Article 30 EC and barriers to trade
- definitions and examples of quantitative restrictions and measures having equivalent effect
- the *Dassonville* formula

- the principles from *Cassis de Dijon*
- remedies

Answer

The European Community is based upon a customs union whereby there is a common external tariff for goods coming into the Community and the removal of barriers to intra-Community trade. It has been relatively easy for the Community to deal with the more obvious barriers to trade, such as tariffs. It has been the non-pecuniary barriers, which are more subtle and disguised, that have caused problems, such as those experienced by James. Article 30 EC provides that barriers to trade which amount to quantitative restrictions and all measures having equivalent effect are prohibited. Such quantitative restrictions have been interpreted by the ECJ in *Riseria Luigi Geddo v Ente Nazionale Risi* (1974) to cover any measure which amounts to a total or partial restraint on trade between Member States.

The concept of measures having equivalent effect to quantitative restrictions has been given a wide interpretation by the Court of Justice. It is much wider than mere quantitative restrictions. To assist with the application of the concept it is divided into those measures which are indistinctly applicable and those which are distinctly applicable. Indistinctly applicable measures are often introduced by governments for seemingly the most worthy of purposes. As such measures are applied to both imported and domestically produced goods alike, they are often thought by the government concerned not to discriminate in any way and not to fall within the prohibitions of Article 30. Such measures include regulatory controls designed to enforce minimum standards such as price, which occurs in James's problem. Distinctly applicable measures are those which are applicable only to imported goods.

In the problem the French government has introduced standards for packaging in that any meat product must not be weighed in kilos and not pounds. This was introduced to protect consumers. This measure comes within the category of indistinctly applicable measures since it applies to both French and imported products of this type. It was the Directive 70/50 which introduced the categories of measure having equivalent effect to quantitative restrictions in order to help Member States to identify and eliminate such measures in the transitional period. Although this period has passed, the Directive is still seen as providing non-binding guidelines to the interpretation of Article 30. It is Article 3 of the Directive which deals with indistinctly applicable measures. Such measures are said to be only contrary to Article 30 EC if they do not satisfy the principle of proportionality, ie if the same objective cannot be attained by other measures which are less of a hindrance to trade.

However, it is the case law of the European Court which is of most importance to James. Building upon the Directive, the court has made some very important judgments in this area of Community law. The first case was *Procureur du Roi v Dassonville* (1974), which led to the development of the Dassonville formula. Dassonville had imported some Scotch whisky from France. Under Belgian law it was necessary to have a certificate of origin from the State in which the goods had been manufactured. As the seller did not have such a certificate he produced one of his own. When he was subsequently charged with forgery, he claimed that the Belgian law was contrary to Community law. From its answers to the Article 177 reference made by the Belgian court, the Dassonville formula was developed which stated that the Belgian measure was capable of breaching Article 30. The formula is that all trading rules enacted by Member States which are capable of hindering, directly or indirectly, actually or potentially, intra-Community trade are to be considered as measures having an effect equivalent to quantitative restrictions.

In the *Cassis de Dijon* case (1978) the *Dassonville* formula was extended. In this case a German law required the minimum alcohol content of cassis to be 25%, whereas that imported from France was 15-20%. When it was challenged by the importer the court applied the *Dassonville* formula and held that the German law contravened Article 30. In rejecting the claim that they were protecting public health and the consumer, the court stated that this could be achieved by the alcoholic content of the different products being stated on the label. Under the first principle, certain measures which may fall within the *Dassonville* formula but will not breach Article 30 if they are necessary to satisfy mandatory requirements of the public interest. These include protection of public health and the defence of the consumer and are wider than those listed in Article 36 EC. This principle has become known as the 'rule of reason'. However, the national measure must be proved to serve a purpose which is in the general interest and as to take precedence over the requirements of the free movement of goods. Thus, if the measure is necessary in order to protect mandatory requirements, it will not breach Article 30.

The second principle derived from the *Cassis de Dijon* case gives rise to a presumption that goods which have been lawfully marketed in one Member State will comply with the 'mandatory requirements' of the importing State. This presumption can be rebutted but it is very difficult to do so. The burden of proving that the measure is necessary to protect the interest concerned falls on the Member State which imposed it. Although the measure maybe justifiable in principle, such measures clearly operate as a hindrance to intra-Community trade.

Obviously, James wishes to challenge the French law and obtain a judgment that it is contrary to Community law. The most direct way to do this is to seek to sell a quantity of his meat and sausages in France and to be charged with contravening the domestic legislation. Once the case is before a court he can request them to declare the legislation to be contrary to the provisions of Community law. The court will probably be reluctant to do this without a reference being made to the ECJ under Article 177 EC. The discretion to make such a request under Article 177(2) belongs to the court alone, but having raised the matter of Community law, the court can either decide the point itself or make a reference. It maybe in James's interest for the court to decide the matter itself, since a reference can take up to 18 months even though *Francovich* (1992) may provide him with a remedy in damages. Whatever the court decides to do, it is the principles of Community law outlined above which will be applied. It will be necessary to apply the principle of proportionality to ensure that the measures that go beyond what is strictly necessary to achieve the desired end are held to be contrary to Community law. It is therefore important to see how the ECJ has dealt with cases similar to James's.

With regard to the fact that the meat is labelled in English and not French, although this may be a marketing disadvantage for James it should not stop him selling it in France. His meat is marketed in the UK and therefore under the second *Cassis* principle it must be admitted to the French market. For the second point listed by the official, an obvious question is why it is a requirement of French consumer protection that meat must be packed in kilos? This measure appears to be indistinctly applicable and since the *Cassis* case it is necessary for any court hearing the case to apply the rule of reason to Article 30. Is the measure necessary to protect the mandatory requirement of consumer protection? If it is then it will not breach Article 30. However, the ECJ case law has shown that the word 'necessary' has been interpreted to mean no more than is necessary by applying the principle of proportionality. As indicated above, the German government in the *Cassis* case did not succeed with their defence because the consumer could have been protected by some other means. For example, in *Commission v Germany* (1989) German law on the meat content of sausages could not be enforced against imported sausages where there was no threat to health to invoke Article 36 EC. This was held to be in breach of Article 30 because the objective could have been achieved by other means, such as labelling, which would be less of a hindrance to trade. Here again it would seem that James can defeat any attempt by the French government to justify the measure as being a mandatory requirement.

In *Commission v Germany* (1988), a case was brought against the German prohibition of additives in imported beer. The European Court held that the prohibition of marketing products containing additives authorised in the Member State of production but prohibited in the Member State of importation is permissible only if it complies with the requirements of Article 36. But the court emphasised the last sentence of Article 36 which states that such prohibitions should not constitute a means of arbitrary discrimination or a disguised restriction on trade between Member States. The court concluded that the use of a specific additive which is authorised in another Member State must be authorised in the case of a product imported from that Member State.

It would seem that the French government cannot use the domestic law to stop the importation of James's sausages.

In *Keck and Mithouard* (1993) the European Court had to deal with a reference concerning the prohibition in France of resale at a loss. Although the facts are not exactly as those affecting James, the court's judgment is applicable. In clarifying its case law the court said that the application to products from other Member States of national provisions restricting or prohibiting certain selling arrangements were not such as to hinder directly or indirectly, actually or potentially, trade between Member States within the meaning of the *Dassonville* judgment. This was provided that those provisions applied to all affected traders operating within the national territory and affected them the same way, both legally and factually. In these circumstances Article 30 EC is not breached and James can raise his prices to conform to the set minimum.

Question 25

WH Davis plc are in a very worrying position. Five years ago they developed a new pharmaceutical product to relieve cold congestion and granted the right to sell under the Davis trademark to two companies; one in Germany and one in the Netherlands. WH Davis plc kept the UK market and exports outside the European Community.

Three months ago the German company reported to WH Davis that their products were appearing on the German market. The goods had been purchased in the UK from pharmaceutical wholesalers and transported to Germany where the packaging had been altered to conform with German drug laws. The German price for the Davis product is 30% higher than the price in the UK.

WH Davis plc have discovered that an English company, Stoob Ltd, are responsible for the exports to Germany. They have complained to the UK government, as have the German company to their government, and a joint approach was made to the Commission to stop this movement under Article 36 EC. WH Davis plc have also contacted Stoob Ltd direct, but their response was that any action against them would be contrary to the free movement of goods.

Advise WH Davis plc.

Answer plan

As you read this type of question you should mark those passages which you feel cover those facts which are relevant to the law and make sure that you deal with them in your answer.

The main points to cover are:

- Articles 30 and 34, stating the policy of free movement for imports and exports
- the principles from *Cassis de Dijon* case
- derogation under Article 36 EC
- rights associated with trademarks

Answer

This question concerns the free movement of goods, one of the fundamental principles of the European Community. The Community is based upon a customs union which provides for a common customs tariff to goods coming from outside the EC and the removal of barriers to the free movement of goods within the EC. This applies to both imports (Article 30 EC) and exports (Article 34 EC) between Member States. These Articles are aimed at the governments of Member States but have implications for individual business organisations. The EC does not want to have the situation where governments remove barriers, only for companies to organise their operations so as to set up new ones. If a number of companies operate in this way competition policy under Articles 85 and 86 may be involved. However, in this problem WH Davis do not appear to be acting in agreement with other undertakings or in a dominant position, so I will not look at the competition aspects of this problem in detail. What is more applicable is Article 36 which allows derogation from Articles 30 and 34 on specific grounds with the overall requirement that there is not an arbitrary discrimination or a disguised restriction on trade between Member States.

There is a presumption in favour of goods lawfully marketed in one Member State of the Community being accepted in another Member State. This was clearly stated in the second principle identified by the court in the *Cassis de Dijon* case (1978). If a company or State is seeking to rebut that principle it must prove that the conditions are such that Article 36 is applicable. This Article gives a number of grounds which are only available to the government of Member State. For example where it is claimed that restrictions are justified on the grounds of public policy or public security. However, it is possible for a business to seek derogation under Article 36 on the ground of 'protection of industrial and commercial property'. This includes such intellectual property rights as patents, copyright and trademarks. This supports the recognition given in the treaty that property rights have not been affected by the establishment of the EC. Article 222 EC states that the treaty shall in no way prejudice the rules in the Member States governing the system of property ownership.

If WH Davis plc are to achieve a solution to their problem they must seek assistance from Article 36. How much protection will Article 36 give to them?

In *Deutsche Grammophon* (78/79) concerning copyright, the ECJ stated that Article 36 permitted prohibitions or restrictions on the free movement of goods only to the extent that they were justified for the protection of the rights that form the specific subject matter of the property. In other words, it is necessary to look at what the owner of the property right is seeking to protect. Given that Article 222 clearly states that property rights have not been affected by the Community, the court could not dispute this. However, the court went on to draw a distinction between the existence of industrial property rights and their exercise. It was this latter aspect of property rights which could interfere with the free movement of goods and which the court wanted to ensure was not in conflict with the integration of the 'common market'. This principle does not only apply to copyright but to all intellectual property.

In the pharmaceutical case of *Centrafarm BV v Winthrop BV* (16/74) a claim was made by Winthrop that their trademark had been infringed. What right did the trademark-holder have? The court held that they had the exclusive right to use the trademark for the purposes of putting into circulation products protected by the trademark for the first time. They might either do this themselves or transfer that right to a third party by way of licences, etc. Once the protected product had been put onto the market in a particular State by or with the consent of the owner, he can no longer be allowed to rely on his national property rights to prevent the importation of that product from that State into other Member States. The rights that are associated with the trademark are exhausted. This doctrine of exhaustion of rights has been applied by the court to all types of property rights, including trademarks, patents and copyright.

In this problem WH Davis are the owners of the trademark and therefore have the rights described above. They exercise these rights themselves in certain countries but have consented to two companies exercising this right on their behalf in Germany and Holland. If a product like the cold remedy has been lawfully put onto the market with the owner's consent in one Member State, the importation of that product into another Member State can not be restricted.

This will apply even if, as in WH Davis' case, the purpose is to prevent parties taking advantage of price differences in different Member States. This is after all what was attempted in *Centrafarm v Winthrop*. (The emphasis in that case was to ask what makes a trademark valuable - the reservation to the owner, through his exclusive right to put marked products into circulation, or the goodwill associated with the trademark.)

There have been cases where importers have sought to take advantage of the price differentials which apply in different Member States and the exhaustion principle but the product has had to be re-packaged or labelled to meet the requirements of that particular market. This is what has happened in this problem to meet the specification of the German drug laws. In the case of *Hoffman-La Roche v Centrafarm* (102/77) a similar situation arose regarding the product 'valium'. In the UK a subsidiary of the Roche group marketed the product in packages of 100 or 500 tablets at lower prices than in Germany.

Centrafarm purchased these UK products and re-packaged them in 1,000 tablets, affixed the Hoffman-La Roche trademark and sold them in Germany. Obviously, Hoffman-La Roche sought to protect what they saw as an infringement of their trademark. In this important case the ECJ laid down certain conditions which, if met by the importer, means that the re-packager cannot be restrained by the trademark holder from importing the product. The conditions illustrate the possibility that the holder of the trademark may seek to organise the marketing of his product so as to constitute a disguised restriction on trade between Member States. In *Centrafarm v American Home Products* (3/78) the court recognised this danger even though the use of different marks in the UK and Netherlands could be justified under Article 36. The importer in *Pfizer Inc v Eurim-Pharm Gmbh* (1/81) followed these guidelines when importing Vibramycin tablets manufactured by Pfizer in the UK into Germany. In this case the court held that the plaintiff company could not rely on its trademark and Article 36 to prevent the importation under these circumstances.

My advice to WH Davis is that they have a difficulty in the sense that the ECJ have given a very narrow interpretation to Article 36 because they have given greater significance to the last sentence of the Article. They are seeking to protect their trademark whose essential function is to guarantee to consumers or final users the original identity of the marked product, so as to avoid confusion. They could bring an action in the national court seeking to enforce this right by a request for an injunction against Stoob Ltd and damages for the infringement of their right. However, as has been shown above the ECJ has developed a clear principle in these cases in such cases as *Hoffman-La Roche v Centrafarm*. Whether the national court decides or makes a preliminary reference to the ECJ, it is this principle which will be applied. The problem does not indicate the form of the re-packaging or what information is printed on it. However, it is clear from the question that Stoob Ltd did not communicate with WH Davis about their intention to re-package and import into Germany. This is one of the conditions laid down in *Hoffman-La Roche v Centrafarm* and met successfully in *Pfizer* case. It is possible that on Stoobs Ltd failing to meet all the conditions, WH Davis may be able to protect how they currently operate if it is not considered to be a means of arbitrary discrimination or a disguised restriction on trade between Member States.

However if Stoobs gave the appropriate notice, assuming the packaging is acceptable, they will then meet all the conditions laid down by the ECJ.

Question 26

Analyse TWO of the following cases which came before the European Court of Justice and explain their importance in the development of Community law:

(a) *Cassis de Dijon* - Case 120/78

(b) *Commission v Ireland* - Case 249/81

(c) *Centrafarm v Sterling Drug* - Case 15/74

Answer plan

When approaching a question like this the temptation is to produce too descriptive an answer. The facts are important but are only one element of the answer. You should seek to deal with:

(a) the facts, the legal points raised and the Decision of the court

(b) what kind of case was it? A preliminary reference or a direct action? What Article of the Treaty was it based upon?

(c) the cases chosen for this type of question have usually played their part in developing or reinforcing European Court judgments - what part has this case played?

Answer

(a) *Cassis de Dijon* - Case 120/78

This action was brought in German court because of the application of a German law which forbade the marketing of liqueurs with a low alcohol content. The French liqueur called *Cassis de Dijon* had a maximum strength of 20% alcohol by volume whereas German law required a minimum content of 25%. The French company claimed that the German law was contrary to Article 30 EC as it interfered with the free movement of goods. Although the German authorities were not affecting the free movement of goods by imposing quotas, their actions were still covered by Article 30. This is because the Article also forbids measures having an equivalent effect to quotas.

The German authorities claimed that the law did not discriminate against the French liqueur as the same minimum content also applied to German producers. To allow the 'milder' French drink to be treated as a liqueur would lead to a reduction in alcohol content applied to German producers and thus a lowering standard. In order to avoid the application of Article 30 the German government had to plead Article 36 EC. This Article allows a government of a Member State to derogate from its obligations under Article 30 on such grounds as public policy, public morality, public security or the protection of the health and life of humans, animals and plants. Specifically the German government argued that its minimum standard law was aspired by the wish to protect the consumer from alcoholism, ie public health. However Article 36 ends by saying that it may be used as a means of disguised restriction or trade.

The Court of Justice said that in the absence of common rules to the production and marketing of alcohol, it is for the Member State to regulate in that they are necessary to satisfy fiscal supervision, the protection of public health the defence of the consumer and the fairness of commercial transactions. These points were raised by the German government. They said that public health was protected by fixing a minimum alcohol content as beverages with a low alcohol content more easily induce a tolerance towards alcohol. There would be a general lowering of standards with the lowest alcohol content permitted in any Member State becoming the Community standard. This was rejected by the court as stronger beverages were generally consumed in a diluted form. They also rejected the claim that lower alcohol contents would lead to unfair practices against consumers.

As far as the court was concerned the requirements set by the German government relating to the minimum alcohol content did not serve the general interest and interfered with the fundamental principle of the free movement of goods. It would be a much more simple matter to ensure that suitable information is conveyed to the purchaser by requiring the display of an indication of origin and of the alcohol content on the packaging of products.

(b) *Commission v Ireland* - Case 249/81

Faced with economic problems the Irish government announced in 1978 a programme to create jobs in Ireland's manufacturing and service industries. The main platform for this policy was to persuade individuals to purchase Irish goods. Supported by public funds a 'Buy Irish' campaign was launched involving the Irish Goods Council and the use of a 'Guaranteed Irish' symbol. In 1981, the European Commission delivered its reasoned Opinion that the campaign was equivalent to a quantitative restriction on imports and in breach of Article 30 EC. Article 30 EC prohibits all quantitative restrictions on imports and all measures having equivalent effect. The concept of measures having an equivalent effect has been interpreted very generously by the court to include any activity capable of influencing the behaviour of traders.

The reasoned Opinion is a requirement when the Commission is seeking to exercise its powers under Article 169 EC against a Member State which is failing to fulfil its obligations under the Treaty. It is the final step in the administrative stage before the Commission decides whether to take the Member State before the European Court of Justice. The reasoned Opinion has to provide details of the failure on the part of the Member State, the action required to be taken and the time-scale in which this must be done.

The Irish government argued that the campaign was not contrary to Article 30. They did so by arguing that the prohibition only applies to measures which are binding. All that the campaign did was to give moral support and some financial aid for advertising the activities pursued by the Irish industries. The aid was compatible with Article 92 EC, which permits State aids to industry for such purposes as to combat unemployment. They also claimed that there had been no restrictive effect on trade as the campaign had failed. During the campaign the proportion of Irish goods to all goods sold on the Irish market fell from 49.2% to 43.4%!

The court rejected these arguments because they believed that the Irish government's considered intention was to substitute domestic products for imported products on the Irish market and thereby to check the flow of imports from other Member States. Even though the campaign did not have any significant success, the court could not overlook the fact that the activities form part of a government programme which is designed to achieve this substitution of domestic products for imported products and as such is liable to affect the volume of trade between Member States. The 'Buy Irish' campaign was discriminatory and had the potential effect on the imports from other Member States as if it was one of a binding nature.

A measure like this cannot escape the prohibition laid down in Article 30 EC solely because it is not based on Decisions which are binding on businesses. Even measures which are not binding may be capable of influencing the conduct of traders and consumers and thus of frustrating the aims of the Community set out in Articles 2 and 3 EC. The action of the Irish government was a restrictive practice which represented the implementation of a programme defined by the government and which affected the economy as a whole by encouraging the purchase of domestic products. Given that the Irish government had provided some financial funding for the campaign they were in breach of their obligations under the Treaty. The judgment in this case should not have come as a surprise to the Irish government as they had already been the subject of an Article 169 EC action by the Commission in Case 113/80. In that case the court had held that the Irish government had broken Article 30 EC by imposing a legal requirement that imported 'souvenirs of Ireland' should bear either the name of their country of origin of the word 'foreign'.

(c) *Centrafarm v Sterling Drug* - Case 15/74

Sterling Drug was the parent company holding a number of patents in several countries including the Netherlands and the United Kingdom, for a treatment of infections of the urinary passages. The trademark 'Negram' is used for this product. In the United Kingdom the trademark was the property of Sterling-Winthrop Group Ltd and in the Netherlands by Winthrop BV a subsidiary of the UK company.

Centrafarm imported into the Netherlands from England and Germany some of the medicinal preparations manufactured according to the patent method and put onto the market by subsidiaries of Sterling Drug, some of which carried the trademark Negram. They did this without the agreement of Sterling Drug. By importing from the United Kingdom, Centrafarm had been able to take advantage of a considerable price differential. This was almost 50% of the price charged in the Netherlands.

In June 1971 Sterling Drug submitted an application to a Dutch judge sitting in chambers requiring Centrafarm to refrain from any further infringement of their patent. The judge refused on the basis of his interpretation of the patent law. Sterling Drug succeeded on appeal and the case finally came to the Dutch Supreme court on appeal by Centrafarm. This court used the preliminary reference procedure of Article 177 EC to ask certain questions on patent rights in relation to the provisions of the Treaty.

The European Court accepted that the main issue was whether

the Treaty rules on the free movement of goods prevented the patentee from ensuring that the product protected by the patent is not marketed by others. It referred to Article 30 EC and the prohibition on quantitative restrictions on imports and all measures having equivalent effect. However, it recognised that Article 36 EC did allow such restrictions or prohibitions on the grounds justified for the protection of commercial or industry property, which would include patents. This had to read in conjunction with the last sentence of Article 36 EC which states that such restrictions shall not constitute a means of arbitrary discrimination or a disguised restriction on trade between Member States.

Given that the EC Treaty does not interfere with property rights, the court looked at the exercise of those rights. Article 36 EC allows for the derogation from one of the fundamental principles of the Community, but only where the derogation is justified for the purposes of safeguarding rights which constitute the specific subject matter of the property. What are these rights in relation to patents? The court answered that the specific subject matter of a patent was the guaranteed right of the patentee, as a reward for their creative effort, to manufacture and put into circulation for the first time their product. This could be done directly by the company or by the grant of licences to third parties. In relation to this right the patent-holder could seek enforcement of their rights.

What the court was concerned to do was not to allow the exercise of a patentees right to interfere with the development of the Community. If the patentee could prevent the importation of protected products marketed by him or with his consent in another Member State, he would be able to partition off national markets and thereby restrict trade between Member States. Therefore the action of Sterling Drug, given that it was not necessary to protect their exclusive rights flowing from their patent, was incompatible with the Treaty provisions concerning the free movement of goods. This principle has been applied in subsequent cases, especially where drug companies have sought to use their property rights to block parallel imports from other Member States.

Chapter 7

Competition Policy

Introduction

The competition policy of the European Community is seen as a very important safeguard to the development of the European Community. Many of the questions set on this topic are of the problem-type, notably on the application of Articles 85 and 86.

However, there are possible essay questions on the main principles, as illustrated by some of the questions in this chapter. It is also possible for questions to be set which have a competition element and the free movement of goods, for example the WH Davis problem in Chapter 6. In such circumstances you can either split your answer between the topics or indicate the possible involvement of one but concentrate on the other.

Checklist

Students should have a clear knowledge of the differences between Articles 85 and 86, and the role each plays in the competition policy of the EC.

More specifically you should understand the following points:

- The type of agreements dealt with by Article 85(1)
- The possible exemptions under 85(3)
- The meaning of dominant position under Article 86
- The control of mergers within the EC
- The sanctions for anti-competitive behaviour
- The control of public anti-competitive behaviour under Articles 92 and 93
- The role and powers of the European Commission
- The remedies available, including those provided by the national courts

Question 27

Dicero plc have been purchasing large quantities of manopull textiles from Smart International, a German company, for five years. They are the only manufacturers of this product and they control world sales by a system of licensing agreements.

Two years ago they began imposing retail prices on all purchasers, including Dicero, and restricted the distribution areas any company could control. Dicero were allocated the UK market, whereas companies in France and Italy were given their domestic market plus a share of the world market. For the last twelve months Dicero have had discussions with Smart International to try to obtain some of the necessary export markets to allow for viable production levels. They have conceded nothing. In fact they have stated that unless we sign a new agreement with them they will give the UK market to the French company.

Advice Dicero.

Answer plan

This traditional problem question requires the application of Article 85 EC, and the following specific points:

- the relationship between community and national competition law
- a definition of 'dominance' within the meaning of Article 86
- factors associated with dominance in fact
- abuse of a dominant position
- remedies

Answer

This problem is concerned with one undertaking, Smart International, acting in a way which appears to be anti-competitive. The European Community, having as one of its objectives the removal of barriers to trade between Member States, takes a strong policy against any undertaking which seeks to exercise economic power in the market in a way which sets up barriers to such trade.

Under Article 86 EC monopolies in themselves are not prohibited, but it does prohibit certain anti-competitive conduct by such organisations. The Article applies to either goods or services and has a scope which is not limited to those businesses which are established in the European Community.

It would seem that Dicero Products may have a remedy under this provision of the Treaty. If it can prove that Smart International are acting in breach of Article 86, such action is prohibited by the Article. In order to satisfy Article 86, three essential ingredients must be proved. The undertaking must have a dominant position in the market, there must be an abuse of that position and that abuse must affect trade between Member States. If this last requirement is not met the matter is left to be dealt with by the national competition laws of the Member State concerned.

In order to prove that Smart International are in a dominant position Dicero need to satisfy the definition of dominance laid down by the Court of Justice in *United Brands Co v Commission* (1976). This case involved United Brands' position in the banana market. The court said that dominance means a position of economic strength enjoyed by an undertaking which enables it to prevent effective competition on the relevant market because its strength allows it to act independently of its competitors, customers and ultimately of its consumers. The Commission added to this in the *AKZO Chemie BV* case (1986) that it may also involve the ability to eliminate or seriously weaken existing competitors or to prevent potential competitors from entering the market.

Although this is the principle of dominance it has to be looked at more closely if the rules of the court are to be satisfied.

It may be possible to say that this is the way that Smart International are acting, but are they in a dominant position?

Specifically what is the market in which Dicero are claiming that Smart International are dominant? This is not as straightforward as it may appear, as the European Commission has found when seeking to apply Article 86 EC. It is necessary to identify the relevant market. As far as the court and Commission are concerned this is a matter of product substitution. In the *Continental Can* case (1972) a large Dutch packaging company were being taken over by a subsidiary of the Continental Can company based in the USA.

The Continental Can company was a large organisation in the packaging industry, controlling 86% of a German metal containers company which it intended to transfer to the Dutch company if it acquired it. This would have meant that Continental Can would have had significant market power in Europe and specifically in Germany. However, although the court agreed with the Commission that the takeover could be an abuse, the Commission had not looked at the relevant market. It had not taken into account product substitution. In other words alternative suppliers of cans could adapt their production to produce cylindrical cans suitable for fish or those who purchased the cans could swop to a different shape or design. Such product substitution can be assessed by reference to the characteristics of the product, its price or the use to which it may be put. Are there any substitutes for manopull? What market is it in?

Although the Commission got the market wrong in *Continental Can*, in the bananas case of United Brand's, they satisfied the court that the banana market was distinctive. In that case United Brands had argued that the correct market was the fresh fruit market, in which they were not dominant. However, by means of information about buying habits of consumers and the special characteristics of bananas, the Commission were able to defeat this argument. Could Smart International argue that the consumer had alternative textiles to select from and therefore would not be disadvantaged by their actions? In the *Commercial Solvents* case (1974) the court stated that Article 86 was not concerned only with abuses which prejudiced consumers directly but also those abuses which impair the competitive structure of the market and thus affect consumers indirectly. It would appear that Smart International's action falls into this type of category. The Commission, supported by judgments of the court, takes a hard line in seeking to protect competition in manufacturing and in particular to prevent smaller firms suffering at the hands of more powerful competitors. We are not told the size of Smart International or Dicero, but even where the relevant market has been quite small, as in the *Hugin Cash Registers* case, Article 86 has been applied provided an undertaking has been dominant in the particular market.

If it is assumed that it is possible to identify the relevant market, are Smart International behaving in a way which does not need to take into account their competitors, purchasers or consumers? In other words are they dominant in fact? This requires a wide ranging economic analysis of the market and Smart International. Following previous Commission Decisions four factors are taken into account. The first of these, and the most important, is market share. How much share of the market does Smart International have? Secondly, how long has Smart International held this position in the market? Obviously the longer the period of time, the greater the barriers to entry for new competitors or entrants to the market will be. Thirdly, the financial and technological resources of Smart International. Can they use their resources to use predatory pricing to undercut potential rivals or to maintain their technological advantage? Lastly, access to raw materials and outlets may give Smart International more power. Does it control not only raw materials and production but also applications or retail outlets? This form of vertical integration within their business will be evidence of a dominant undertaking.

4. barriers for Cp or to enter the market

Finally in order to come within Article 86, it must also be proved that Smart International are dominant within the common market or in a substantial part of it. We are told that Smart International control sales in the world but more importantly within the European Community by means of licensing agreements.

It is clear, therefore, that this criteria is satisfied.

Having identified that there is a dominant position, this does not mean that Article 86 has been satisfied. It is not the fact that an undertaking being in a dominant position which is sufficient, Dicero must show that there has been an abuse.

Article 86 itself provides a number of examples of abuse. This list is not to be considered exhaustive, but it does illustrate what Dicero could prove. The problem states that Smart International are restricting the distribution area of each company granted a license. More importantly they have threatened to refuse to supply Dicero if it refuses to sign the agreement.

The refusal to supply in *United Brands* was found to be an abuse. *May affect*

In *Commercial Solvents* the anti-competitive refusal to supply also *trade bt* amounted to an abuse. This will not always be the situation of the *MS* refusal is based on objective criteria and is non-discriminatory. It does not appear that this would be the case with Smart International. *Consequen*

If an undertaking is found to be abusing its dominant position, there is no possibility of exemption as there is with restrictive practices under Article 85. Fines can be imposed by the Commission for breach of Article 86, ranging from one thousand to one million ecus or 10% of the undertaking's turnover.

Substantial fines have been imposed in the past, for example 60 million ecu in the *Polypropylene* case (1986). The threat over Dicero may make them reluctant to wait for action to be taken by the European Commission against Smart International. Article 86 is directly effective and can be applied in the national courts.

There has been some reluctance in national courts to do this because of the detailed economic analysis indicated above which is often necessary with Article 86 cases. However, breach of Article 86 should lead to the application of the same remedies as are available for similar breaches of national law. Therefore, it would be appropriate for Dicero to seek an injunction or a declaration in interlocutory proceedings. As was indicated in *Garden Cottage Foods* (1984) by the House of Lords, English courts are reluctant to award damages in such cases.

Question 28

Jamesons Ltd are a small chain of retail chemists. Until five years ago they owned 8 shops, but they now have 30. As they have expanded in number they have also increased the size of the shops. This allows them to offer a greater selection of merchandise for sale.

Recently a problem has developed concerning the supply of perfume. Oddwax SA (Paris) refuse to supply any of their exclusive brands of perfume because they claim that Jamesons Ltd are not one of their recognised distributors, and secondly that when supplies of Oddwax products have been obtained from third parties Jamesons have sold them below the prices indicated by Oddwax. fixed price

Jamesons have written to Oddwax stating that they consider the refusal to be contrary to EC competition law, and that legal action will be taken, if necessary, to obtain supplies from Oddwax.

Oddwax have replied that they received a letter from the Commission three years ago about these matters which stated that 'on the information available the Commission can see no reason to intervene under Article 85(1)', and had 'consequently closed the file'. Oddwax considered that this legitimised their activities.

Advise Jamesons.

Answer plan

This question concerns Article 85 and the kinds of restrictive practices which have been identified under EC competition policy as being anti-competitive.

You should cover the following points:

- relationship between Articles 85 and 86
- types of agreements covered by Article 85(1)
- the affect of Article 85(1), ie 85(2)
- possible exemption under Article 85(3)
- comfort letters
- the role of the national courts
- remedies

Answer

In the context of European Community law a possibility for Jamesons Ltd is to seek to utilise the competition policy of the Community. Under Articles 85 and 86 certain action is considered anti-competitive and therefore contrary to EC law. The Community is very concerned to safeguard legitimate competition undertaken by businesses such as Jamesons. It does this by dealing specifically with restrictive trade practices (Article 85) and monopoly situations (Article 86). The latter deals with 'an undertaking which is in a dominant position' in the market for particular goods and abuses that position. As Oddwax SA (Paris) do not appear to have such a position in the market, I will concentrate on Article 85 EC.

Article 85 provides a very broad base of liability subject to the possibility of exemption under Article 85(3). It covers agreements which have as their object or effect the prevention, restriction or distortion of competition within the Common Market. Is there an agreement between Oddwax and its distributors which is making it difficult for Jamesons to get supplies? The agreement does not have to be a formal written one to fall within Article 85, because it also covers concerted practices which includes 'gentlemen's agreements'. In *ICI v EC Commission* (1972) the ECJ defined such practices as a form of co-ordination between enterprises that has not yet reached the point where there is a contract in the true sense of the word but which in practice consciously substitutes a practical co-operation for the risk of competition. Therefore because there is a number of recognised distributions for Oddwax products, there must be an agreement between the parties even if we are not told what form it takes.

It is clear that such agreements come within the scope of Article 85 but are they amongst those which are identified as being incompatible with the Common Market? Article 85(1) lists a number of examples of such agreements which impede the free movement of goods or services throughout the Community and thus distort competition with the market. The list is not exhaustive but it does include one which seems to apply to the situation facing Jamesons Ltd.

This is where the agreement directly or indirectly fixes purchase or setting prices or any other trading conditions. It would seem from this that there is one aspect of the problem facing Jamesons which is covered, namely selective distribution agreements. This is the term used by the European Commission for sales conducted through a network of authorised dealers or outlets. Only certain selected dealers are admitted to the network and only they may receive supplies. This type of agreement is often very attractive to manufacturers because, quite legitimately, it gives them control over the way in which their product is sold, and can help them maintain an up-market image. However, it is also a way of maintaining high retail prices. It is stated in the problem that one of the reasons for Oddwax refusing to supply Jamesons is the fact that they had sold the products before at below the price indicated by Oddwax. If an agreement comes within Article 85(1) it is automatically void under 85(2). This means that the agreement can only be implemented at the risk of the parties to it. It can also mean that if action is taken by the European Commission under the procedure of Regulation 17/62, the parties to the agreement, notably Oddwax in this problem, could be heavily fined by the Commission. The fine could amount to one million ecu or 10% of the companies worldwide turnover, which ever is the greater.

However, although Article 85(2) states that all such agreements are void, Article 85(3) gives the power to the Commission to grant exemption so that 85(1) does not apply. What the Commission look for in the agreement is a contribution to the improvement of production or distribution of goods, or the promotion of technical or economic progress with the proviso that customers are allowed a fair share of the resulting benefit. It is also necessary that the restrictions in the agreement go no further than is necessary for the objectives to be achieved and it does not provide the possibility of eliminating competition in respect of a substantial part of the products in question. If Oddwax had sought an individual exemption it would have had to prove that the agreement with the outlets met these conditions. However, it is a long process to obtain an individual exemption so that the European Commission introduced various block exemptions which allow the parties to draft their agreements to fall outside the scope of Article 85(1). However, although there have been eight Regulations issued granting exemptions, none would apply to this problem. In the letter received by Jamesons from Oddwax, reference is made to the comment from the Commission that on the information available, they saw no reason to intervene under Article 85(1) and had closed the file. This does not mean that an exemption has been granted. It is more likely to be what is termed a 'comfort letter'. These were introduced by the Commission in an attempt to reduce its workload and to speed up the decision-making process. However, it has been held by the ECJ to be merely an administrative letter and not binding on the national courts because it is outside the framework of Regulation 17/62. This was stated by the court in a number of judgments referred to as the 'Perfume cases' (1980). The file indicated to be closed three years ago by the Commission can be re-opened, especially when new information or a change in circumstances is brought to their attention.

It would seem that the refusal by Oddwax to supply Jamesons is contrary to Article 85(1) and does not fall within any possible exemption. Under European Community competition law the court has introduced the *de minimis* principle. This states that to come within Article 85(1) competition must be affected to a noticeable extent, judged by taking into account the position of the parties indicated by their size and share of the market. If the principle apples then Article 85(1) will not be breached and Jamesons must look to national law to provide a remedy. However, it is unlikely on the facts in the problem that it will apply in this case. Is there any action open to Jamesons? It would be possible to complain to the European Commission on the expectation that they will utilise the machinery under Regulation 17/62 to enforce Article 85. However, this will be a lengthy business and a speedier remedy should be considered. Jamesons has threatened legal action so this may be a possibility. As the 'comfort letter' mentioned above is not legally binding, it is not possible to go to the ECJ to seek its annulment under Article 173, but national courts are required to apply Article 85(1) as it is directly effective, thus providing the best course of action for Jamesons. The national court will be able to use the European rule of reason devised by the ECJ to decide if the agreement is compatible with 85(1). If it is found to be incompatible by the court, then it is void because only the European Commission can grant exemption, not the court. Thus the remedies available in national courts for breach of Article 85 are those remedies available for similar breaches of national law (Rewe-Zentralfinaz 1976). Although the court will not have the power to order fines. In the case of Jamesons the remedy will be an injunction or a declaration in interlocutory proceedings. In the UK the possibility of the court awarding damages to Jameson is unclear. In *Garden Cottage Foods Ltd v Milk Marketing Board* the House of Lords left it unclear as to whether a breach of Article 85 could give rise to a remedy in damages.

Question 29

Critically review the powers of the Commission under the Competition law of the EC.

Answer plan

This straightforward essay-type question requires the following points to be covered:

- what is the basis of the EC competition policy
- Articles 85 & 86 - 90 EC
- procedures under Regulation 17/67
- power to issue Decisions and levy fines
- control of Commission's exercise of powers via actions for annulment (Article 173) and damages (Article 215)

Answer

According to the European Commission, competition is the best stimulant of economic activity since it guarantees the widest possible freedom of action of all. The Treaty does not define the concept of 'competition' but refers to certain measures which interfere with competition and are therefore prohibited, subject to exemptions granted by the Commission. Thus Article 3(f) sets as one of the objectives of the Community, the institution of a system ensuring that competition in the Common Market is not distorted. Competition policy is another instrument which the Community can use to ensure that objectives set out in the Treaty are obtained. For example, that economic integration will take place to produce 'one common market'.

The chapter of the Treaty dealing with competition contains mainly two sets of rules, reflecting the private and public economic activity which takes place. Articles 85 and 86 apply to enterprises which might be involved in restrictive practices or who are abusing a dominant position within the market. Articles 92 and 93 cover aid granted by Member States. The European Commission has a central role in enforcing Community competition policy. They have the power to issue Decisions which, under the definitions in Article 189 EC, are binding upon those to whom they are addressed.

The Commission's powers relate to four main areas. They have the power to collect information, to grant exemption under Article 85(3), to impose fines and to make interim measures. The powers it has and the procedures it must follow are laid down in Regulation 17/62. These substantial powers are necessary if the Commission is to fulfil its role. However, the procedural requirements are strict under Regulation 17/62 and there is a general duty of confidentiality. A breach of these duties or procedures can result in an action being brought under Article 173 before the Court of Justice, and ultimately the Commission Decision can be annulled. It is also possible for an action for damages to be brought against the Commission, as happened in the *Adams* case (1986). Adams brought an action under Article 215 against the Commission for breach of confidentiality when they allowed to be disclosed to his employers, Hoffman-La-Roche that he had assisted them.

With regard to Article 85, dealing with restrictive practices, the Commission's task is to monitor agreements with a view to granting negative clearance or exemption. This is done on the basis of information supplied by the applicant and other parties.

The Commission has the power to impose fines of up to ecu 5,000 where applicants intentionally or negligently supply incorrect of misleading information. The power of granting exemption under Article 85(3) is only given to the Commission. Before doing so the Commission must publish a summary of the relevant application or notification and all interested parties must be invited to submit their comments. If the final Decision is adverse to the applicant the Commission must give him an opportunity to be heard on the matters to which he objects. Due to the need to speed up the process of considering applications for exemption, the Commission has issued a number of block exemptions which allow undertakings to arrange their business affairs so as not to be in breach of competition policy.

In order to make a Decision related to Community competition policy, the Commission normally needs further information in order to come to an opinion on the legality of the behaviour in question. There are two basic ways to obtain this information, by either investigations or written requests for information. For example if the Commission is investigating the behaviour of a dominant firm it may write not only to the company concerned but to the smaller undertakings who have dealings with the company.

If the replies from the undertakings are incorrect or incomplete, the Commission has the right to impose fines of up to ecu 5,000. On some accessions it is necessary to undertake detailed market analysis and to this end the Commission has been given exhaustive powers. The Commission may conduct general enquiries into whole sectors of the economy if economic trends suggest that competition within the Common Market is being restricted or distorted. To achieve this task the Commission may request every undertaking in a particular sector to supply details of agreements or concerted practices considered exempt. Undertakings or groups which may be in a dominant position may also be required to supply information concerning their structure and practices. Additional information may be requested from governments or competent authorities in Member States. In all these instances the Commission can request any information which it considers 'necessary' to enable it to carry out its tasks. In addition to requesting information, the Commission can seek it by carrying out on-the-spot investigations. These include the power to enter premises, examine books or business records, to copy such records and to conduct oral examinations. These investigations may be 'voluntary' or 'compulsory'. Where they are compulsory Commission officials are required to produce written in the form of a Decision specifying the subject matter and purpose of the investigation. Normally, the Commission will resort to an unannounced visit where a serious risk exists that the undertakings, if forewarned of the inspection, will destroy any incriminating evidence. In *National* (1980), a 'dawn raid' had taken place at its offices, with a search and seizure operation taking place before the company's lawyers could arrive. National claimed that although the raid was authorised by a Decision under Regulation 17/62, some prior warning should have been given. The Court of Justice, hearing an action under Article 173 to have the Decision annulled, disagreed. They held that under the Regulation the Commission was entitled to undertake such investigations as are necessary to bring to light any breaches of Articles 85 and 86. However, it is for the court to control the investigative powers of the Commission as was stated in another case involving a 'dawn raid (*Hoechst* (1989)). In some instances the Commission may request the competent authority of the Member State, such as the Office of Fair Trading, to carry out necessary investigations on its behalf. All undertakings are bound to comply with the legitimate demands of the Commission even if the information is self-incriminating. If they fail to co-operate or give false or misleading information they are liable to penalties.

Obviously in the exercise of its powers to collect information a great deal of commercially sensitive data comes before the Commission officials. The Commission has a general duty of confidentiality and must have regard to the legitimate interests of undertaking in protecting their business secrets. However, the Court of Justice held in *AKZO Chemie v Commission* (1986) that it is for the Commission to decide which particular documents contain business secrets. The Commission has to issue a Decision informing the undertaking, if it intends to communicate documents containing alleged secrets to third parties. This allows the undertaking to challenge the Decision before the European Court of Justice.

The Commission has the power to impose fines of up to ecu 1 million or 10% of the world annual turnover of the undertaking, whichever is the larger, where Article 85(1) or Article 86 has been infringed. This applies whether the infringement has arisen intentionally or negligently. The amount of the fine will depend upon the seriousness of the behaviour, its duration and the size of the undertaking involved. A deliberate infringement will normally deserve a heavier fine than where an undertaking has been purely negligent. The Commission has not been hesitant in using its power to impose fines. In the *Pioneer Hi-Fi* case (1980), a fine of almost 7 million ecu's was imposed for breach of Article 85(1), although it was subsequently reduced on appeal to the court. Any fine levied is paid to the Commission and no amount of it goes to the injured victim of the anti-competitive practice. They must seek a remedy in their national courts. The Court of First Instance, under Article 172 has unlimited jurisdiction with regard to fines. Where the amount of the fine is being challenged this will normally be done by way of proceedings under Article 173 to annul the Decision imposing it.

The work of the Commission with regard to competition policy raises complex issues which may take up to two years before they are resolved. In some instances such a delay may cause irreparable damage to some of the undertakings. To deal with this possibility the Commission is given the power to take immediate action in the form of interim measures to stop objectionable behaviour. This power was implied by the court under Regulation 17/62 in the *Camera Care* case (1980). These measure are of a temporary nature aimed at safeguarding the *status quo*.

It can be seen that in relation to the competition policy of the European Community the Commission does have very wide powers. In the exercise of these powers the Commission is subject to the law of the Community, including the general principles of Community law which have been identified by the court. The Court of First Instance has the power to confirm, reduce, cancel or increase fines and penalty payments imposed by the Commission. As all legally binding actions by the Commission are required to be made by Decisions, these can be challenged before the Court of Justice via an action under Article 173. There is, therefore, clear judicial control of the Commission to ensure that it exercises its powers within Community law. Given the identified need in Article 3(f) EC to have a machinery to ensure that competition within the Community is not distorted, the powers given to the Commission are necessary to achieve this.

Notes

This answer concentrates on the powers associated with Articles 85 and 86. It would be possible to concentrate more on Articles 92 and 93, although most of the powers of the Commission are exercised against private undertakings.

Question 30

What is meant by 'an abuse of a dominant position'?

Answer plan

This is a very popular type of question. It is straight forward, but you should cover the following points:

- Article 86 EC & the EC competition policy
- the role of the Commission
- definition of 'dominant position' from *Continental Can*
- the Decision in *United Brands*

Answer

The term 'dominant position' is associated with Article 86 EC and the policy against anti-competitive behaviour by businesses. There is nothing in Community law which does not allow for a dominant position to be established. What Article 86 is concerned with is the abuse of that dominant position within the common market or a substantial part of it. It is designed to restrain the conduct by a dominant firm that harms those with whom it deals. Such an abuse is prohibited in so far as it may affect trade between Member States.

In *Continental Can* (1972) the Commission defined its view of a dominant position. They said that undertakings were in a dominant position when they have the power to behave independently without taking into account their competitors, purchasers or suppliers. This arises due to the undertakings share of the market or because of the availability of technical knowledge, raw materials or capital in addition to market share. It does not mean that there should be an absolute domination in the sense that the undertaking can eliminate all other competitors. It is enough that their market strength allows them an overall independence of behaviour. The concept of dominance was developed further in *AKZO Chemie BV* (1986) in which the Commission stated that the ability to eliminate or seriously weaken existing competitors or to prevent potential competitors from entering the market may be involved in a dominant position.

In *Continental Can* the court insisted that the Commission analyses an undertaking's market power in two steps. First it needs to define the relevant market and secondly it should assess their dominance within that market. This is not an easy exercise because markets are not always easy to identify. If the market is given a narrow definition, perhaps ignoring the possible substitutes available, it may indicate a large market share which overstates the market power of the undertaking's product. If a wide definition is given to the market the undertaking's market share is understated. The court is quite stringent in requiring the Commission to define the relevant market and to give reasons for its definition. In the *Continental Can v Commission* case the Commission's finding that the Continental Can company was in a dominant position over the supply of cans and closures used for meat and fish products was not accepted by the court.

The main problem was that the Commission had not paid sufficient attention to substitute products. The meat and fish suppliers could turn to glass or plastic containers. Or the manufacturers of cylindrical cans could move towards the production of the flat cans traditionally used for meat and fish products. In the *United Brands* case the company sought to prove that the Commission had got the market wrong once more. However, the court accepted that the Commission was right in identifying the relevant market as that of bananas. Although *United Brands* said that the relevant market was that of fresh fruit, in which they were not dominant, the Commission showed that bananas were consumed particularly by the very young, the old and the sick and was little affected by the pricing and consumption of other fruit.

It is clear that to establish dominance within a particular product market requires detailed economic analysis. From this analysis a number of factors are used to determine dominance. The market share held by the undertaking is a crucial factor when determining dominance. In the *Continental Can* case for example the company had 80% of the German market. *United Brands* had 45% of the bananas market, so it is possible to see the wide variation in market share which can be involved. The Commission considers that a share of between 20-40% may amount to dominance in certain markets. The period of time in which the undertaking has held its position in the market will be important. What are the financial and technical resources of the 'dominant' undertaking? Can it eliminate competitors by intensive advertising campaigns or by predatory pricing? The access to raw materials and markets can also be important. In the *United Brands* case the company was vertically integrated, owning plantation, shipping, storage and distribution businesses for bananas. In *Commercial Solvents* the company which refused to supply another Italian company with aminobutanol had a near-monopoly in its production. The refusal to supply in this case is an example of the final factor which may determine dominance, namely the behaviour of the firm. A firm's behaviour may indicate that it is dominant within the definition given above from the *Continental Can* case, ie it is able to act independently of its competitors, customers, and ultimately, of its consumers. Another example would be the discriminatory pricing system used by United Brands.

Article 86 is only infringed where dominance is within the common market or a substantial part of it. It is not entirely clear how large an area or what proportion of supply amounts to a 'substantial part of the common market'. In *Sugar* (1975) the court stated that the pattern and volume of the production and consumption of a particular product as well as the habits and economic opportunities of vendors and purchasers must be considered. The Commission provided some useful guidance on the relevant geographical market in its Notice on Agreements of Minor Importance, where it noted that the cost of transport is particularly important. It is also necessary to consider the temporal aspect when looking at the question of dominance. The time of year can have a large impact on a particular market, especially when looking at fresh produce.

As indicated earlier it is not the dominance in fact which Article 86 is designed to deal with but the abuse of that dominant position. What amounts to an abuse under Article 86? The Article itself does give some examples of anti-competitive behaviour, but the list is not intended to be exhaustive. There are two main categories of abuse, exploitative or anti-competitive abuses. Exploitative abuses arise where the dominant undertaking takes advantage of its position by imposing harsh or unfair trading conditions. The most common examples of these are unfair prices, unfair trading conditions, discriminatory treatment and refusal to supply. Unfair prices were defined in *United Brands* as a price which bears no reasonable relation to the economic value of the product. Although the court did not state its opinion on the point, the Commission argued that United Brands were charging excessively high prices for its Chiquita brand of bananas. When United Brands refused to allow importers to sell the bananas when they were still green, they were found to be imposing unfair trading conditions. This was despite United Brands' argument that they imposed this requirement to ensure that the consumer obtained a better product. Some of the prices charged by United Brands differed by up to 100% in different Member States. Such was their power to impose discriminatory pricing. Finally United Brands refused to supply one of its main customers who had invested heavily in the appropriate plant and buildings because it had taken part in an advertising campaign for a competitor. Such is the power of the undertaking in a dominant position.

Anti-competitive abuse is less easy to prove than exploitative abuse. They are not usually so harsh but they have the same affect in that they reduce or eliminate competition. For example the tying-in agreement which came before the court in *Hoffman-La Roche* (1977). This undertaking had a dominant position in seven separate vitamin markets. Customers undertook to buy all or most of their requirements from La Roche as part of tying-in agreements. As a 'reward' such companies received fidelity rebates in the form of discounts. The agreements also included 'English' clauses which allowed a customer who found suppliers offering similar products elsewhere, to ask La Roche to match these prices. If La Roche failed to do so the company was free to purchase the products elsewhere. Although not oppressive for the companies concerned, the Commission found these tying-in agreements limited their customers freedom to buy from alternative suppliers. Once the alternative suppliers had been identified, La Roche was of a size to be able to take pre-emptive action to remove its competitor. Both the Commission and the court found these practices to be abusive.

The kind of predatory pricing used by La Roche is another example of anti-competitive abuse. In *AKZO Chemie BV* (1986) a firm in a dominant position in the production of organic peroxides used this strategy where prices are reduced below cost, in order to drive potential competitors out of the market. Other examples of anti-competitive abuse includes refusal to supply, exclusive reservation of activities and import and export bans. In *Continental Can* the Commission applied Article 86 in the context of a proposed merger or takeover. The Commission's decision said that the proposed takeover constituted an abuse of their dominant position within the common market, ie Germany. Such a case is unlikely to happen now under Article 86 EC as there is now Regulation 4064/89, a special measure to deal with mergers and acquisitions.

Question 31

Analyse TWO of the following cases which came before the European Court of Justice and explain their importance in the development of Community law:

(a) *Consten & Grundig* - Cases 56 & 58/64

(b) *ICI (Dyestuff)* - Case 48/69

(c) *United Brands* - Case 27/76

Answer plan

When approaching a question like this the temptation is to produce too descriptive an answer. The facts are important but are only one element of the answer. You should seek to deal with:

(a) the facts, the legal points raised and the decision of the court

(b) what kind of case was it? A preliminary reference or a direct action? What Article of the Treaty was it based upon?

(c) the cases chosen for this type of question have usually played their part in developing or reinforcing European Court judgments - what part has this case played?

Answer

(a) *Consten & Grundig* - Cases 56 & 58/64

This case concerns attempts by private traders to carve up the internal market when one of the fundamental objectives of the Community was to remove national barriers to trade. Consten was a French firm which specialised in acting as wholesalers for electrical products. Grundig was a German firm which manufactured radio, television sets and similar products in Germany. The reason the two cases are joined is because they both arise from the exclusive distribution contract made between the two businesses in 1957. Under this contract Grundig promised not to deliver to any other French distributor and to include in any contract they entered into with other firms elsewhere a clause preventing their goods from being transferred to France. Consten promised in return to buy Grundig's products and not from any other competitors and not to deliver outside France. One final fact was that the products subject to the contract all carried the trademark GINT, ie Grundig International. Consten registered this mark in France with Grundig's consent.

Two important factors happened subsequent to this contract in 1957. Firstly, in 1958 the Treaty of Rome setting up the European Community came into force and with it the Articles dealing with anti-competitive activity. In 1962 Regulation 17 was adopted which provided the machinery for the Commission to deal with any anti-competitive behaviour. Under this Regulation agreements like the one between Grundig and Consten had to be registered. This was done by Grundig. Secondly, also at this time French competitors were getting Grundig products into France and selling them at lower prices. Consten had sued a number of these businesses in the French courts for unfair competition and infringement of their trademark.

Acting under Regulation 17 the Commission in 1964 took a Decision addressed to Grundig and Consten stating that their contract was in breach of Article 85(1). They were forbidden to hinder the acquisition by competitors of the goods covered by the contract for resale in France. The firms wished to challenge these Decisions, which they did under Article 173 EC in an action for annulment. Article 85(1) prohibits agreements which may affect trade between Member States and which have as their object or effect the prevention, restriction, or distortion of competition within the common market. Grundig and Consten claimed that they were not competitors and so there was never any question of them promising not to compete with each other. Supported by the Italian government they argued that the word 'agreement' in Article 85 EC only applied to contracts between competitors at the same level - horizontal agreements. However, the court held that Article 85 refers in a general way to all agreements which distort competition within the common market. Therefore as the Treaty does not make a distinction between the level at which the firms operate or whether they are competitors or not, such a distinction can not be implied into the Treaty. Competition can be distorted within the meaning of Article 85(1) by agreements which prevent or restrict the competition between one of them and third parties. The contract created an unjustified advantage at the expense of the consumer, contrary to the aims of Article 85(1).

The firms also argued that Article 85's reference to 'affect' meant affect in a detrimental way, for the worse. The contract they argued strengthened Grundig and allowed for greater competition between them and their rival manufacturers. The court held that what is important is whether the agreement is capable of constituting a threat, either direct or indirect, actual or potential, to freedom of trade between Member States in a manner which might harm the attainment of the objectives of a single market between States. Thus the fact that the agreement encouraged an increase in the volume of trade between States is not sufficient to exclude the possibility that the agreement may 'affect' such trade, especially as Consten were prohibited from re-exporting to other Member States.

The final argument put forward against the Commission's decision was that Consten owned the trademark in France. Under Article 222 EC it is stated that the Treaty does not prejudice the rules in Member States governing the system of property ownership. Yet the Commission's decision had stopped Consten's use of its trademark protection to prevent parallel imports of Grundig products. The court's view was that the GINT trademark was intended to place an obstacle in the way of parallel imports. As the agreement is void under Article 85(2), this would be ineffective if the trademark could still be used by Consten to achieve the same objective. There is a distinction between the rights inherent in a trademark, which are recognised by Article 222 EC and the exercise of those rights. The rights of the owner of a trademark are limited to the extent that the exercise of those rights may infringe Article 85(1).

(b) *ICI Ltd v Commission* - Case 48/69

This case, which is often called the *Dyestuff* case, involves the competition policy of the European Community and in particular Article 85 EC. This Article is concerned with restrictive practices arising from agreements and concerted practices which affect trade between Member States. However, what amounts to a concerted practice was one of the key questions in this case.

ICI was among the undertakings producing aniline dyestuffs, who together accounted for 85% of the market. There had been three uniform price increases introduced almost simultaneously in 1964, 1965 and 1967. The increases covered the same product. In January 1964 there was a 10% increase followed in autumn 1964 a 10-15% increase which was to come into effect in January 1965. At a meeting in Basle in August 1967 one of the producers announced an 8% increase and two other producers subsequently announced a similar increase. The Commission concluded that there had been a concerted practice between the undertakings and using its powers to enforce the Community's competition policy it imposed a fine on all the undertakings involved. The undertakings challenged the Commission's decision by a direct action before the European Court under Article 173 EC. They claimed that the price increases merely reflected parallel behaviour associated with an oligopolistic market, where each producer followed the price-leader.

The court upheld the Commission's decision. In its judgment the court stated that the inclusion of concerted practices in addition to agreements between undertakings in Article 85 EC was for a specific purpose. The object is to bring within the prohibition of the Article a form of co-ordination between undertakings which, without having reached the stage where an agreement properly so called has been concluded, knowingly substitutes practical co-operation between them for the risks of competition. The behaviour of the participants is therefore important because it is that which is identified as the concerted practice. However, the court recognised that this behaviour could not be conclusive but it was strong evidence to suggest that the market was not 'operating normally', having regard to the nature of the products, the size and number of undertakings involved and the market volume they controlled. This idea of the 'normal conditions' of the market has been criticised as it does not take into account the type of activity which occurs in oligopolistic markets. Although on the facts of the case it is very difficult to find any support for the dyestuff producers.

The identification of a concerted practice requires the evidence provided by the Commission to be considered as a whole, taking into account the parties involved and the specific features of the market for the product in question, ie the freedom of the consumers to choose their supplier. In this instance the general and uniform increase in prices can only be explained by a common intention on the part of the undertakings. This intention was to adjust the price level and to avoid the risk which could accompany such price increases of changing the conditions of competition.

(c) *United Brands* - Case 27/76

United Brands Co. is a conglomerate owned by a company based in the USA. It is the world's largest seller of bananas. In the opinion of the European Commission, United Brands holds a dominant position in the banana market in a substantial part of the European Community. This is based upon the fact that it handles 40% of the trade in bananas in the EC and has overwhelming economic power based upon the vertical integration of its banana business. United Brands owns numerous plantations in tropical banana-growing countries and a fleet of refrigerated banana boats. In addition it controls banana ripening in consumer countries and takes direct charge of the advertising campaigns and sales promotion activities related to its brand, Chiquita. It is the only firm to have all these advantages in the banana market and is thus in the position to use them to place major obstacles in the way of effective competition in the banana market.

The European Commission reached the decision that United Brands was abusing its dominant position, contrary to Article 86 EC. This was based upon a number of points, including:

(i) UB prohibited its distributors and ripeners from reselling green bananas, which meant there was market fragmentation;

(ii) It charged its customers prices which differed according to the Member State in which they were located. Such differences could amount to 100%, although there were no objective reasons for this discrimination;

(iii) It charged unfair prices for sales to its customers in Germany, Denmark and the Benelux countries;

(iv) Finally, for no objectively valid reason, it refused for nearly two years to supply one of its main Danish customers.

The Commission considered these to be serious violations of Article 86 EC and imposed a heavy fine of one million ECU and ordered United Brands to put an end to its infringements. The importance of this case lies in the fact that the Commission investigated United Brands entire marketing policy in the light of Article 86, perhaps because of the problems it had experienced in the *Continental Can* case (1972). They were not attacking the commercial dynamism of United Brands which is not contrary to Article 86, but because a dominant firm has an obligation not to indulge in business practices which are at variance with the goals of the Community's competition policy. It is not being in a dominant position which is contrary to Article 86, but the abuse of that position.

United Brands appealed to the European Court against the decision of the Commission, seeking its annulment under Article 173 EC. They claimed that the 'relevant market' identified by the Commission was too narrow and should have been the fresh fruit rather than the banana market. The court upheld the Commission's choice of bananas as the relevant market. However, they quashed the Commission's decision that UB's prices were excessive because the Commission should have at least have asked United Brands about its costs. Overall the court upheld the Commission's Decision, including its condemnation of UB's refusal to supply, although the fine was reduced to 850. The definition of a dominant position given in the court's judgment has been followed very closely in subsequent cases involving infringements of Article 86. The definition is that a dominant position involves economic strength which enables an undertaking to prevent effective competition and to act independently of its competitors, customers and ultimately of consumers.

Question 32

Critically review the development and operation of the EC merger policy.

Answer plan

It is quite rare to have a problem question set on mergers, although this may change as case law on merger regulation develops. Where questions are set they are generally of an essay-type. The main points which should be covered in your answer are:

*   the role of Articles 85 and 86 EC in merger policy
*   the need for a specific merger policy
*   the Merger Regulation 4064/89
*   the requirements of the Regulation
*   the benefits of the Regulation

Answer

When the European Community was established there was no specific Treaty provision dealing with mergers within the Community. Under the EC competition policy it was assumed that Article 86 EC, which applies to the abuse of a dominant position, would be used to deal with mergers. There was the question of whether the Article would only apply once the merger had taken place. However, in the *Continental Can* case (1973) the European Commission had applied Article 86 EC in the context of a proposed merger involving firms producing metal containers. On appeal the ECJ said that Article 86 EC can be used to stop mergers which eliminate competition. It would not be necessary to prove a causal link between the dominance and the abuse. If there was dominance in fact then the proposed takeover was an abuse. However, the ECJ went on to annul the Commission's Decision in this case on the grounds that they had not identified the dominance in the relevant product market. This is a problem with the proof required under Article 86 EC.

This problem was lessened to a certain extent when in the *Philip Morris* case (1980) the court decided that mergers also fell within the scope of Article 85(1) EC. This Article deals with restrictive practices between undertakings. The Commission had been notified of the proposed merger of Philip Morris and Rothmans Tobacco (Holdings) Ltd which would result in Morris acquiring a controlling interest in the EC cigarette market. The agreement had been notified to competitors of Philip Morris and Rothmans in the EC cigarette market. Two of these competitors, BAT and Reynolds were not satisfied with the action of the Commission and brought an action under Article 173 EC to challenge it. The court held that a purchase of a company's shares by one of its major competitors came within Article 85 EC. However, one of the problems with this method of control of mergers was the delay caused by the Article 85 EC procedure and the affect this could have on the market share price. In addition there was the problem of the relationship between the Community competition policy and the policing of mergers in the Member States. Thus although both Articles 85 and 86 EC had been used to deal with merger situations, they were not very satisfactory.

For many years the European Commission had been making proposals concerning the Community control of mergers on the basis of a 'one-stop procedure'. This would provide a business with clear reporting requirement showing the distinctive involvement of the European Commission as against the various merger bodies in the Member States. In 1989 the Council of Ministers finally adopted Council Regulation 4064/89, known as the Merger Regulation. It came into force on the 21 September 1990. Under the Regulation, which has direct effect, those mergers with a Community dimension are subject to examination by the European Commission. There is thus a shared jurisdiction concerning mergers in the sense that those mergers which do not have a Community dimension remain within the control of the national authorities of the Member States. In the UK this is the Office of Fair Trading.

As mentioned above only those concentrations or mergers with a Community dimension will come within the scope of the EC Regulation. The meaning of 'concentration' is defined by Article 3 of the Regulation in terms of the acquisition of sole or joint control. Thus it may occur by two or more previously independent undertakings merging to become a new independent undertaking or where one undertaking acquires direct or indirect control of the whole or part of another undertaking. This latter situation is quite common in the UK when one undertaking buys a controlling interest of the shares in another company. The first case to be considered by the Commission concerned the two companies Renault and Volvo. The two companies had agreed to exchange 25% of their respective equities in their car businesses and 45% of their truck and bus divisions. In both exchange agreements, management committees were established to decide on 'all matters from research and development to production and purchasing, including co-operating with third party producers'. The Commission decided that the agreement concerning the car activities did not amount to a concentration because neither party had control of the other. However, the truck and bus venture did constitute a concentration due the permanent joint-control, even though it amounted to less than 50% of their equities.

If a proposed merger qualifies as a concentration, the next question is whether it has a 'Community dimension'. The test for this is one of sales or turnover. This means under the Regulation that those mergers involving enterprises with an aggregate world-wide turnover of more than 5 billion ECU and where the aggregate Community turnover of each of at least two of the enterprises concerned is more than 250 million ECU will be subject to examination by the European Commission. Such mergers must be notified to the Commission. The failure to notify or to supply incorrect information may result in a fine of between 1,000 to 50,000 ECU.

Once a transaction is found to be within the scope of the Merger Regulation, the European Commission must then decide whether or not it raises serious doubts as to its compatibility with the Common Market. The vast majority of the fifty or so transactions so far have not raised such doubts and so have been cleared by the Commission. This would seem to indicate that the Commission has established a high threshold for the opening of formal proceedings. The reason for this is that Article 2(3) of the Regulation establishes a two-stage test of compatibility. The initial consideration is whether the concentration 'creates or strengthens' a dominant position within the Common Market or a substantial part of it. This reflects the importance to merger transactions of the case law developed by the court and the Commission when applying Article 86 EC. If this first stage is satisfied, the Commission will then go on to assess whether the transaction 'significantly impedes' effective competition within the market. Another possible reason for the high threshold for the formal proceedings is that the European Commission has to reconcile its competition policy as it applies to mergers and its industrial policy. One of the recitals to the Merger Regulation indicates that mergers are to be welcomed as a way of increasing the competitiveness of European industry, improving the conditions of growth and raising the standards of living in the Community.

Although the Commission has cleared a few mergers with conditions, it has banned one altogether. This was the controversial Decision in the case of *Aerospatiale - Alenia and De Havilland*, where the Commission flatly prohibited the merger. The criticism of the Decision centred on the Commission's definition of the relevant product market. Those who supported the merger claimed that the Commission had taken too narrow a definition of the market as 20-70 seater aircraft. However, the Commission has resisted all attempts to re-open the case.

The early history of the Merger Regulation has proved that such a measure was necessary. The Regulation has provided the 'one stop' approval procedure that undertakings wanted. Also the Commission has kept to the tight time-scale set by the Regulation. The main criticism that has been encountered concerns the definition of the relevant product market. This also arose when Article 86 EC was the main Community vehicle for dealing with mergers. However, the Merger Regulation offers much more flexibility than that provided by Articles 85 and 86 EC.

Free Movement of Workers

Introduction

This is perhaps the most developed area of mobility within the Community, apart from the free movement of goods. Very often there are problem questions associated with the rights of workers and their dependants to move around the Community in order to search for work or take up offers of employment. The starting point on this topic should be Article 48 EC, the Directives and regulations adopted to provide the detail for this Community freedom and the judgments of the European Court of Justice which have developed the principles of interpretation and application of Community law.

Checklist

You need to put this free movement policy for workers within the context of the development of a 'common market for labour' as a necessary factor of production. In particular you should understand:

- The right given to workers under Article 48 to enter and remain in a Member State
- The possible derogation by Member States under Article 48(3) and Directive 64/221
- The possible reservation of 'public service' jobs under Article 48(4)
- Directive 68/360 and Regulation 1612/68 on the rights of entry and the right to remain
- Regulation 1251/70 and the right to remain after employment

Question 33

Maria is a Spanish single parent living in Madrid with her young daughter and mother. She has recently lost her job due to redundancy. While she was a student Maria had spent some time in England on an exchange programme. Remembering the vacancies she had seen advertised in the newspapers, she decided to travel to London to seek employment.

Unfortunately she finds it hard to find employment and is considering seeking help from the social security. She was informed at the social security office that her child and mother must return to Spain immediately if she cannot support them. If she cannot find a job after three months she will have to return to Spain herself.

Advise Maria.

Answer plan

This questions requires you to apply the principles of free movement of workers to a problem involving Maria. What are we going to do about Maria? It is necessary to state the law affecting her, her daughter and her mother and then apply them to the specific information in the problem. Obviously the bulk of the answer will centre on Maria because generally the rights of the daughter and mother are derived from hers. You should cover the following points:

* Article 48(3) EC and the right to accept offers of work

* Directive 68/360 and the case of *Procureur du Roi v Royer* on search for work

* time limitation on searching for work and the factor of social security

* Regulation 1612/68 on dependants

Answer

Maria only needed a valid passport or identity card to enter the UK. No visa or equivalent documentation could have been demanded from her or her family. However, if she wishes to remain in the UK to look for work she will have to meet certain requirements. As there is no indication in the problem that Maria is contemplating setting up her own business or wishes to practise a profession, it is assumed that she comes within the category of 'worker' as far as the European Community is concerned. Articles 52 or 59 EC will not be considered as they refer to the right of establishment and the right to provide services on a temporary basis.

Article 48(3) EC gives an individual who is a worker in one Member State the freedom to move to another Member State to accept offers of employment actually made. There is no definition of worker in the Treaty but subsequent secondary legislation and case law has provided such a definition. In the *Lawrie-Blum* case (1987) the Court of Justice suggested that the essential characteristics of a worker are of someone who performs services for another during a certain period of time and under the direction of another in return for remuneration. Unfortunately Maria has not received such an offer of employment before coming to the UK and therefore does not come within the definition of either 48(3) or of a worker. However, does she have any rights as an individual who is seeking employment as a worker?

In 1968 the Council adopted Directive 68/360 which deals with the abolition of restrictions on the movement and residence of workers and their families. Although this Directive does not specifically cover those who enter another Member State in search of employment, it has been generously interpreted by the Court of Justice to facilitate such a search. In the case of *Procureur du Roi v Royer* (1976) the court held that Article 3 of the Directive included the right to enter a Member State to search for work. When the Directive was being adopted it had been minuted that individuals who moved to another Member State without a specific job offer should be allowed to enter that Member State in order to look for work. This had been pointed out in the *Levin* case (1982). However, this right was to be for a limited period of three months on the proviso that the individual could support themselves without recourse to public assistance. Although this minute had no legal effect the court held in *Antonissen* (1991) that Community law gives immigrants seeking employment the right to enter another Member State and stay there for a sufficient period of time to find out about the job market opportunities and if appropriate to find employment.

Thus from the case law of the court, Maria does have the right to enter the UK for the purpose of seeking work, but what time period does she have? In the cases above the period of three months was indicated. This was perhaps due to the reference in the EC legislation on social security in Regulation 1408/71, to the fact that payment of unemployment benefit for up to three months could be paid in another Member State while the claimant is looking for work. In fact under UK law the period is stated to be a period of six months. However, in the *Antonissen* case mentioned above the court went on to say that if after this period the immigrant provides evidence that they have a genuine chance of obtaining employment, they should not be subject to immediate deportation. The corollary of this is that if they have not found employment and can not satisfy the authorities that they have any genuine job opportunity they can be deported.

It would appear that Maria does have a period in which she can seek employment in the UK, but what of her mother and daughter. Obviously the daughter does not come within the category of someone seeking to exercise her rights as a worker within the Community. The mother may be of such an age that she too could claim the same right as Maria, ie to remain for six months whilst she is seeking employment. However, if we assume that she is dependent on Maria, what are her rights? The situation seems to be a little complicated in that the rights of members of a worker's family and dependants are dependent upon the status of worker being granted to an individual, such as Maria. Those who maybe identified as having the right to install themselves with the worker are defined in Article 10(1) of Regulation 1612/68. It includes the worker's spouse and descendants who are under the age of 21 or dependant relatives. There is no difficulty in concluding that the mother and daughter come within this definition in relation to Maria. However, as indicated above, Maria is not yet a worker within the Community definition. The concern that those who are seeking employment and their dependants should not become a burden on another Member State would indicate that the rights of someone seeking employment could be terminated if they become such a burden. Therefore, if this is what is happening the case of Maria and her family's rights are terminated and they could be deported.

The only way that Maria and her family can remain in the UK is if she can find employment. It is worth Maria or even her mother considering part-time employment if full-time employment is not available, however if her mother obtained employment it may not be so easy to prove that Maria and her daughter are dependant upon her. This is because it was held in the *Levin* case mentioned above that the term worker and its associated rights applied to those who only worked part-time provided the work was 'real' work and not nominal or minimal. In *Kempf* (1986) a part-time music teacher from Germany was working in the Netherlands and receiving supplementary benefits from the Dutch government due to her low income from teaching. When she claimed a residence permit as a worker it was refused, even though such a permit is a recognition of the workers rights under the Treaty and not a prerequisite for finding employment.

However, the court held that a person who pursued a genuine and effective activity as an employed person, even on a part-time basis, could have the status of a worker. If Maria can gain this status she will be granted a residence permit for at least five years and which will be automatically renewable. The rights and benefits associated with such a status, such as not to be discriminated against on the grounds of nationality with regard to education, social advantage, access to employment and training and housing will also apply to her mother and daughter as long as she remains as a 'worker'. This is because their rights depend upon the national of another Member State pursuing an activity as an employed or self-employed person in the territory of another Member State.

Question 34

'The European Community is concerned with encouraging the freedom of economic activity within the Community associated with the employed, the self-employed and business organisations'.

Discuss.

Answer plan

This essay-type question allows you to demonstrate your knowledge and understanding of the wider perspective of the free movement of workers and the right of establishment and the right to provide services discussed in the following chapter. However, this question is in this chapter because as you will see the free movement of workers forms the bulk of the answer. Depending upon your preparation you could expand on the right of establishment etc, and still provide a good answer to the question.

The main points you should cover are:

• Article 48 EC - free movement of workers

• Article 52 EC - freedom of Establishment

• Article 59 EC - freedom to provide services

• Restrictions on mobility - not a general mobility right

• power of derogation under the Treaty

• policy of the EC to remove barriers and widen the scope of free movement

Answer

The main treaty establishing the European Community is the European Economic Treaty, which as its title suggests is predominantly concerned with economic activity. Although many areas of economic policy are covered by the Treaty, it does deal specifically with the economic activity of individuals with regard to the free movement of workers, the right of establishment and the right to provide services. The philosophy of a common market requires the removal of all obstacles to the free movement of the factors of production in the form of labour and enterprise. Thus rather than provide an absolute freedom of migration, for example, the Treaty confines itself to specific economic situations, although as the Community has matured as an organisation, this has been relaxed to a certain extent as recent Directives illustrate.

One of the objects of the Community is to establish a 'common market in manpower', which would serve the purpose of moving labour or workers around the Community. Formalities at borders and points of entry are kept to a minimum. No visas are required from EC nationals, only an identity card or passport. Under Article 48 EC workers who are nationals of a Member State are free to move to another Member State to accept offers of employment actually made and to remain in Member State for the purpose of carrying on employment. There is no definition of 'worker' in the Treaty. There is no definition of 'worker' in the Treaty but subsequent secondary legislation and case law has provided the following characteristics. A worker is someone who performs services for another during a certain period of time and under the direction of another in return for remuneration (*Lawrie-Blum* case (1987)). It was also decided by the court that it included those workers who are 'part-time' as long as the work was 'real' work and not nominal or minimal (*Levin* case (1982)). In addition it was held in *Antonissen* (1991) that those individuals who move to another Member State to seek employment have a temporary right to remain in a Member State to search for work. This should be for a minimum of three months, although in the UK it is in fact six months. Having gained employment a worker has a right to a residence permit in that Member State, valid for five years and automatically renewable. The freedom of movement of workers is mainly based on the principle of non-discrimination on the grounds of nationality, although it is possible for a Member State to derogate from this obligation Article 48(4) is applicable and the work is in a public service where the individual would be exercising discretion and authority affecting the State. However, it can be seen from the main provision of Article 48 and its extension by the case law indicated above, that it is confined to those who are seeking to take part in economic activity. If the worker loses his job voluntarily and is unable to find another, his residence permit may not be renewed and he may be deported if he is no longer involved in economic activity. This occurred in *Williams v Dutch Secretary of State* (1977) where a British subject was continuously unemployed in the Netherlands.

In addition to the worker, under Directive 68/360 members of his family and other dependants also obtain rights of entry and residence in the Member State as the principle of non-discrimination must be extended to them. This is an essential requirement as it would otherwise make the practical implementation of mobility of labour meaningless. Those who can join the worker are defined by Article 10(1) of Regulation 1612/68. Family rights terminate with the primary rights of the worker and also when a dependant ceases to be a member of the family. The death of the worker will not deprive members of his family of their right to remain in the Member State. If they have not acquired their own right to remain, they are given preferential treatment if the death of the worker is associated with his employment, such as an occupational disease or an industrial accident.

Freedom of movement could prove illusory if by moving from one Member State to another the worker loses the rights acquired under social security Regulations, notably those associated with the pension entitlement of the worker and his dependants. The Treaty has therefore provided for the adoption of a system ensuring that all of employment periods are taken into account under the laws of several Member States where the beneficiary has worked. These periods will be added together for calculating the amount of any benefits and they will be paid to him in whichever Member State he resides. Overall, therefore, the freedom of movement for the worker means applying the same treatment to the migrant worker and his dependants as the nationals of the Member State of residence.

Although a worker is an individual, the right of establishment necessary to exercise a profession or to render a service is not confined to individuals but also includes companies. There is no definition of the group of persons entitled to the right of establishment. The rules of entry and residence are broadly the same as for workers discussed above. Article 52 EC contemplates a group of people who, in principle pursue activities as self-employed persons or set up and manage undertakings within the meaning of Article 58 EC. Such persons belong, as a rule, to recognised professions whose status and membership is regulated by law. Therefore the full enjoyment of the right of establishment depends upon the recognition of professional qualifications. Without this recognition the mobility of this part of the 'common market in labour' would be severely restricted. Therefore, the European Commission has concentrated on this recognition of professions as the main barrier to such mobility. Initially the Commission attempted to compare various professional qualifications and training in the Member States and aimed at harmonisation through Directives. However, this was a very slow process with limited success. For example the Directive on recognition of qualified architects took over thirteen years to reach agreement. There has been some success with a number of sectoral Directives being adopted including doctors, nurses, dentists and veterinary surgeons. The change in policy was reflected in the Mutual Recognition Professional Qualification Directive 89/48 which came into force in April 1991. Basically this Directive requires a Member State to recognise someone who has qualified to practice a profession in one Member State to be able to do so in another Member State. This right is subject to the power of the host Member State to require some additional training but within specific limits of time and assessment. The underlying philosophy of the Directive is that professional education and training may vary in detail between Member States, but that any fully trained professional in a given field is likely to have the same knowledge as that required of his counterpart in a different Member State.

To complement the right of establishment there is also the freedom to provide services under Articles 59-66 EC. The provision of services is often connected with the exercise of a profession and in this respect is inseparable from the right of establishment. The services are provided for remuneration or payment. The main difference is that the individual who is providing the service remains resident in another Member State and temporarily pursues his activity where the service is provided. Again, the individual must be allowed to do this without discrimination and on the same conditions as the State imposes on its own nationals.

It can be seen from this discussion of the rights of workers, the self-employed and companies that the Treaty does give priority to the mobility of 'labour' and 'enterprise' for economic purposes. Although the European Court has held that Articles 48, 52 and 59 EC are based on the same principles as far as entry and residence and non-discrimination on the grounds of nationality are concerned, reference is often made in the judgments of the court to 'economic activity'. However, in three Directives adopted in 1990 there does seem to be a recognition that the scope of mobility needed to be widened. Directive 90/364 gives rights to persons of independent means and Directive 90/365 covers retired persons, whereas Directive 90/366 provides rights to students undertaking a vocational course at a university in another Member State for the duration of the course. These examples do not detract from the fact that generally mobility is associated with economic activity.

Question 35

Alfonse is a German national who qualified as an accountant and has been working in Germany where he was trained. He recently applied for a job with Wessex local authority in England, which had advertised for accountants. Although they had already filled the post, Wessex offered him an associate contract which amounted to two-thirds of a full-time post. Alfonse wishes to accept this offer of employment, but he has been informed by the British immigration authorities that he can not take up this post because:

(a) UK legislation requires that posts with local authorities must be filled by UK nationals only, and

(b) that as the post is not full-time it does not come within EC legislation and has to be based on UK law alone.

Advise Alfonse.

Answer plan

As Alfonse is an accountant this question could have been worded differently so that it came within the context of the right of establishment dealt with in the next chapter. This illustrates the need to read any question, especially a problem question like this one, very carefully. The main points to cover in this question are :

- Article 48 EC and Regulation 1612/68 on the rights of workers
- what is a worker? - *Levin*'s case and *Lawrie-Blum*
- restrictions under Article 48(4) and the *Belgium* case 1981

Answer

Under EC law there is a freedom of movement for workers to move around the Community to take up offers of employment. This is based upon Article 48 EC and the associated secondary legislation which has been issued to provide the detail necessary to identify the specific rights of the Community worker. The main question in this problem is whether Alfonse comes within this category of worker and whether there are any specific characteristics of the post which could deprive him of the ability to exercise his rights.

Article 48 EC is quite clear in providing the right for workers who are EC nationals to accept offers of employment actually made. This is confirmed by Article 1 of Regulation 1612/68 on freedom of movement of workers within the Community which refers to the right to 'take up an activity as an employed person'. Unfortunately neither give a definition of worker, but the European Court of Justice has decided that the words should be given their ordinary meaning and should not be interpreted restrictively. However, the concept only covers pursuit of effective and genuine activities. In *Levin*'s case (1982) the court held that the concept of 'worker' is a Community concept and is not dependent for its meaning on the laws of the Member State. How does the court decide if someone comes within this Community concept of worker? In *Lawrie-Blum* (1986) the court suggested that the essential characteristics which should be identified in a 'worker' is that he performs services in a particular time period for and under the direction of another in return for remuneration. Obviously Alfonse satisfies the basic requirement under Community law in that he is a national of a Member State, but does he come within the definition in *Lawrie-Blum*? From the facts given in the problem it would seem that he is going to perform the service of an accountant for Wessex local authority, in return for which they are going to pay him a salary as remuneration. Does the fact that he is only employed on a two-thirds contract affect his position? In the *Levin* case mentioned above, the court held that the term worker applied even to those who worked to a limited extent, ie part-time, provided that the work was real. There has to be some economic activity on the part of the person who claims to be a worker. This was confirmed in *Kempf* where a music teacher was working part-time in the Netherlands and applied for a residence permit. In normal circumstances all those who are workers exercising their rights under Article 48 have a right to such a residence permit which must be valid for at least five years and automatically renewable. This permit is proof of the right granted by the Treaty itself and which exists independently of the document.

The definition of 'worker' in the Community sense rarely causes difficulty in practice because if an economically active claimant under Article 48, like Alfonse, is not a worker he is probably self-employed in which case Articles 52 or 59 come into play. Article 52 EC deals with the right of establishment, including the right to take up and pursue activities as a self-employed person or to set up a business. Article 59 deals with the freedom to provide services. The European Court has held that Articles 48, 52 and 59 EC are based on the same principles as far as entry and residence and non-discrimination on the grounds of nationality are concerned. Therefore categorisation under Article 48, as opposed to Articles 52 or 59, will rarely be crucial.

However, even if Alfonse does have a right to enter the UK to take up his post, albeit part-time, does the second point mentioned by the Immigration authorities raise any obstacles for him? Under Article 48(4) it is specifically recognised that Article 48 will not apply to employment in the public sector. In other words it is possible for a Member State to discriminate in favour of its own nationals on the grounds of nationality for certain jobs. This appears to provide a wide discretion to Member States but it has been given a very narrow interpretation by the European Court of Justice. In *Sotgui v Deutsche Bundespost* (1974), Sotgui was employed as a postman. His employers, the German post office, paid an extra allowance to workers living apart from their families in Germany, but refused it to Sotgui an Italian national working in Germany. The court held that the exemption provided by Article 48(4) did not apply to all employment in the public service as this was too wide a definition. Rather it applied to those activities in the public service which were connected with the exercise of discretion or official authority involving the national interest. On the specific point of discrimination raised by *Sotgui* the court went on to say that Article 48(4) only applied to access to employment and did not permit discrimination once a person had been employed in that occupation.

In another case, *Commission v Belgium* (1981), which is similar to that facing Alfonse the court held that a Belgian law which stated that posts in the public service could be limited to Belgian nationals was declared to be contrary to Article 48. As with the term 'worker', the concept of 'public service' is a Community concept and is not to be interpreted only on national terms. It should apply only to those exercising official authority, as it was intended to apply only to employees safeguarding the general interests of the State. Does this mean that Alfonse can take up his post? It would appear that he will not be a position to exercise official authority. He will not have the status of a civil servant, although this has been held by the court in *Lawrie-Blum* not to mean that Article 48(4) applies.

To enter the UK to take up this offer of employment all Alfonse needs is a valid passport or identity card and a letter from Wessex local authority offering him the job. If as indicated in the problem he is refused entry by the Immigration Officer he is entitled to have access to the normal rights of appeal available under national law. If he is successful, as he should be, in obtaining entry to take up his post he is entitled to a residence permit, renewable automatically at the end of five years, and not to discriminated against on the grounds of nationality with regard to conditions of employment, housing, social security, etc.

Question 36

Analyse TWO of the following cases which came before the European Court of Justice and explain their importance in the development of Community law:

(a) *Lawrie-Blum* - Case 66/85

(b) *Rutili* - Case 36/75

(c) *Bonsignore* - Case 67/74

Answer plan

When approaching a question like this the temptation is to produce too descriptive an answer. The facts are important but are only one element of the answer. You should seek to deal with:

(a) the facts, the legal points raised and the decision of the court

(b) what kind of case was it? A preliminary reference or a direct action? What Article of the Treaty was it based upon?

(c) the cases chosen for this type of question have usually played their part in developing or reinforcing European Court judgments - what part has this case played?

Answer

(a) *Lawrie-Blum* - Case 66/85

Deborah Lawrie-Blum was a British national who passed the first examination at the University of Freiburg to become a teacher at a gymnasium. She was refused admission to the probationary service leading to the second examination, which qualifies successful candidates for appointment as teachers. The law of the Land Baden-Wurttemburg required the possession of German nationality for admission to probationary service. Mrs Lawrie-Blum contended that this refusal on the grounds of nationality had infringed her rights under Article 48(2) EC, whereas the Land argued that a probationary teacher is not a 'worker' within the meaning of Article 48 EC. During the proceedings which followed in the German court, a preliminary reference was made to the European Court under Article 177 EC.

The Land claimed that since a trainee teacher's activity falls under education policy, it is not an economic activity within Article 2 of the Treaty. The term 'worker' within the meaning of Article 48 EC and Regulation 1612/68, they argued, covers only those persons whose relationship to their employer is governed by a contract subject to private law and not persons whose employment relationship is subject o public law. The period of preparatory service should be regarded as the last stage of the professional training of future teachers.

The European Commission took the view that the criteria for the application of Article 48 EC is the existence of an employment relationship, regardless of the legal nature of that relationship and its purpose. The fact that the period of preparatory service is a compulsory stage in the professional development of a teacher and that it is spent in the public service is not relevant if the objective criteria for defining a 'worker' are satisfied. This criteria would include such things as the existence of a relationship of subordination *vis-à-vis* the employer, the actual provision of services by the employee and the payment of remuneration.

The Court of Justice said that the freedom of movement for workers was one of the fundamental principles of the Community. Therefore the term 'worker' should not be left to be defined by the individual Member States but should have a Community meaning. Given its fundamental importance the Community concept of 'worker' must be given a broad interpretation. The essential feature of an employment relationship is that for a certain period of time a person performs services for and under the direction of another person in return for which he receives remuneration.

Applying this concept to the facts of Mrs Lawrie-Blum's case, for the entire period of preparatory service she is under the direction and supervision of the school to which she is assigned. It is the school that determines the services to be performed by her and her working hours and it is the school's instructions that she must carry out and its rules which she must observe. The amounts she receives may be considered as remuneration for the services provided and for the duties involved in completing the period of preparatory service. Consequently, the three criteria for the existence of an employment relationship are fulfilled in this case.

The argument put forward by the Land that services performed in education do not fall within the scope of the Treaty because they are not of an economic nature was rejected. The court said that all that was required for the application of Article 48 EC is that the activity should be in the nature of work performed for remuneration, irrespective of the sphere in which it is carried out. The economic nature of someone's activities cannot be denied merely because their activities are governed by public law. The court had already stated in *Sotgui* (1974) that the nature of the legal relationship between employee and employer is immaterial as regards the application of Article 48 EC.

(b) *Rutili* - Case 36/75

Roland Rutili was an Italian national although he had lived in France since birth. He had married a French woman and until 1968 had held a privileged resident's permit. He was resident in the department of Meurthe-et-Moselle, where he worked and engaged in trade union activities. As a result of Rutili's alleged political actions during the Parliamentary elections in March 1967 and the events of May and June 1968 and his participation in a demonstration during the celebration of 14 July 1968, the Ministry for the Interior made a deportation order against him. On 10 September 1968 an order was issued requiring Rutili to reside in the department of Puy-de-Dome. In November 1968 the Minister for the Interior revoked the deportation and residence orders affecting Rutili, but decided to prohibit him from residing in particular departments. In January 1970 Rutili applied for a residence permit for a national of a Member State of the EC. In October 1970, following an appeal by Rutili, he was issued with a residence permit by the Prefect of Police valid for five years, but restricting his residence in line with the views of the Minister for the Interior. In December 1970 Rutili brought proceedings seeking the annulment of the Decision limiting the territorial validity of his residence permit.

The Tribunal Administratif, Paris, decided to stay the proceedings under Article 177 EC so that questions could be put to the Court of Justice. The first question concerned the interpretation of 'subject to limitations justified on grounds of public policy' in Article 48 EC. The court said that this concerns both those legislative provisions adopted by each Member State to limit the freedom of movement and residence within its territory, and the individual Decisions taken in application of such provisions. The object of the provisions of the Treaty and secondary legislation is to regulate the situation of individuals and to ensure their protection, thus the national courts must examine whether individual Decisions are compatible with Community law. The second question asked for the precise meaning of the word 'justified'. The freedom of movement of workers is one of the fundamental principles of the Treaty and therefore any derogation must be strictly interpreted so that its scope cannot be determined unilaterally by each Member State. Therefore the word 'justified' seeks to limit the discretionary powers of Member States and to protect the rights of those who are seeking to exercise their rights under Article 48 EC.

The duty imposed upon Member States is to base the measure adopted exclusively on the personal conduct of the individuals concerned, as required by Article 3 of Directive 64/221. To refrain from adopting any measures which are not related to the requirements of public policy or which adversely affect the exercise of trade union rights. They should immediately inform anyone against whom a restrictive measure has been adopted of the reasons in which the Decision is based so that they can consider an appeal.

In particular, measures restricting the rights of residence which are limited to part only of the national territory may not be imposed by a Member State on nationals of another Member State who are subject to Article 48 EC except in the case and circumstances in which such measures may be applied to nationals of the State concerned. Therefore the judgment in Rutili reinforces the non-discrimination approach of the Treaty. A Member State does not have the power to restrict the movement of nationals of other Member States within its territory unless it has the power in similar circumstances to restrict its own nationals.

(c) *Bonsignore* - Case 67/74

Carmelo Angelo Bonsignore was an Italian national residing in Germany. He was convicted of a firearms offence in that he was in unlawful possession of a firearm which accidentally caused the death of his brother by his careless handling of the firearm. The local German criminal court found him guilty of possession of the firearm and imposed a fine for breach of the firearms legislation. The court also found him guilty of causing death by negligence but imposed no penalty on this count, considering that no purpose would be served in the circumstances, notably the mental suffering caused by the death of his brother. Following this criminal conviction, the Aliens Authority ordered that he be deported. Bonsignore appealed against this Decision, during which a reference was made to the European Court under Article 177 EC.

The reference was required because the German court wished to know the interpretation of Articles 3(1) and (2) of Directive 64/221 which dealt with the co-ordination of special measures concerning the movement and residence of foreign nationals which are justified on the grounds of public policy, public security or public health. These are the grounds available under Article 48 EC which allow a government of a Member State to derogate from their obligations under the Treaty.

The German court hearing the appeal was of the view that deportation was not justified because of the special circumstances of the case. There was no special preventive characteristic of Bonsignore in the case. The only reason could be to deport Bonsignore as a general preventative measure, as an example to others who may also be in illegal possession of firearms. The Directive had been introduced into German law by a special Law on the Entry and Residence of Nationals of Member States of the European Community passed in 1969. The German court wanted to ensure that the German legislation was applied in accordance with the requirements of Community law, hence its request for interpretation.

The first question refers to whether Articles 3(1) and (2) of the Directive are to be interpreted as excluding the deportation of a national of another Member State as a deterrent to other foreign nationals from committing criminal offences of the type committed by the person to be deported. The second question posed the alternative meaning of these Articles in the Directive, namely that the EC national to be deported will commit further offences if he remains in the Member State.

The European Court of Justice said that according to Articles 3(1) and (2) of Directive 64/221, measures taken on grounds of public policy or of public security shall be based exclusively on the personal conduct of the individual concerned and that previous criminal convictions shall not in themselves constitute grounds for the taking of such measures. These Articles have to be interpreted in the light of the objectives of the Directive and the need to ensure the uniform application of Article 48 EC, without discrimination between nationals and non-nationals of a Member State.

Article 3 of the Directive provides that measures adopted on grounds of public policy and for the maintenance of public security against nationals of Member States cannot be justified on grounds outside the personal conduct of the individual involved. This has to be the situation where a government is seeking to depart from one of the fundamental principles of the Community, ie the free movement of persons. Thus we have the requirement that a deportation order may only be made for breaches of the peace and public security which might be committed by the individual concerned. Therefore the outcome for Bonsignore was that the European Court said in answer to the Article 177 reference that Directive 64/221 prevents the deportation of a national of another Member State if the purpose is solely to deter other aliens, ie of a preventative nature.

Chapter 9

The Freedom of Establishment and the Freedom to Provide Services

Introduction

Very often these topics are joined with the free movement of workers and therefore a good understanding of all three aspects should be obtained. This is especially true as the court has held that the principles of non-discrimination, etc, are the same whether it is Article 48 EC (the free movement of workers), Article 52 EC (the freedom or right of establishment for the self-employed and companies) or Article 59 EC (the freedom to provide services). Problem questions are very popular on this area of Community law, although in law degrees it is not uncommon to have an essay question on the freedom of establishment for lawyers.

Checklist

- Article 52 EC and the freedom of establishment
- Article 59 EC and the freedom to provide services
- Article 60 EC and what constitutes a service
- The right to receive services
- Derogation under Article 56 EC and Directive 64/221
- Directive 73/148 on rights of entry and residence
- Directive 75/34 on the right to remain after employment for the self-employed and their families
- The special problems of 'professionals' and the Mutual Recognition Directive
- The special measures to deal with companies operating within the Community

Question 37

Pierre is a fully qualified engineer in France. As a result of attending the 'Engineering 2000 Fair' in Paris, he applied for a two year post-graduate course at a British university. He was accepted onto the course and arrived at Dover with Anne-Marie, his Canadian

non - eEC.

co-habitee. His luggage was searched and found to contain pornographic videos, which were confiscated. The Immigration Officer checked the Home Office computer, which indicated that the French police had reported that Pierre was a member of an anarchist organisation. On the basis of this information the Immigration Officer refused them permission to enter the UK on the grounds that their exclusion would be conducive to the public good.

Advise Pierre and Anne-Marie of their rights, if any, under EC law.

Answer plan

This question deals with the mobility of students within the Community. It concentrates on the right of individuals to move to another Member State to receive services as against the provision in the Treaty which deals the right to provide services. This should be discussed and applied, along with the following points:

- Articles 48, 52 and 59 EC to identify if Pierre is covered by any of these provisions
- case of *Luisi* which identified rights of recipient of services
- meaning of vocational courses - *Gravier v City of Liège*
- Directive 64/221 on derogation
- Directive 90/366 for students

Answer

The EC Treaty has as one of its basic freedoms that of the ability of individuals to move between Member States in order to carry out certain activities. The Treaty specifies three situations, namely the free movement of workers, the right of establishment and the freedom to provide services. As Pierre does not seek to establish a business in the UK the Treaty provisions associated with establishment have no application to the problem. Is he a worker? The concept of worker is a Community concept and is not dependant for its meaning on the laws of any particular Member State. The essential characteristic of a worker, according to *Lawrie-Blum* (1986), is that he performs services during a particular time period for and under the direction of another in return for remuneration. This concept has been generously interpreted by the Court of Justice in *Procureur du Roi v Royer* (1976) to include the right to enter another Member State in order to search for work. However, although he is a qualified engineer, Pierre is not seeking to enter the UK as a 'worker', but to take up his place on a two year postgraduate course. Article 48, specifying the rights of workers does not provide any assistance to him. It is the last category associated with services which needs to be considered if the EC law is to provide any assistance to Pierre and Anne-Marie.

Articles 59 and 60 EC provides for the removal of restrictions on the freedom to provide services. More importantly for Pierre they have been interpreted by the European Court of Justice to embrace the freedom to receive services. This would include the postgraduate course which he wishes to take. It was stated by the court in *Luisi v Ministero del Tesoro* (1983), following the Commission's view in *Watson and Belman* (1976), that there was a freedom for the recipient of services to go to another Member State, without restriction, in order to receive a service there. Although the case involved the transfer of money out of Italy in breach of Italian currency law for the purpose of tourism and medical treatment, the principle in the judgment included persons travelling for the purpose of education. The right of residence exists during the period for which the service is provided, which in Pierre's case would be the two years duration of the course. Any breach of this freedom would be *prima facie* a breach of Articles 59 and 60 EC.

Would Pierre's course qualify under this right to receive services? As an economic orientated Treaty, the main concern would seem to be education or training of a vocational kind. However, the court has given a wide definition to the meaning of vocational education. In *Gravier v City of Liège* (1984) it was held to include all forms of teaching which prepares for and leads directly to a particular profession or which provides the necessary skills for such a profession. Although Pierre is already a qualified engineer, the postgraduate course he has applied for would seem to satisfy this definition in that it deals with a specialist area of engineering skills. Thus he may claim equal access and on the same basis as nationals of the Member State, ie UK nationals. This was confirmed in *Blaizot v University of Liège* (1987), which involved a university veterinary studies course. However, as with all the freedoms arising from the Treaty there are exceptions where the Member State may derogate from their obligation under the Treaty. These are specifically those in Articles 56 and 66 EC, which allow for derogation on the grounds of public policy, public security and public health. As there is no indication that Pierre offers any threat with regard to public health, it is public policy or public security which maybe used by the UK government to justify its actions. The public policy provision has been interpreted strictly by the European Court to ensure, as it stated in *Van Duyn* (1975), that its scope is not unilaterally determined by the Member State without control by the European Community institutions. In *Rutili v Ministre de l'Interieur* (1975) the court held that restrictions on the movement of an EC national on the grounds of public policy could only be accepted where the behaviour of the individual constitutes a genuine and sufficiently serious threat to public policy.

Article 3(1) of Directive 64/221 states that any exclusion on the grounds of public policy or public security must be based exclusively on the personal conduct of the individual. Is Pierre's membership of an anarchist association sufficient personal conduct to exclude him? In *Van Duyn v Home Office* (1975) a Dutch national was refused entry to the UK to take up employment with the Church of Scientology because the UK regarded the activities of the Church as objectionable and socially harmful. The court held that although past association with an organisation does not count as personal conduct, present association does and the activities in question must constitute a genuine and sufficiently serious threat to public policy affecting one of the fundamental interests of society. Do French anarchists pose such a threat, given that there are probably British anarchists? In *Van Duyn* mentioned above, the court allowed the UK to apply a stricter standard on an EC national than the one it applied to its own nationals because the UK deemed that it was necessary. It would appear that if Pierre is a member of such an organisation and the UK government do believe that he constitutes a genuine and sufficiently serious threat to society they can exclude him. If they do it must be on the membership of the anarchist association because the pornographic videos would not in themselves amount to a reason to exclude him. In the *Bonsignore* case (1975) it was accepted that the concept of personal conduct expresses the requirement that a deportation order may only be made for breaches of the peace and public security which might be committed by the individual concerned.

Under Article 6 of Directive 64/221 Pierre is entitled to know on which ground, ie public policy or public security, the Decision is based, unless this information contravenes state security. This allows the individual to prepare his defence. If the UK fails to comply with Article 6 it may lead to the quashing of a deportation order, as happened in *R v Secretary of State for the Home Office, ex parte Dannemberg* (1984). Under Article 8 Pierre is entitled to the same legal remedies in relation to a Decision on entry. In the UK an immigrant normally has a right of appeal against immigration Decisions to a person called an adjudicator and then to the Immigration Appeal Tribunal. Such appeals cover issues of fact, law and the exercise of discretion, so the merits of the Decision would be fully reviewed.

In June 1992 a Directive specifically issued to cover the situation of students came into force. This Directive 90/366 only applies if the person concerned does not come within one of the categories in the free movement provisions of the Treaty. The Directive is purely supplementary and the case law indicated above still applies to Pierre. What about Ann-Marie? She is a Canadian national and as such does not receive the benefits associated with the European Community which are for EC nationals only. However, does her relationship with Pierre provide her with any rights of entry? If Pierre was allowed entry to take up his place on the postgraduate course would she be able to enter with him? Perhaps due to the limited duration of a course, under Directive 90/366 there is a narrow definition which only includes the student's spouse and dependent children and not family members. If Ann-Marie was married to Pierre there would be no problem in that the nationality of the spouse does not need to be one of the Member States. However, she is his co-habitee and is not included in the Directive. In *Netherlands State v Reed* (1986) the court held that the term 'spouse' included co-habitee. Although this case was concerned with the mobility of workers, it will not help Ann-Marie even if the court applied its principles of interpretation across the mobility categories. The Decision was on the basis of non-discrimination in that the Dutch authorities were required to give Reed the right of residence as they recognised the rights of co-habitees under Dutch law. Therefore the judgment will not assist migrants in a similar situation unless the State they wish to enter has the same rule as the Dutch. The UK does not have such a rule.

It would seem that if the court is satisfied that there are grounds for the UK government to derogate from the Treaty, they will uphold the refusal to allow Pierre to enter the UK to take up his postgraduate course. If they are not satisfied and Pierre is allowed to enter the UK as a student he must be given a residence permit for the duration of the course. However, whatever happens to Pierre it can be seen from the *Reed* case above that Ann-Marie will not be allowed to benefit from the rights given to him. She must seek a visa in her own right as a Canadian national.

Question 38

'As long as a lawyer is qualified in one Member State, he has a right to practise in any Member State.'

Discuss.

Answer plan

This essay question requires a discussion of the development of the Community law on the right of establishment and the provision of services. In particular the following should be raised:

• freedom of establishment under Articles 52 - 58 EC

• Directive 77/249 and the right to provide services

• problems of lawyers and other professionals

• the impact of the Mutual Recognition Directive

Answer

The European Community principle of equal treatment is not always sufficient to ensure that the immigrant is able to practise his profession in another Member State. In the case of lawyers it is obvious that recognition of his professional qualifications and admission to the appropriate professional organisation is also required and can cause problems.

There is no directly applicable provision in the EC Treaty requiring Member States to recognise qualifications acquired in another Member State or obliging them to allow immigrants to practice a profession without the appropriate qualifications (*Auer* (*No 1*) (1979)). This seems reasonable given that the services of such professionals have a big impact of those who seek their advice and services. However, Article 57(1) EC requires the Council to adopt Directives on the mutual recognition of diplomas, certificates and other evidence of formal qualifications. Without a relevant Directive the migrant is likely to find that Community law is of limited assistance to him. The Commission had attempted to remedy the situation by promoting separate Directives for each profession, such as medicine, dentistry, veterinary medicine and midwifery. The objective of these Directives has been to make it easier for a person practising a profession in one Member State to practise that profession in another Member State. However, the important difference between these professions and lawyers is that although the principles of medicine or dentistry are much the same in every Member State, those of law differ. It is therefore hardly surprising that the progress on facilitating the free movement of lawyers has been very slow. Directive 77/249 was specifically aimed at lawyers but it is only concerned with the provision of services and not the right of establishment. It makes provision for lawyers to carry out their profession in another Member State on a temporary basis. 'Lawyer' under this Directive is defined by a list of terms to reflect the diversity in the European Community. The function of the list is to indicate those practitioners who are able to benefit from the rights conferred by the Directive and the activities to which it applies. Thus anyone who is recognised as a 'lawyer' for the purpose of the Directive can perform the work of a lawyer in another Member State but only on a temporary basis. While he is performing this work he must use the title of his home country, as it would appear in that country. Thus a French lawyer must call himself '*avocat*' even when he is working in the UK or Germany. This avoids any misunderstanding and indicates the specialism of the lawyer in the law of the appropriate Member State. In this capacity the foreign lawyer can do all the work of a local lawyer, unless the national law of the Member State reserves certain activities for its national lawyers and on the proviso that he represents a client in court work in conjunction with a local lawyer. This has meant in the UK that such foreign lawyers cannot undertake probate or conveyancing work, which is reserved for UK lawyers.

It could be expected that in time the European Commission would issue a Directive which would widen the scope of recognition for lawyers of one Member State to establish themselves and practise in another. However, recognising the time involved in such a process as producing specific Directives the Commission changed its strategy and concentrated on producing a general Directive that would apply to all professions. This Directive applies to the legal profession and is the Mutual Recognition Directive 89/48. Like all Directives on establishment Directive 89/48 benefits Community citizens with regard to qualifications awarded in a Member State. Under this Directive recognition is to be given to diplomas as defined by Article 1(a). There must be three essential characteristics for such 'diplomas': it must be awarded by a competent authority in a Member State following the successful completion of a course lasting at least three years at a university or equivalent institution plus professional training. Finally such a 'diploma' must qualify the holder for the pursuit of a regulated profession in a Member State. The profession of a lawyer is in the list of regulated professions. Article 3 of the Directive provides the basic rule that if a Member State requires a 'diploma' as a condition for exercising a regulated profession, it must accept a 'diploma' obtained in another Member State. In contrast to the situation where a lawyer is providing a 'service' of a temporary nature, when he is exercising the right of establishment the lawyer is entitled to use the professional designation of the Member State in which he practises. Thus a French *avocat* who establishes himself and practices in the UK can call himself a solicitor.

This would seem to make it straight-forward for a lawyer qualified in one Member State to practise in another. However, the Directive does recognise that professional training does vary between Member States and allows the Member State where the individual wishes to practise to set certain conditions. This may involve an adaptation period during which supervision by a qualified practitioner is required of the foreign national or an aptitude test of professional knowledge. In England the test for foreign lawyers wishing to practise as solicitors is called the Qualified Lawyers Transfer Test. Having successfully passed this test the normal rules concerning registration and admission to the appropriate professional body will apply. However, such registration or admission cannot be refused on any grounds contrary to Community law. As with any member of the legal profession, once registered or admitted the migrant lawyer must obey the rules of professional conduct laid down by the Member State in which they practise. Should these rules be incompatible with the Treaty's freedom of movement principles they will not be applied. For example a French rule requiring migrant doctors to give up their registration in their country of origin before being allowed to register in France was contrary to the Treaty. Although it happened before this general Directive came into effect, the case of *Ordre des Avocats v Klopp* illustrates this point with regard to the legal profession. This case involved a French rule that an *avocat* cannot establish chambers in more than one place. Klopp was a German who qualified as a lawyer in Germany and opened an office there. He then re-qualified in France and applied for admission as an *avocat*, but his application was refused because he was not prepared to give up his office in Germany. The court held that such a requirement was contrary to the Treaty.

Question 39

'Company law is one of the most important and active areas in the harmonisation of the national laws of the Member States. The European Community's objective is to create a uniform system of company law.'

Discuss.

Answer plan

Although it is not very common to get examination questions on European Community policy towards company law, it does form part of the syllabus of most European law courses as part of the freedom of establishment. Where questions do arise they are generally of this essay-type. The best way to approach these questions is on the basis of freedom of establishment and the right to provide services and the implications these have for the recognition of companies in the various Member States. The answer will use authority based on the Treaty as there are very few cases on these aspects of company law. The main points to cover are:

- Article 52 EC and the right of establishment
- Article 58(1) EC and the meaning of company
- Article 54(3)(g) and the need for safeguards
- Articles 59 and 66 EC and the provision of services by companies
- Article 220 EC and negotiations of conventions
- Directives adopted for harmonisation, with examples
- European Economic Interest Groupings
- the European company

Answer

Although there are many developments associated with the rights of workers and the self-employed within the European Community, it must be remembered that companies play the predominant part in any modern economy. It is to be expected therefore that provision should be made for companies to move around the Community to take part in economic activities. The main provisions of the EC Treaty concerned with the right of establishment and the freedom to provide services apply to companies. However, one of the main problems encountered is that whereas individuals, whether as workers or self-employed, are uniform in their identity across the Community, this does not apply to companies. Member States have different requirements with regard to such matters as incorporation, registration and liability. If there is to be true mobility for companies, action has to be taken to make sure that these differences are not used to create barriers to the mobility of companies. This was re-enforced in the build-up to the completion of the Single Market policy in 1992 when the European Commission said that such an internal market cannot exist unless companies incorporated in one Member State are permitted to do business in another.

The EC Treaty identifies two rights for companies, namely establishment and provision of services. Under Article 52 EC companies have the right to establish themselves in another Member State by setting up agencies, branches or subsidiaries. Having so established themselves, the companies have the right not to be discriminated against and must be treated under the same conditions as those laid down by the Member State for its own nationals. What companies can benefit from this freedom? The same rule applies to companies as it does to individuals, who must be nationals of a Member State if they are to benefit from the freedom specified in the Treaty. Article 58(1) specifies that as far as companies are concerned they must be formed in accordance with the law of a Member State and have their registered office, central administration or principal place of business within the Community. The Court of Justice held in the *Segers* case (1986) that to allow a Member State in which a company carried on its business to treat that company in a different manner solely because its registered office was in another Member State would render Article 58 valueless. Just as there is a requirement that workers and the self-employed should receive remuneration in order to satisfy the Treaty, so companies which are non-profit making do not come within the definition of Article 58(1). The remuneration requirement is repeated in Article 59 dealing with the right to provide services. This provision deals with a company established in one Member State providing service of an industrial, commercial or professional nature in another Member State. The main difference with services is that in contrast to establishment the company is entering another Member State only temporarily to pursue this activity.

As indicated above companies should be able to establish themselves or provide services on the basis of non-discrimination on the grounds of nationality. They should also not be subject to more burdensome rules in the host Member State than are absolutely necessary. The European Community has attempted to deal with this last point by seeking uniformity in the whole Community or at least on the basis of 'equivalents'. Article 220 EC requires the Member States to negotiate conventions with each other in order to secure uniformity of recognition of business practices across the Community. The Article specifically mentions the mutual recognition of companies within the meaning of Article 58(2). As a result of this requirement, a Convention on the Mutual Recognition of Companies and Bodies Corporate was signed in 1968 by the six founder members of the European Community. However, it is not in force as it was not ratified by the Member States. Given this failure but recognising the importance of company law, the policy of the EC has been to move forward on the basis of Directives dealing with specific matters.

The company law of each Member State has developed through its own legal and political traditions and hence there are wide variations not only in terms but also in concepts. It was thought necessary, if the freedom of establishment was to be a reality, that there should be a minimum safeguard to protect the shareholders or members of companies and others who enter into transactions with the company. This is specifically mentioned in Article 54(3)(g) EC. If companies in the EC are to deal across national boundaries, it is important that investors, customers and creditors are able to deal with confidence with enterprises from other Member States, whether directly or through their subsidiaries or agencies. The fact that over thirteen Directives have been proposed reflects the extensive programme of harmonisation of company law embarked upon by the European Community. Although not all of these Directives have been adopted, those which have cover such technical matters as company capital, company accounts, appointment of auditors and disclosure of information. These are important because companies established or providing services in different Member States facing the need to adjust to different regulatory regimes may lead to duplication of accounting, licensing and other requirements. This would act as a disincentive to penetrating other national markets. It may also reduce the opportunities for benefiting from economies of scale.

Another way of seeking to reduce the problems for companies operating in more than one Member State is to establish EC corporate structures. The first step was taken in this development with the establishment of European Economic Interest Grouping by Regulation 2173/85. These EEIGs permit companies and others to co-operate within the Community on a cross-border basis, and thus provide a vehicle for joint-ventures. EEIGs have the mixed characteristics of companies and partnership. They are not separate in the sense that the companies are still liable for the debts of the EEIG but they do have a separate legal capacity. Such groups have to be registered, which in the UK is a requirement to register with the Registrar of Companies. An EEIG cannot have more than 500 employees or offer any share participation to the public. Obviously there are certain limitations with EEIG but they do provide a flexible vehicle for economic activity.

The ultimate aim of the Community is to have a new company formation which will have legal capacity throughout the Community. This is to be the European Company or Societas Europaea (SE) which will be established by registration with the European Court in Luxembourg under a distinctive European Community company statute. Even though registration would be with the court, the SE would be domiciled in a particular Member State. The intended role of the SE is to facilitate cross-border co-operation by means of large-scale mergers and associations. It can be seen that this is perhaps the natural extension from the EEIG which facilitates such ventures but on a smaller scale. There have been some criticisms of the establishment of SEs which has led to delay in the adoption of the necessary Community legislation.

It can be seen from the points discussed above that the Treaty clearly identified the need to harmonise areas of company law if companies were to exercise the rights of establishment and provision of services. However, Community legislation has progressed slowly as the national requirements of the Member States varied widely. The Directives which have already been adopted have helped companies involved in cross-border activities but the ultimate establishment of the European Company has not been achieved. The Regulation allowing for EEIGs was a major advance but is aimed at smaller joint-ventures. The objective of the Community is to ensure that company law across the Community does not act as a barrier to economic activity by companies and provides safeguards for those who are doing business with them. To this end the Community seeks to provide a minimum standard of uniformity in company law across the Member States.

Question 40

Analyse TWO of the following cases which came before the European Court of Justice and explain their importance in the development of Community law:

(a) *Reyners* - Case 2/74

(b) *Van Binsbergen* - Case 33/74

(c) *Walgrave & Koch* - Case 36/74

Answer plan

When approaching a question like this the temptation is to produce too descriptive an answer. The facts are important but are only one element of the answer. You should seek to deal with:

(a) the facts, the legal points raised and the Decision of the court

(b) what kind of case was it? A preliminary reference or a direct action? What Article of the Treaty was it based upon?

(c) the cases chosen for this type of question have usually played their part in developing or reinforcing European Court judgments - what part has this case played?

Answer

(a) *Reyners* - Case 2/74

Although born and bred in Belgium, Jean Reyners was of Dutch nationality. Although resident in Belgium, where he had been educated and been made Docteur en Droit Belge, it had not been possible for him to be admitted to the practice of the profession of avocat in Belgium. The reason for this is that the Belgian Code Judiciaire provides that no one may hold the title of avocat or practice that profession unless he is a Belgian and holds the docteur en droit. Having previously obtained this qualification, it was the nationality requirement which was impeding Reyners. It was possible to obtain dispensation from the condition of nationality in cases determined by the King, on the advice of the General Council of the Ordre of Avocats. This was provided for in a Decree of 1970, but was limited to the nationals of countries which themselves admitted Belgians to the profession. Unfortunately the Netherlands Bar was only open to the Dutch.

Reyners had made a number of applications for dispensation from the nationality requirement, but they had all been refused. He finally applied to the Conseil d'Etat of Belgium, the highest public law court, to have this provision of the decree quashed on the grounds of its incompatibility with the EC Treaty. To enable it to decide the case the court stayed the proceedings and a reference was made for a preliminary ruling under Article 177 EC. The main questions under the 177 procedure was whether Article 52 EC on the right of establishment became directly applicable at the end of the transitional period and whether the 'official authority' exception in Article 55 EC applied to avocats.

The governments of Member States were divided on the direct effect of Article 52 EC. Although the German government supported the possibility of direct effect in its intervention, the governments of Belgium, Ireland, Luxembourg and the UK disagreed. They based their views on the fact that Article 52 was wider and vaguer than the prohibition of non-discrimination on the grounds of nationality and the fact that it was to be enforced by Directives left discretion to Member States. The view of the German government was that the provisions which impose on Member States an obligation which they have to fulfil within a particular period, become directly applicable when, on the expiration of this period, the obligation has not been fulfilled.

The court held that the rule on equal treatment with nationals is one of the fundamental legal provisions of the Community. Therefore, if there is a set of legislative provisions effectively applied by the country of establishment to its own nationals, these are capable of being directly invoked by nationals of all the other Member States. The fact that the freedom of establishment should have been attained at the end of the transitional period is made easier but is not dependent on the implementation of a programme of measures. The fact that the progression has not been made leaves the obligation itself intact beyond the end of the period provided for its fulfilment. After the expiry of the transitional period the right of establishment is sanctioned by the Treaty itself with direct effect.

Article 55 EC provides for a derogation from the right of establishment when the activities which are involved in that State are connected, even occasionally, with the exercise of official authority. Given that the freedom of establishment and the rule on equal treatment are fundamental to the Community, the court stated that Article 55 cannot be interpreted so as to defeat the objective of the Treaty. It wanted to avoid the effectiveness of the Treaty being defeated by unilateral provisions of Member States. Although each Member State must be looked at individually, the professional activities of avocats do not constitute, as such, the exercise of official authority. For Article 55 to apply there has to be a direct and specific connection with the exercise of official authority.

This Decision does not mean that any citizen can simply move to another Member State and set up in business or a profession. Each Member State has its own rules which applies to its own nationals covering such matters as qualifications. However, if the professional or other qualification is already recognised in the host country as being equivalent, Article 52 forbids the refusal of permission on the grounds of nationality (*Patrick* (1978)) or a requirement that the arrival obtain the national qualification (*Thieffry* (1977)).

(b) *Van Binsbergen* - Case 33/74

Van Binsbergen was a Dutch national who wished to challenge a social security Decision against him. He had authorised M Kortman, a Dutch national established in the Netherlands, to act on his behalf and bring an appeal against the Decision. Kortman was an experienced legal adviser and representative in social security matters. However, during the case Kortman moved his home to Belgium and it was there that he corresponded with the Dutch court. The court concluded that Kortman was now practising from Belgium. Under a Netherlands statute on procedure in social security cases legal representation could only be provided by persons established in the Netherlands. They therefore said that he could no longer act for Van Binsbergen.

Kortman invoked Articles 59 and 60 EC providing for the progressive abolition, during the transitional period of restrictions on freedom to provide services within the Community. The Dutch court made a preliminary reference to the European Court under Article 177 EC. There are some similarities with *Reyners* case 2/74 only here it is a question of services rather than establishment. In fact, after *Reyners* case it should be quite straightforward to hold Articles 59 and 60 EC to have become directly effective at the end of the transitional period, at least as regards discrimination on the grounds of nationality.

The problem was to identify the discrimination involved in the case. Kortman, Van Binsbergen, the social security court and the domestic law in question were all Dutch. However, the fact that the Dutch law did disqualify any legal adviser of any country who was not established in the Netherlands was relevant. The establishment requirement is a restriction within Article 59 EC, but does the

Article have direct effect in the sense of providing a right which the national courts must enforce?

The European Court said that the restrictions to be abolished under Articles 59 and 60 EC included any requirements imposed upon the person providing the service on the basis of nationality or residence which do not apply to persons established within the Member State. This latter requirement of habitual residence could have the result of depriving Article 59 of all useful effect, as its object is to abolish such restrictions.

However, this has to be balanced against the possibility of the person providing the service taking advantage of his right to avoid professional rules of conduct which would be applied if he was established in that State. Therefore a residence requirement could be imposed if the desired ends could not be achieved by less restrictive means. Such rules must be considered objectively and would be permissible provided they satisfied certain criteria. These are that they are non-discriminatory, objectively justified and not disproportionate.

Following the principles in *Reyners* case the court held that Articles 59 and 60 EC did have direct effect. However, the importance of Van Binsbergen is that it shows that the ECJ were careful to limit the area in which Article 59 EC works directly, namely with restrictions based on nationality and residence.

(c) *Walgrave & Koch* - Case 36/74

Bruno Walrave and Norbert Koch are both Dutch nationals who offer their services for remuneration to act as pace-makers on motorcycles in medium distanced cycle races. They provide these services under agreement with the 'stayers', who cycle in the lee of the motorcycle, or the cycling associations or with sponsors. Competitions in which their services are requested include the world championships. Under the rules for the world championships to apply after 1973 the pace-maker must be of the same nationality as the stayer. Walrave and Koch considered that this rule is incompatible with the EC Treaty as it prevents a pace-maker of one Member State from selling his services to a stayer of another Member State. They therefore brought an action against the Association Union Cyclists Internationale which was the body that made the rule.

The national court made a reference to the European Court under Article 177 EC relating to the interpretation of Articles 48, 59 and 7 EC. Article 48 EC provides for the free movement of workers, whereas Article 59 EC deals with the freedom to provide services. Article 7 EC is one of the fundamental principles of the Community in that it prohibits any discrimination on the grounds of nationality. However, the rules in question were not made by a government of a Member State but an international sporting federation which is not subject to public law. Could the prohibition be applied to them was the important question raised by this case.

The practice of sport is subject to Community law only in so far as it constitutes an economic activity within Article 2 EC. The court stated that the activities referred to in Article 59 EC are not to be distinguished in their nature from those in Article 48 EC merely because of the form of the Regulation covering employment. The prohibition of discrimination found in these Articles do not only apply to public authorities but extend to rules of any other nature aimed at regulating gainful employment and the provision of services.

The abolition by Member States of obstacles to the freedom of movement for persons and the freedom to provide services are fundamental objectives of the Community contained in Article 3(C) EC. This abolition would be compromised if barriers of national origin could be neutralised by obstacles resulting from autonomous associations or organisations which do not come under public law. Therefore these Articles may be taken into account by the national court in judging the validity or the effects of a provision inserted in the rules of a sporting organisation.

The national court had anticipated this possible answer, so it asked whether the fact that this was an international organisation made any difference. The key point for the court was where the relationship governed by the rules was entered into or the place where they took effect. If these were within the territory of the Community, then the Community view on non-discrimination would apply. Thus any races, for example, which took place in a Member State could not do so under rules prohibited by the Treaty.

Chapter 10

Freedom from Discrimination

Introduction

The main focus of this freedom from discrimination is based on the economic aspect of employment and discrimination based upon sex. However, you should look at Chapter 2 where the protection of fundamental rights was identified as one of the general principles of Community law. That general principle has a wider meaning than merely discrimination based upon sex. This chapter concentrates on the general principle of equal pay for equal work for men and women laid down in article 119 EC and the directives issued to provide the detail required for the full implementation of this principle. Generally the questions asked on this topic are of an essay type because of the wider knowledge normally required of national employment law for problem questions. Such questions are more likely to arise in employment or industrial law papers. However, it is possible for questions to be constructed which deal specifically with Community law.

Checklist

Following on from the general principle of Community law of non-discrimination, you should understand the following points and the appropriate cases:
- Article 119 EC on the principle of equal pay for equal work for men and woman
- The meaning of 'pay' within Article 119
- The extent of the direct effect of article 119 EC
- Directive 75/117 on equal pay for work of equal value
- Directive 76/207 or the Equal Treatment Directive for men and women in employment
- Directive 79/7 with regard to equal treatment in matters of social security
- Directive 86/378 regarding equal treatment for occupational pension schemes
- Directive 86/613 which provides for equal treatment in self-employment

Question 41

'Equality between men and women in employment is a fundamental right under Community law.'

Discuss.

Answer plan

This question deals with the specific area of employment in relation to the principle of equality derived principally from Article 119 EC. This should therefore be the starting point and the essay should then be developed to include the following points:

- *Defrenne* judgment in 1976
- scope of Article 119 EC through the meaning of pay and worker
- Equal Pay Directive 75/117
- Equal Treatment Directive 76/207

Answer

In part one of the EC Treaty, where the underlying principles of the Community are listed, reference is made to the principle of equality. This indicates the special status given by Community law to the principle of equality. This principle has been repeated in secondary legislation, mainly directives, and the case law of the European Court. In fact, it has been principally the judgments of the court which has elevated the principle to its special status.

The consequence of this special status accorded to the principle of equality can be seen through the case law relating to equal treatment of men and women in terms and conditions of employment within the European Community. It is the cases associated with Article 119 EC which show this development clearly. Article 119 requires each Member State to ensure that men and women should receive equal pay for equal work. Equal pay, under this article refers not only to wage levels but also to any payment in kind in respect of remuneration for employment. In its judgment in the *Defrenne (2)* case (1976), the court held that article 119 has a double aim which covers both economic and social aspects of employment. It seeks to ensure that States which have implemented the equality principle do not suffer a competitive disadvantage and to achieve social progress. In 1978 when it was delivering its third judgment associated with Madame Defrenne's case the court expanded the principle of equal pay into a general fundamental right of equality which required the elimination of discrimination based on sex.

With regard to the application of the principle of equality in employment it is not only article 119 which is important, as there have been a number of important directives adopted which have expanded the application of the principle. Article 119 itself refers expressly to pay but the European Court of Justice has adopted a liberal interpretation to the question what constitutes pay. In *Garland v BREL* (1982) the court held that the grant of special travel facilities to former employees after retirement constituted pay, even in the absence of any contractual entitlement to such facilities. Mrs Garland had been employed by British Rail Engineering Ltd before her retirement but complained that, whereas a male employee would receive special travel facilities for himself and his spouse, a female employee only received them for herself and not her husband. Her employer was held to be acting contrary to Article 119 because the legal nature of the facilities is not important for the purpose of the application of Article 119 provided that they are granted in respect of the applicant's employment.

In *Bilka-Kaufhaus v Weber von Harz* (1985), Weber was a female part-time worker who was seeking to challenge her employer's occupational pension scheme. Although the scheme was non-contributory for full-time employees with the employer paying all the contributions, this was not the case with part-timers. Under the scheme, only part-time employees who had been employed by the company for at least 15 out of a total of 20 years could qualify. The court held that the benefit constituted consideration paid by the employer to the employee in respect of her employment and thus came within Article 119. In this case the court seemed to draw a distinction between contractual and statutory pension schemes. However, Article 119 was held to be applicable to a statutory social security benefit in *Rinner-Kuhn v FWW Spezial Gebeaudereiniging GmbH* (1989). This case also included a part-time employee who was employed as a cleaner. She challenged the German legislation which permitted employers to exclude workers who worked less than 10 hours per week from entitlement to sick pay. Despite statements in *Defrenne* and *Newstead v Dept of Transport* (1986) that social security schemes were outside the scope of Article 119, the court held that sick pay fell within the article. Therefore, the German legislation was contrary to Article 119.

However, it is not only cases brought by female employees which have allowed the European Court to develop the application of the principle of equality to employment. In *Barber v Guardian Royal Exchange Assurance Group* (1989) a group of male employees challenged their employer's contracted-out pension scheme. The employer's scheme was a substitute for the statutory scheme and was payable at different ages for men and women. The court held that since the worker received these benefits from his employer as a result of his employment, the fact that the benefits were payable at different ages for men and women resulted in a difference in pay. Following this case it would appear that the only social security pension schemes provided for workers which fall outside of Article 119 are those which provide for workers in general, as a matter of social policy.

It is not only the case law associated with Article 119 that the principle of equality in employment has been applied. As indicated above, a number of directives have been adopted to implement or supplement Article 119. The Equal Pay Directive 75/117, for example, requires the elimination of all discrimination on the grounds of sex with regard to all aspects and conditions of remuneration. In *Jenkins v Kingsgate (Clothing Productions) Ltd* (1981) the court held that this Directive restates the equal pay principle of Article 119 without altering its scope. However, the judgment in this case allowed for the possibility of a 10% difference in pay between full-time and part-time workers without infringing Article 119 providing that the difference in pay was 'objectively justified' and did not discriminate on the basis of sex. Guidelines were provided in the later case of *Bilka-Kaufhaus* mentioned above, to assist in identifying what might constitute objective justification for such differences in pay. The onus is on the employer to prove that the difference in treatment corresponded to a genuine need of the enterprise, was a suitable way to obtain the objective pursued by the business and was necessary for that purpose. This could perhaps be described as the application of a principle similar to proportionality.

Another important Directive was that dealing with Equal Treatment (76/207). This Directive dealt with access to employment, vocational training, working conditions and social security. In the UK this Directive has been used in the context of different retirement ages for men and women. Although the UK legislation implementing this Directive excluded provisions for death and retirement benefits from its scope, the Directive itself contained no such exclusion. The UK legislation therefore had to be amended. The most important case in this respect was *Marshall v South West Hampshire Area Health Authority* (1985), when Marshall successfully challenged her employer's decision to force her to retire at an earlier age than that of male employees. The important factor in the case was acceptance by the court that this Directive had direct effect. Article 2 of this Directive allows the possibility of derogation from the equal treatment principle on specific grounds. This was raised in *Johnston v the Chief Constable of the RUC* (1986) by the police employers as a defence to their refusal to renew Johnston's contract of employment due to the special requirements of policing in Northern Ireland and the need for the police to carry firearms. The court held that there was no general public safety exception to the equal treatment principle available under the EC Treaty and that it was for national courts to decide whether the conditions specified in Article 2 are satisfied.

There are many other directives, many with the words 'equal treatment' in their title. In all cases it can be seen that the court has attempted in its judgments, notably those arising from 177 references, to apply the principle of equality which it now considers to be a general principle of Community law. In the context of employment relations, however, it has recognised that there is an economic impact to its judgments. By the principle of direct effect applying to Article 119 and some of the directives, notably the Equal Pay and Equal Treatment Directives, the court has recognised that a great burden could fall onto employers. For this reason the court has limited the retrospective effect of its judgments such as *Defrenne* and *Barber*. However, as can be seen by the cases mentioned above, the court has moved the principle of equality in employment forward to a new base line.

Question 42

To what extent does Article 119 give workers in the Member State directly effective rights to equality irrespective of sex?

Answer plan

This question is on the more narrow area of Article 119 EC, but it must be remembered that this Article is very important in the development of equal pay and non-discrimination on the grounds of sex. Particular reference should be made to the following cases:

* *Defrenne* (1976)
* *Macarthys v Smith* (1980)
* *Bilka-Kaufhaus v Weber von Harz* (1985)
* *Rinner-Kuhn* (1989)
* *Enderby v Frenchay Health Authority* (1994)

Answer

Article 119 EC requires each Member State to ensure the application of the principle that men and women should receive equal pay for equal work. Although this is an instruction to the Member States, by stating in the *Defrenne* case (1976) that the Article has direct effect the court has identified a right which can be enforced by the individual employee in the courts of the Member State. Under the principle of direct effect three conditions have to be satisfied, namely that the provision must be clear and unambiguous, it must be unconditional and it must take effect without further action by the EC or Member States. Once these conditions are met the individual is not dependent upon the Member State or the institutions of the Community for the right granted by the Treaty or other source of Community law.

The principle of equal pay was said by the court in *Defrenne* (1976) to form one of the foundations of the Community. Its role was seen as a way of achieving one of the social objectives of the Community, namely the improvement of living and working conditions for men and women. This requires a levelling up of pay for women, rather than a levelling down of that of men. As was restated in *Enderby* (1994), the purpose is to remove obstacles which disadvantage women in employment. If this was to be achieved, the Community was conscious of the need to ensure that those States which had incorporated such equality principles were not disadvantaged in a competitive sense as against those States whose undertakings were not obliged to meet such an objective.

In *Defrenne v Sabena* (1976) the Court of Justice had upheld the direct effect of Article 119. Madame Defrenne had been employed by the Belgian airline Sabena as an air hostess. She complained of being paid a lower salary than her male colleagues although the work they did was the same. In a 177 reference the Belgian court asked if Article 119 could be relied upon before national courts. In its judgment the court said that discrimination on the grounds of sex could be indirect and disguised discrimination or direct and overt discrimination. The latter type of discrimination was more easily identified and could be based solely upon the criteria of equal work and equal pay referred to in Article 119. In such cases Article 119 was directly effective and gave use to individual rights which national courts must protect. It was necessary for additional measures to be taken with regard to indirect discrimination. This was achieved by the Equal Pay Directive 75/117 which supplements Article 119. Article 1 of this Directive provides for the elimination of all discrimination on the grounds of sex with regard to all aspects and conditions of remuneration. It must be remembered that Article 119 on its own is not sufficient to cover all aspects of equal pay, although this has not stopped the court extending the scope of the Article through a number of very important judgments.

In the course of the 177 reference in *Defrenne*, the UK government and the European Commission submitted that Article 119 would only have direct effect as between individuals employed by the State and not those employed by a private employer. In other words, they were claiming that it should only have vertical and not horizontal direct effect. The court rejected this argument claiming that Article 119 is mandatory in nature and must extend not only to the action of public authorities but to all contracts between individuals. This judgment made the way clear for individuals to challenge their employers directly on the basis of the EC Treaty in national courts where they believed themselves to be victims of sex discrimination in matters of pay.

Article 119 requires that men and women should receive equal pay for equal work. In *Macarthys Ltd v Wendy Smith* (1980) the court held that a requirement of contemporaneity of employment is not to be read into the Article. Smith was paid £50 per week whereas her male predecessor had received £60. Under UK legislation the requirement was for the male and female workers to be doing the same job at the same time if a comparison was to be made. However, the Court of Justice held that the only issue was whether or not the work was 'equal' and it did not matter whether or not the man and woman whose work and pay were to be compared were employed at the same time in the undertaking or not.

Although it was initially thought that 'pay' in Article 119 was limited to the wages or salary received by the employee, it has been given a much wider interpretation by the European Court. For example, in *Garland v BREL* (1982) the special travel facilities granted to former employees on retirement were held to constitute pay, even if there was no contractual obligation to make such facilities available for those who had retired. Mrs Garland therefore had a right not to be discriminated against on the grounds of sex in comparison with a retired male employee.

There have been a number of cases involving pension schemes, including those where the claimant has been a part-time employee. In *Bilka-Kaufhaus v Weber von Harz* (1985) Weber claimed that the pension scheme of her employer infringed Article 119. Under the scheme part-timers had to be employed by the business for at least 15 out of the last 20 years, whereas full-time employees benefited from the non-contributing scheme without any time requirement. As the contributions paid by the employer were to supplement existing social security schemes, they amounted to consideration paid by the employer to the employee with the meaning of Article 119. Perhaps the most important case in pensions is the case of *Barber v Guardian Royal Exchange* (1989). Under the employer's scheme the normal pensionable age for women was 57 and for men 62 years of age. The court held that since the worker received these benefits from his employer as a result of his employment they constituted 'pay' with Article 119. The immediate impact of the *Barber* case has been that employers have been required to harmonise pension ages for men and women in contracted-out schemes. The limitation to contracted-out schemes reflects the judgment of the court that State pensions are not 'pay' within Article 119. This was applied in *Roberts v Birds Eye Walls Ltd* (1990).

Sick pay has also been held by the court to come within the meaning of Article 119. In the *Rinner-Kuhn* case a part-time office cleaner challenged the German legislation which permitted employers to exclude part-time workers from entitlement to such pay. This discretion given to employers brought the payment of sick pay to part-timers within Article 119. Lastly, redundancy payments were held in the *Barber* case, mentioned above, to be pay with Article 119, irrespective of whether payment is made under a contract of employment, on an *ex gratia* basis or under statute.

It can be seen from the cases above that Article 119 EC has been interpreted by the court to give workers in the Member States directly effective rights to equality irrespective of sex. Cases have been brought mainly by female workers, but males in the *Barber* case successfully used the Article to obtain equality with regard to redundancy and occupational pension payments. The direct effect of the Article has been limited by the court restricting it to direct discrimination but with the support of the directive's adopted on equality, notably the Equal Pay Directive, the court has not limited the extensive application of the Article as a basic principle. This is illustrated by the way that the court has given a wide interpretation to the meaning of 'pay' within Article 119 EC.

Question 43

'Direct and indirect discrimination law in the Community is to remove sex-related pay discrimination.'

Critically discuss this statement, drawing on recent judgments of the European Court of Justice.

Answer plan

This question deals with the general topic of discrimination but offers the opportunity to display knowledge of recent cases. In this case it is *Enderby v Frenchay Health Authority* (1994). However, in addition to Article 119 EC you should make reference to the following cases:

- *Bilka-Kaufhaus v Weber von Harz* (1985)
- *Defrenne* (1976)
- *Nimz v Freie und Hansestadt Hamburg* (1992)
- *Danfoss Case* (1989)

Answer

In the case of direct discrimination sex is the cause of the less favourable pay or treatment, but there must also exist a causal connection between the sex of the worker and the lower pay. The allocation of particular wages or salary scales to particular jobs can result in direct discrimination. Since that form of direct pay discrimination is not expressly based on the sex of the worker, a female worker claiming equal pay encounters evidential problems if she has to prove the causal connection between her sex and the lower pay for particular types of jobs. Thus, when all the objective elements of discriminatory pay (work that is the same or of equal value, lower pay for a woman when compared with a man in the same undertaking) has been proved, there should be a rebuttable presumption of sex-discrimination. It would be sufficient for the plaintiff to prove an example of the same (or equivalent) work by a man being better paid than that of a woman, leaving it for the employer to furnish counter-evidence, for example by adducing objective grounds for the unequal pay which are not based on the sex of the recipient.

Indirect discrimination is a legal concept which enables cases of unequal treatment, for which there is an objective justification but which in fact result in the woman being disadvantaged, to be included as an instance of unlawful sex discrimination. In the recent case of *Enderby v Frenchay Health Authority* (1994) Dr Enderby brought proceedings against her employer before an industrial tribunal, claiming that she was involved in work of equal value to that of a principle clinical psychologist and a grade 3 principle pharmacist. Her annual pay was £10,106, while those of employees in the other two professions taken as comparators were respectively £12,527 and £14,106. In the *Enderby* case her professional group is characterised as a 'purely female profession'. Enderby's counsel put forward the argument that in a purely female profession the membership of that profession can have effects which are similar to a link with part-time work. The fact that speech therapists are almost exclusively women is also at least partly due to the connection between the social role of women and work (ie difficulties encountered by women in working full-time – see case 170/84 *Bilka*). The opportunities of working part-time and flexi-time are particularly attractive to women.

Advocate General Lenz in the *Enderby* case stated that the purpose of a conceptual scheme is to comprehend methods by which women are placed at a disadvantage in their working lives and not to create additional obstacles to claims being made before the courts in respect of sex-related pay discrimination. In accordance with the result-orientated line taken by the Court of Justice in the past, a pragmatic approach ought to be pursued. The problem with UK legislation and legal tradition is that it does not readily allow for such an approach. However, Lenz warned that the historical and social context of a 'purely female profession' is most probably sex-related, and if an explanatory approach were accepted as sufficient justification, that would lead to the perpetuation of sexual roles in working life. Instead of the equality of treatment which is sought, there would be afforded a legal argument for maintaining the status quo.

Thus, a collective agreement, which in these circumstances includes rules applying exclusively to that professional group, may also represent rules specifically relating to women. In these proceedings what is called for is a comparison between representative groups of employees, each doing work of equal value. If this comparison reveals that the group consisting principally of women suffered a significant disadvantage when compared with the male group comparator, a presumption of indirect sex discrimination will arise. In such circumstances the employer, in order to avoid the charge of sex discrimination, would have to show that this was due to objectively justified factors unrelated to any discrimination on grounds of sex.

Thus, with both direct and indirect discrimination the claimant can raise a rebuttable presumption of discrimination, in the first case with a specific comparison and in the other by a comparison of groups, which places the onus on the employer to adduce evidence rebutting that presumption or to produce a justification. Article 119 EC requires the employer to justify objectively the difference in pay between job A and job B.

The principle of equal pay under Article 119 EC, and repeated in Article 1 of Directive 75/117, has been held by the court to be directly applicable (see *Defrenne* (1976)). It can not be ignored by collective agreements as it has affects on the relations between employer and employee. Moreover, it should not be open to an employer to conclude various collective agreements with different groups in order to limit the impact of the principle of equal pay, even if each agreement individually applies the principle. This applies in particular in the case of collective agreements within the same firm where one element in the principle of equal pay is present in so far as the employer is the same.

What other reasons can be put forward by an employer to justify objectively the difference in pay? In some circumstances, the employer maybe compelled by the state of the labour market to offer higher remuneration for members of a particular professional group in order to attract suitable applicants. The only question then is the extent to which the objective reason can serve to justify the difference in pay. In *Nimz* (1992) the court held that collective agreement which allows employers to maintain a distinction as regards overall pay between two categories of workers who are both performing the same type of work but part-time and full-time, does constitute discrimination against female workers vis-à-vis male workers, if in fact a much lower percentage of men work on a part-time basis than women. Such an agreement must therefore in principle be regarded as contrary to Article 119 EC, unless the difference in treatment between the two categories of workers can be shown to be based on objectively justified factors unrelated to any discrimination on grounds of sex. In *Bilka-Kaufhaus* (1986) the employer argued that full-time employees gained experience and thus skills and abilities more quickly than part-timers working less than three-quarters of normal hours. However, the court held that this was not sufficient to justify objectively the difference in treatment. However, it is important to remember that when the national court is reviewing these factors that it is applying Community law. This requires them to take into account such general principles of Community law as proportionality, ie whether and to what extent there is a shortage of candidates for a job and whether the need to attract them by higher pay constitutes an objectively justified economic ground for the difference in pay between the jobs in question.

In the *Enderby* judgment the Court of Justice held that the shift of onus of proof takes place when that is necessary to avoid depriving workers who appear to be the victims of discrimination of any effective means of enforcing the principle of equal pay. There can be no doubt that the employer applied a system of pay which was not lacking in transparency since the rates of pay of NHS speech therapists and pharmacists are decided by regular collective bargaining processes in which there is no evidence of discrimination as regards either of these two professions. However, if the pay of speech therapists is significantly lower than that of pharmacists and if the former are almost exclusively women while the latter are predominantly men, there is a *prima facie* case of sex discrimination, at least where the two jobs in question are of equal value and the statistics describing that situation are valid. It is for the national court to assess whether it may take into account those statistics.

In the *Danfoss* case (1989) the employees union produced statistics relating to the wages paid to 157 workers between 1982 and 1986 which showed that the average wage paid to men was 6.85% higher than that paid to women. The employers claimed that these differences were due to the application of criteria for additional payments based upon mobility, training and length of service. The Court of Justice held that the employer had to justify these criteria, with the exception of length of service.

As Article 119 EC is mandatory in nature, the prohibition of discrimination between male and female workers not only applies to the action of public authorities, but also extends to all collective agreements designed to regulate employment relationships and to contracts between individuals. In a successful action the remedy available is to set aside that provision of the collective agreement which is contrary to Community law because of indirect discrimination. This can be done without requesting or awaiting its prior removal by collective bargaining or any other procedure and to apply to members of the group disadvantaged by that discrimination the same arrangements as are applied to other employees, arrangements which, failing the correct application of Article 119 EC in national law, remain the only valid system of reference. There also remains the possibility of a *Francovich* action against the government.

Question 44

Analyse TWO of the following cases which came before the European Court of Justice and explain their importance in the development of Community law:

(a) *Defrenne (No 2)* - Case 43/75

(b) *Marshall* - Case 152/84

(c) *Barber* - Case 226/88

Answer plan

When approaching a question like this the temptation is to produce too descriptive an answer. The facts are important but are only one element of the answer. You should seek to deal with:

(a) the facts, the legal points raised and the decision of the court

(b) what kind of case was it? A preliminary reference or a direct action? What Article of the Treaty was it based upon?

(c) the cases chosen for this type of question have usually played their part in developing or reinforcing European Court judgments - what part has this case played?

Answer

(a) *Defrenne (No 2)* - Case 43/75

Madame Defrenne was employed as an air hostess by Sabena, a Belgian airline company. She claimed that in paying their male stewards more than their air hostesses, even though they were performing identical tasks, Sabena was in breach of Article 119 EC. It was conceded by the employer that Defrenne did the same job as that done by male stewards, but until 1966 she was paid less than them under the terms of a collective agreement negotiated between Sabena and the unions. She began her action in 1968, claiming the difference between her remuneration and that of men from 1963 to 1966. Under Belgian law there is a five year limitation rule so that she was taking her claim as far back as she possibly could. She began her action in a Belgian Labour court, which made a reference to the European Court under Article 177 EC, seeking the interpretation of Article 119 EC.

Article 119 EC provides that equal pay for work of equal value will be ensured during the first stage of the Community. This period expired at the end of 1961 without any action being taken by the Member States to implement Article 119 EC and the Commission made a recommendation on the issue. As a result of this the Member States adopted a resolution which purported to give themselves more time, ie extending this first stage. When this period also expired the European Commission failed to use the procedure under Article 169 EC against defaulting States, something they were criticised for by the court. However, what Madame Defrenne is claiming is that this failure on the part of the Member States does not affect her rights under Article 119 EC, because it has direct effect. The Member States and the Commission did not consider that the Article had in fact become directly effective at the end of the first stage, when the Member States had failed to fulfil their obligations under the Treaty.

The Court of Justice had found Articles of the Treaty to have direct effect before this case, as in *Van Gend en Loos* (1963), but generally this was in cases where the Articles involved a cross-border or transnational element. In the case of *Van Duyn* (1975) Article 48 EC which deals with discrimination on the grounds of nationality was found to have direct effect. But that concept of discrimination is straight forward when compared with Article 119 which requires 'equal pay for equal work'. However, the court identified that discrimination could be direct or indirect. With direct or overt discrimination it was possible for an individual to make a challenge without the need for further supplementary measures to identify what the term means. With regard to such actions the court held that Article 119 EC was directly effective because the criteria set for the principle of direct effect to apply were present.

It was necessary for Directives to be issued to deal with the more disguised indirect discrimination but Madame Defrenne was successful in her action for equal pay. As part of the social policy of the Community, the court believed that the principle of Article 119 EC was a fundamental right of Community citizens. This 'social' right was supported by the economic fear on the part of some Member States that the failure to have equal pay would lead to variations in business overheads and thus competition between the Member States. However, the court recognised the financial impact of its judgment that Article 119 EC would have direct effect in both the public and the private sector. The court limited its ruling by stating that anyone who had not already initiated an action in their Member State would not be able to claim 'back pay' in the way that Madame Defrenne had. All future cases would not be able to claim for a period dating back to before the judgment in this case.

(b) *Marshall* - Case 152/84

Miss Marshall was employed by the Southampton Area Health Authority as a senior dietician, until she reached the age of 62. When she reached this age she was dismissed, even though she had expressed the wish to continue in employment until she was 65 years of age. The sole reason for her dismissal was that she was a woman who had passed the retirement age applied by the Health Authority to woman. The Authority's general policy was that its employees should retire when they reached the age at which state retirement pensions became payable. This was 60 years of age for woman and 65 for men. The Authority was willing to waive its general policy for particular individuals in particular circumstances. This it had done for Miss Marshall by employing her for two more years after she reached 60 years of age. Marshall complained to an industrial tribunal against her dismissal which she claimed was contrary to the Sex Discrimination Act 1975 and Directive 76/207, in that it unlawfully discriminated against her on the grounds of her sex.

The Health Authority claimed that in laying down the retirement ages for its employees it was merely reflecting the different retirement ages for state pensions. These differences in age were permitted by Article (1)(2) of Directive 76/207. In addition, they argued that an EC Directive could never impose obligations on individuals and could only have direct effect against a Member State in its capacity as a public authority and not as an employer. The case reached the Court of Appeal where a reference was made under Article 177 EC to the European Court of Justice. The Court of Appeal asked two questions on the interpretation of Directive 76/207. The European Court's answer was that the principle of equality of treatment was one of fundamental importance, and therefore Directive 76/207 was to be strictly interpreted. Thus the exception to the prohibition of discrimination on the grounds of sex in relation to the granting of old-age pensions and retirement ages was in this category. Article 5(1) of Directive 76/207 was to be interpreted as meaning that a general policy dismissing women when they reached the state pension retirement age constituted discrimination on the grounds of sex, contrary to the Directive.

Although the Court of Justice accepted the principle that a Directive could not impose obligations on an individual, ie horizontal direct effect, this was not true where the state was involved. It did not matter in what capacity the state was involved, in that it could be as an employer or as a public authority. In this case Miss Marshall was able to invoke Directive 76/207 against her employer, the Health Authority, since this Authority was an 'emanation of the State'. The main point was to stop a Member State taking advantage of its own failure to comply with Community law.

(c) *Barber* - Case 226/88

Barber was an employee of Guardian Royal Exchange (GRE). He was a member of a contracted-out pension scheme established and wholly financed by his employer. Under this scheme the normal pensionable age was 62 for men and 57 for women. In the event of redundancy the scheme provided for immediate payment of a pension to men aged 55 or woman aged 50. Barber was made redundant at the age of 52, so he did not qualify immediately for a pension but would receive a deferred pension payable when he reached the age of 62. He complained to an industrial tribunal, claiming unlawful discrimination on the grounds of sex. The tribunal dismissed his application, as did the Employment Appeal Tribunal. Barber appealed to the Court of Appeal, which made a reference to the European Court under Article 177 EC. The reference asked whether benefits paid to a redundant employee by his employer were subject to either Article 119 EC, dealing with equal pay, or the Equal Pay Directive 75/117 and the Equal Treatment Directive 76/207. The court answered that Article 119 EC did apply.

The previous case law of the European Court had been uncertain. In *Garland v BREL* (1982) the court had held that certain benefits paid after retirement constituted pay. In *Worrington v Lloyds Bank Ltd* (1981) the court rejected adjustments in gross pay designed to compensate for differential pension contributions as being incompatible with Article 119 EC. In *Bilka-Kaufhaus GmbH v Weber von Hartz* (1986) it had held that a purely contractual pension paid by an employer came within Article 119 EC. Whereas in *Burton v BRB* (1982) the court had held that a man denied access to a voluntary redundancy scheme on account of his age had not been a victim of a breach of Article 119. In addition to this the Community has always made it clear that state pensions are excluded from the scope of Article 119 EC.

The reason underlying the *Barber* judgment was that the private contracted-out occupational pension constituted consideration paid indirectly by the employer and therefore fell within the scope of 'pay' within Article 119 EC. This also applied to any benefit paid on redundancy. Putting these two together it meant that the pension and redundancy payments payable to Barber came within Article 119. As there were different age qualifications for men and women under the pension scheme payable on redundancy, this offended against the principle of equal pay for men and women stated in Article 119 EC.

This was a very important judgment with far reaching implications for individual workers and the administration of occupational pension schemes. Both the Commission and the UK government had mentioned to the court in their interventions that this case would have financial consequences for these pension schemes. They asked the court to limit the impact of its judgment, as the court had done earlier in its *Defrenne* case 43/75. This is what the court actually did. The court ruled that the direct effect of Article 119 EC to such occupational pension schemes would generally only apply to cases arising after the date of the judgment in this case, with one exception. This was that cases already initiated or where claims had already been raised under national law, could proceed on the basis of direct effect of Article 119 EC.

The reason given by the court for this limitation of the impact of its judgment in *Barber* was that Directive 79/7 had authorised Member States to defer from the principle of equal treatment for men and women in certain matters, including contracted out occupational pension schemes. Thus the administrators of such schemes had been entitled to believe that they were not acting contrary to Article 119 EC. In the interests of legal certainty the retroactivity of this judgment would have severe affects on the financial balance of such schemes. Protocol 2 of the Maastricht Treaty reinforces this point by stating that although there is full and immediate acceptance of the implications of the *Barber* judgment, problems have been created for employers, pension funds, insurance companies, etc. Therefore the Protocol confirms that equal treatment in occupational schemes must be applied in respect of employment after 17 May 1990.

Chapter 11

External Relations

Introduction

The external relations of the European Community includes its ability to enter into agreements with third countries and international organisations. Therefore the key point of this topic relates to the competence of the Community to enter into such agreements. Generally speaking the questions which occur on this topic are essay-type, although on very rare occasions the direct effect of a treaty provision may appear in a problem question.

Checklist

Students should ensure that they understand the general point on the legal personality of the Community (Article 210 EC) and the following points:

- The express external competence of the Community, including the Common Commercial Policy (Articles 110-116 EC), Association agreements (Article 238 EC) and agreements with international organisation (Articles 229-231 EC)

- The procedure laid down in the Treaty for negotiating international agreements (Article 228 EC), including the roles of the Council, Commission and the European Court

- The implied external powers of the Community associated with the doctrine of parallelism

- Mixed agreements

- The direct effect of treaty provisions

Question 45

What are the express treaty-making powers of the EC? Do individuals derive any rights from such treaties?

Answer plan

This essay-type question, the most common form of question on external relations, requires an answer which covers the following points:

- express treaty-making powers, including the Common Commercial Policy and association agreements
- Opinion 1/75
- Opinion 1/78
- direct effect of Articles of treaties
- *International Fruit Company* case
- *Bresciani* case
- *Haegeman v Belgium State*

Answer

This question raises two issues for consideration, Community competence and the ability of individuals to enforce any rights arising from these treaties. Express treaty-making power is granted by the EC Treaty in two cases, commercial agreements (Article 113 EC) and association agreements (Article 238 EC). Article 228 EC lays down the general rules regarding the procedure to be followed where the treaty-making power is exercised but does not itself confer such powers on the Community. In addition, Articles 229-231 require the Community to co-operate with international organisations which is generally achieved by international agreements. The general rule is that all such international agreements are negotiated by the Commission and concluded by the Council.

The Common Commercial Policy of the EC is a very important area of Community activity. Although it does not come within Part 2 of the EC Treaty which deals with the foundations of the Community, its appearance in Part 3 dealing with the economic policy reflects its importance. As the Community is based upon a customs union it is necessary for not only a removal of internal barriers to trade but also a common policy towards goods coming from outside the Community. This is where the Common External Tariff is required as well as other measures related to the Regulation of external influences of a commercial character on the internal market and its producers.

The Common Commercial Policy is covered by Articles 110-116 EC. It is Article 113(1) which gives an indication of the scope of the policy. It relates to tariff rates, trade agreements, export policy and measures to protect trade such as are necessary to deal with dumping or subsidies. The European Court of Justice has stated that this list is not exhaustive but merely examples of its scope. In Opinion 1/75 on Understanding on Local Costs Standard the court stated that the commercial policy is made up of a combination and inter-action of internal and external measures. It reflects a progressive development of a body of rules which come together to apply to the field of common commercial policy. In this Opinion it was explicitly stated by the court that the Community had exclusive power in this field of the common commercial policy. If this was not accepted it would allow individual Member States to adopt positions on export credits which may differ from those of the Community and distort the institutional framework in which the Common Commercial Policy should operate. Under Article 113(2) the Commission submits proposals to the Council for implementing the common commercial policy. If negotiations are required with third countries these are authorised by the Council but undertaken by the Commission. Any agreement is concluded by the Council on behalf of the Community under Article 114.

However, in its Opinion 1/78 on the International Agreement on Natural Rubber the court did recognise that in certain circumstances the participation of the Member States in an international agreement was necessary. This Opinion concerned an international agreement designed to achieve a balanced growth between the supply and demand for natural rubber. This required a guaranteed stable export earning for exporting countries whilst ensuring supplies for importing countries at a fair price. In order to achieve this it was decided to establish a buffer stock to even out fluctuations in the market for natural rubber. Although the subject matter of this agreement fell within the common commercial policy of Article 113, the financing of the buffer stock was to be provided by the Member State. If the financing had been provided by the Community, the Community would have exclusive power. Thus as finance was to be provided directly by the Member States they could participate in the agreement together with the Community.

Association agreements are governed by Article 238 EC which provides for such agreements with a non-Member State or an international organisation. Such agreements often act as preliminary to, or substitutes for, membership of the Community.

If the Community enters into agreements with third countries or international organisations, can these be invoked by individuals before their national courts? The effect of treaties on individuals within the European Community varies from one Member State to another, depending upon whether it is a monist or dualist state. For example in Belgium, France, Grece, Luxembourg and the Netherlands treaties can usually be invoked in national courts and are normally given priority over national laws. Whereas in other Member States such as the United Kingdom and Ireland, treaties cannot be invoked at all but are considered to be purely a matter for the executive. In such countries the content of such treaties can only be made binding as to individuals through separate legislation.

In the second *Haegeman* case (1974) the Court of Justice referred to the fact that treaties with third countries are concluded by an act of the Council and that their provisions form an integral part of Community law. The main principle which has to be considered in this respect is the direct effect of these agreements. In dealing with this question there is no indication in the Treaty itself that such agreements may be directly effective and the ECJ has not been wholly consistent in its approach. When deciding questions of direct effect the court is seeking to satisfy three requirements. These are that measures must be clear and unambiguous, it must be unconditional and it must take effect without further action by the EC Member State. These apply to any measure which an applicant claims is directly effective.

In *International Fruit Company's* case (1972) the company claimed that certain EC Regulations violated Article XI of the General Agreement on Tariff and Trade (GATT). The court had to decide whether the international agreement was capable of conferring rights on citizens of the Community which they can invoke before national courts. It was clear that the GATT agreement was binding upon the Community and thus its Member States. However, the general scheme and terms of the General Agreement were such that only the contracting parties or states could act if one of the other contracting parties acted contrary to the agreement. Therefore the GATT was not capable of conferring on citizens of the Community rights which they can invoke before national courts.

However, in the *Bresciani* case (1976) the court did accept that an association agreement did confer rights on Community citizens which the national courts of the Community must protect. In this case Bresciani was importing raw cowhides from Senegal, a state which came within an association agreement under the Yaounde Convention. Under Italian law an inspection fee was charged covering the cost of examinations and laboratory tests. This fee amounted to a charge having an equivalent effect to a customs duty and was prohibited under the Treaty. Also in *Haegeman v Belgian State* (1974) the ECJ accepted that the Association Agreement with Grece was an act of the institutions of the Community and therefore within a 177 preliminary reference for interpretation.

Therefore there are a number of specific subject matters where the Treaty grants express treaty-making powers to the Community, notably under the common commercial policy, the association policy and relationship agreements. In addition, following the *ERTA* case the external competence of the Community has been extended by the doctrine of parallelism whereby an internal power may give rise to an external competence. Whatever the origins of the external power, the approach of the court has not been consistent. The result has made the individual very dependent on occasions on the approach taken by the courts of the Member State towards the recognition of Treaties with third countries.

Question 46

What is meant by the doctrine of parallelism? What has been its impact on the external competency of the EC?

Answer plan

The doctrine of parallelism is derived from the judgment in the *ERTA* case, therefore the answer requires this case to be dealt with and the following points

- the legal personality of the Community under Article 210 EC
- express treaty-making powers
- *Cornelis Kramer* case
- Opinion 1/75
- Opinion 1/76
- Opinion 1/78

Answer

The doctrine of parallelism is associated with the external relations of the European Community. The Community was given its own legal personality, separate from its Member States by Article 210 EC. This meant that it had the power to enter into agreements with third countries or international organisations like GATT. Having been given this authority by the Treaty, there are specific Articles of the Treaty which give express powers to enter into agreements on specific matters. For example the Community may conclude agreements with third countries under Articles 113-114 EC on those matters which come within the Common Commercial Policy enumerated in Article 113 EC.

As far as the Member States were concerned the Community only had those external powers which were expressly conferred by the Treaty. If there were no such express powers, they felt that none were to be implied. The Member States were rudely awakened when the Court of Justice gave its judgment in the *ERTA* case (1971). This case was brought before the court because of a dispute between the Council and the Commission over the division of powers and responsibilities in exercising the external powers of the EC. This agreement provided the power to regulate the maximum driving hours for lorry drivers. The governments of the Member States claimed that as treaty-making power had not been expressly granted to the Community, the competence for such agreements remained with them. The Commission had started proceedings under Article 173 for the annulment of the Council's discussions resulting in a common position.

The Commission failed on the merits of the case because the negotiations for the European Road Transport Agreement were well advanced before the adoption of a Council Regulation on road transport. However, the ECJ laid down the general principle that the existence of Community common rules precludes Member States from undertaking obligations with third countries which affect those rules. The Member States objected to this idea because they said that it ignored the political element of such international treaties. However, the court had reached this conclusion based upon Article 210 EC relating to all the objectives defined in Part One of the Treaty. This means that each time the Community adopts provisions laying down common rules to implement a common policy envisaged by the Treaty, the Member States no longer have the right to undertake obligations with third countries which affect those rules. This applies regardless of whether the Member State is acting individually or collectively with other Member States. They have to operate within the framework of the Community. The result is that the Community has exclusive power in all external matters affecting the application of the Community legal system, as the internal measures are inseparable from the external aspect.

The adoption of internal rules is frequently referred to as conferring Community competence in external relations. In the *Cornelis Kramer* case (1976) proceedings had been instituted in the Dutch courts against fishermen accused of contravening laws limiting catches of certain fish. These laws had been adopted in accordance with a recommendation of the North-East Atlantic Fisheries Commission, a body established by an international convention ratified by all EC states except for Italy and Luxembourg. The Dutch court asked by way of an Article 177 EC reference whether the Community alone has authority to enter into commitments of the kind contained in the international convention. The court held that the Community must enjoy the capacity to enter into international agreements over the whole field of Part 1 of the Treaty. However, the court did concede that transitional interim concurrent rights might be exercised by Member States until such time as the Community itself exercised its own functions. When this happened the power came within the exclusive power of the Community. This case seems to apply the *ERTA* decision.

This was discussed in the Article 228 EC Opinion 1/75 Exports Credits where the Commission argued that the conclusion of OECD Local Costs Understanding was a matter of exclusive Community competence. However, the Member States cited *ERTA* and argued that this could only be true if there were corresponding internal rules. In its judgment the court did not deal with this point but held that the understanding came within the Community's commercial policy under Articles 113 and 114, and was thus within an exclusive Community competence. The court spoke of the impossibility of concurrent powers being exercised at the same time in regard to the subject matter.

In Opinion 1/76 Laying Up Fund the court made it clear that the existence of rules was not necessarily the prerequisite for the existence of Community competence. The power to bind the Community with third countries flows from the implications from the provision of the treaties creating the internal power. Also in Opinion 1/76 the court held that the Community is entitled to co-operate with another country in setting up a public international organisation and in granting powers of decision to that organisation. However, the court stated that the structural elements of the Community cannot be sacrificed by the competence of a new international organisation. This view was repeated in the ECJ's Opinion regarding the European Economic Area (EEA) in 1992. The Opinion of the court (Opinion 1/92) was that the establishment of a joint EEA court was incompatible with the Treaty of Rome 'and would lead to serious legal complications'.

Therefore Community competence in external relations exist where there is an internal power to act, whether or not it has been exercised, and participation in an agreement is necessary. An internal power is therefore parallelled or mirrored by an external competence. This is the basis of the doctrine of parallelism, which has greatly extended the external competence of the European Community. There have been complications on occasions where the agreement with third countries have been 'mixed' agreements. This is where there is some competence with the Community and some within the powers and responsibilities of the Member States. In Opinion 1/78 National Rubber the ECJ accepted participation by the Community and Member States in an agreement which was clearly within the Community's commercial policy. This reflected the pragmatic view often taken by the court. Under the 'economic' clauses of the agreement finance was to be provided by the Member States, hence their participation. However, if the finance was provided by the Community it would have exclusive competence and the participation by the Member States would not be accepted.

Question 47

Analyse TWO of the following cases which came before the European Court of Justice and explain their importance in the development of Community law:

(a) *ERTA* - Case 22/70

(b) *Cornelis Kramer* - Cases 3, 4 and 6/76

(c) Opinion 1/75

Answer plan

When approaching a question like this the temptation is to produce too descriptive an answer. The facts are important but are only one element of the answer. You should seek to deal with:

(a) the facts, the legal points raised and the Decision of the court

(b) what kind of case was it? A preliminary reference or a direct action? What Article of the Treaty was it based upon?

(c) the cases chosen for this type of question have usually played their part in developing or reinforcing European Court judgments - what part has this case played?

Answer

(a) *ERTA* - Case 22/70

In January 1962, under the auspices of the United Nations economic Commission for Europe, the European Agreement concerning the work of drivers of vehicles engaged in cross border journeys (ERTA) was signed by five of the then six Members States of the Community. The agreement never came into effect due to a lack of sufficient ratification. Subsequently negotiations began again in 1967 to revise the agreement. Meanwhile work had been going on within the EC with regard to harmonisation of driving and rest periods of drivers of road transport vehicles, resulting in a 1969 Regulation. At its meeting in 1970 the Council of Ministers discussed the attitude to be adopted towards the forthcoming ERTA negotiations. They agreed a common position, as required by the EC Treaty. However, the Commission disagreed with this procedure because they felt that this was now a matter for the

Community and not the individual Member States. The Commission brought this case before the European Court under Article 173 EC seeking judicial review of the Council's common position and negotiation of the ERTA.

The main point of the case concerned who had competence with regard to external agreements on this policy area. If it was still with the Member States then the Council of Ministers actions would be within the Treaty. However, if was now a Community competence the Treaty specified how the negotiations should take place. The Council claimed that as the Community only had such powers as had been conferred on it, authority to enter into agreements with third countries cannot be assumed in the absence of an express provision of the Treaty. More specifically Article 75 EC, which conferred upon the Community powers defined in wide terms, implementing the common transport policy, relates only to internal measures.

The Court of Justice, however, said that in the absence of specific provisions of the Treaty relating to the negotiation and conclusion of international agreements in the sphere of transport policy, it is necessary to look to the general system of Community law in the sphere of relations with third countries. Article 210 EC provides the Community with legal personality to establish links with third countries over the whole field of objectives defined in Part 1 of the Treaty. Each time the Community, with a view to implementing a common policy envisaged by the Treaty, adopts provisions laying down common rules the Member States no longer have the right, whether acting individually or collectively, to undertake obligations with third countries which affect these rules. This applies whatever form the internal rules may take. Once this happens the Community alone is in a position to assume and carry out contractual obligations toward third countries affecting the whole sphere of application of the Community legal system. The Member States must operate within the institutional framework of the Community, by which the Commission negotiate and the Council conclude such international agreements.

Although on the facts the court found that the Council had not exceeded its powers, the judgment was to have long term implications for the external competence of the Community. The case developed the idea of parallel internal and external Community competence.

(b) *Cornelis Kramer* - Cases 3, 4 and 6/76

Criminal proceedings had been brought against certain Netherlands fishermen who were accused of having infringed the Dutch rules limiting the catches of sole and plaice. These rules had been adopted on the basis of the provisions of the North East Atlantic Fisheries Convention. The Dutch court made a preliminary reference to the European Court under Article 177 EC on the external competence of the Community. In essence the questions asked were on whether Member States retained the power to adopt measures such as those under the Convention, whether such measures are compatible with Community law and whether the Community had exclusive competence in this policy area.

As there was an absence of a specific provision in the Treaty authorising the Community to enter into international commitments in the sphere of conservation of fish, the court looked to the general system of Community law in the sphere of external relations of the Community. The court recited the traditional view that Article 210 EC gave the Community legal personality and therefore the capacity to enter into international commitments over the whole range of Community objectives. The court said that in this specific case it must be recognised that authority to enter into particular international agreements may be express or implied from the provisions of the Treaty. The only way to ensure the conservation of fish, both effectively and equitably, was through a system of rules binding on all the States concerned, irrespective of whether they were members of the European Community. In these circumstances it follows from the duties and powers which Community law has established internally that the Community has authority to enter into international commitments on fish conservation. However, having established that the Community has authority the court needed to look at whether the Community had assumed external responsibility.

The Community had not yet fully exercised its functions in fish conservation and therefore when the Convention arose the Member States had the power to assume commitments, such as the Convention. Having had the power to enter the Convention, the Member State now had the power to enforce it within the area of its jurisdiction. However, the court pointed out quite clearly that the authority of the Member State was of only a transitional nature, until the Community had acted so as to assume exclusive competence in this policy area. This had to happen at the latest six years after Accession as by that time the Council was required under Article 102 of the Act of Accession to introduce measures for fish conservation. Once this had happened the Member States were under a duty to use all the political and legal means available to ensure the participation of the Community in the Convention and similar agreements.

(c) Opinion 1/75

Under Article 228 EC the Court of Justice can be asked to give its Opinion on the compatibility of proposed international agreements with the EC Treaty. This Opinion by the court was on a draft 'Understanding on a local Cost Standard', drawn up under the auspices of the OECD. The key question was whether the Community had the power to conclude such an agreement and whether that power is exclusive.

The Treaty does include in Articles 112, 113 and 114 EC a commercial policy which covers both internal rules and the power to conclude agreements with third countries. The field of the common commercial policy necessarily covers systems of aid for exports and more particularly measures concerning credits for the financing of local costs linked to export operations. These were the main provisions of this draft treaty. The Council had already adopted Directives on credit insurance in 1970 and 1971. Therefore the court concluded that the subject matter of the Understanding on a Local Costs Standard was within the sphere of the Common Commercial Policy and thus within the ambit of the Community's powers.

The court said that a commercial policy is in fact made up by the combination and interaction of internal and external measures, without priority being taken by one over the others. Sometimes agreements are concluded in execution of a policy fixed in advance, sometimes that policy is defined by the agreements themselves. Such agreements may be outline agreements, the purpose of which is to lay down uniform principles. This was the case with the Understanding on local costs.

On the question of exclusive competency the court said that given the Community's commercial policy it would not be acceptable for Member States to exercise a concurrent power in either the internal or the international sphere. Articles 113 and 114 EC show clearly that the exercise of concurrent powers by Member States and the Community is impossible. To accept the contrary view would recognise that in relations with third countries, Member States may adopt positions which differ from those agreed by the Community through its institutions. The court said that it was of little importance that the obligations and financial burdens inherent in the execution of the agreement envisaged by the Understanding are borne directly by the Member States.

The Member States argued before the court that the conclusion of the Understanding was not a matter of exclusive Community competence based upon the Decision in the *ERTA* case. They said that there were no corresponding internal rules so there could not be any parallel external competence. However, the court did not deal with this point in its judgment, but held that the Understanding fell within the Community's commercial policy. Following on from the *ERTA* case this judgment added to the exclusive external powers of the Community.

Chapter 12

The Internal Market and the Treaty on European Union

Introduction

The Internal Market and the 1992 campaign seems to have been with us for some time, and has now been followed by the Maastricht Treaty on European Union. The internal market will always be a topic since the EC is based upon a customs union. Therefore, the problems encountered with the reality of such an organisation will go in and out of fashion. At the moment, the main questions are on the legal implications leading up to the completion of the Internal Market, notably the Single European Act and the important cases on the freedoms associated with the Community. However, these will begin to focus on the Maastricht Treaty, as the next stage in the development of the Community looks towards the inter-government conferences in 1996.

Generally, questions on this topic are essay type questions, simply because, on the whole, problems would have to be very complicated to encompass the topic. As this topic changes so rapidly it is very important to read newspapers to follow the changing political and legal environment in which the Community operates.

Checklist

Your should be familiar with the following:

- the background to the Single European Act 1987, notably the Commission's White Paper on the Completion of the Internal Market
- The Single European Act – Articles 8a and 100a on the internal market, the changes to the voting procedures in the Council of Ministers and the powers of the European Parliament
- The Maastricht Treaty on Economic and Monetary Union, but more importantly on European Union
- the proposed changes to the institutional balance

Question 48

'The 1992 process was necessary because the Treaty of Rome had not been fully fulfilled.' (Sir Leon Brittan)

Discuss.

Answer plan

This question is typical of those which have been developed recently to cover the background to the 1992 internal market campaign. It is possible to answer it as indicated below or you may wish to draw in more cases to illustrate some of the problems encountered before the completion of the internal market. Obviously this would help you utilise those cases you know well from other areas of the syllabus. However, the main points that should be covered are:

- basic principles of the common market, including Articles 2 and 3 EC
- problems with barriers, including non-tariff barriers
- the European Commissions' White Paper
- the Cecchini Report and the identified benefits of completing the internal markets
- the landmark cases of *Van Gend en Loos* and *Cassis de Dijon* as examples of the European Court's contribution towards the reality of a common market

Answer

Article 2 of the Treaty of Rome, signed in 1957, states that the task of the Community is to establish a common market and the progressive approximation of the economic policies of the Member States. This was expected to provide a continuous and balanced expansion of economic activity with associated benefits of stability and the raising of the standard of living of those within the Community. Article 3 EC then goes on to specify the outcomes of the closer relations between the Member States.

Within Article 3 EC are the four 'fundamental freedoms' in Community trade law, namely the free movement of goods, persons, services and capital. Customs duties are outlawed by

Article 12 EC and this prohibition on fiscal barriers is complemented by Article 95 EC, which forbids systems of internal taxation which discriminate against imported goods. Article 30 EC outlaws quota systems and measures having equivalent effect and constitutes the heart of the Treaty rules designed to secure the free movement of goods. Workers are entitled to the freedom of movement between Member States by virtue of Article 48 EC and this right is extended to the self-employed and the provider of services by Article 52 and 59 EC respectively. Companies as well as individuals are beneficiaries of these provisions.

Reference is also made to the need for common policy-making in several areas, including the need for harmonisation of rules. Having been signed in 1957, it would be expected that the customs union or common market would now be complete. In July 1968 the original six Member States proudly announced that they had completed the elimination of tariffs and quota restrictions within the Community and established the Common External Tariff. All this had happened 18 months ahead of the schedule laid down in the Treaty. When the Community was enlarged in the 1970's and 1980's the necessary transitional periods were made to allow the new Member States to make appropriate adjustments to conform to the Community's requirements.

However, it was clear that in practice the European Community in the form of a common market was far from complete. Non-tariff barriers to trade were still operating, even amongst the original Member States. As Member States sought to protect domestic industries in the face of unemployment, there was evidence to suggest that non-tariff barriers were getting larger. They were taking the form of nationalistic public purchasing policies, differences in indirect taxation, differences in standards, monopolies and restrictive practices, State subsidies and frontier formalities.

The European Commission produced its White Paper in 1985 on 'Completing the Internal Market'. This White Paper does not propose the target date of 1992 but spells out the logical consequences of the Council`s commitment to the internal market. It did, however, provide a policy agenda for some 300 measures which needed to be adopted by the end of 1992 in order to make the internal market a reality. The programme leading to the completion of the internal market consists of three parts. Existing physical barriers covering the control of goods and the control of individuals are to be removed. The imposition of veterinary and phytosanitary requirements, the commercial and economic policies of governments and businesses are examples of such physical barriers and are well documented in the cases brought before the national courts and the European Court of Justice. The second part of the programme is the removal of technical barriers. Examples of these barriers include different national product regulations and standards. The third part of the programme is the removal of fiscal barriers, including the approximation of value added tax (VAT) and excise taxes. As Sir Leon Brittan observed 'the 1992 process was necessary because the Treaty of Rome had not been fully fulfilled'.

This view was reinforced by the Cecchini Report on the 'European Challenge: 1992, the Benefits of a Single Market' (published in 1988). The Report profiled the European Community, identifying the costs of the absence of a single market and the gains such a market would provide. These gains would come as benefits to consumers, companies and governments. The potential growth this would generate would provide between four to seven percentage points on the Community's domestic product. The report was based on research projects established in 1986 by Lord Cockfield, the EC Commissioner with responsibility for the Internal Market. This research provided a vivid illustration and rigorous analysis of the costs imposed on Europeans by non-tariff barriers which 30 years after the Treaty of Rome meant that the common market had not been achieved. The costs were estimated at Ecu 200 billions.

The barriers, such as border controls and customs red-tape, divergent standards and technical regulations, conflicting business laws and protectionist procurement practices had to be removed. The start was to be the removal of non-tariff barriers, which would reduce costs. As a result of this prices would fall as businesses were subject to more competition in previously protected markets. The fall in prices would also stimulate demand, giving companies the opportunity to increase output and obtain economies of scale which would allow them to compete better on the world market.

Sir Leon's comment that 'the Treaty of Rome had not been fully fulfilled', indicates that some advances had been made. There had been a number of important judgments given by the European Court of Justice, notably on references made under Article 177 EC.

Two cases in particular are worthy of special mention. The case of *Van Gend en Loos* (1963) provided one of the first landmark judgments on the free movement of goods and the relationship between national and Community law. It also included the basis of the principle of direct effect, which was to be such a powerful weapon for individuals seeking to enforce their Community rights. Van Gend en Loos had been importing glue from Germany and paying customs duties of 3% of its value. In 1959 a Dutch law had ratified a Benelux customs protocol which levied an 8% duty on the glue. Obviously Van Gend en Loos objected because of the impact of this on their business, but could this objection give rise to a right of action? The European Court of Justice stated that the Community constituted a new legal order which not only imposed obligations on individuals but also gave them rights which the national courts must enforce.

The other case is that of *Cassis de Dijon* (1978) which developed the ideas generated by the court in the *Dassonville* case (1974). The case of *Cassis de Dijon* was brought in a German court because of the application of a German law which forbade the marketing of liqueurs with a low alcohol content. The French liqueur called Cassis de Dijon had a maximum strength of 20% alcohol by volume whereas German law required a minimum content of 25%. This case established the principle of mutual recognition whereby products lawfully produced and marketed in one Member State had to be permitted to be marketed in other Member States. This meant that mutual recognition could replace the lengthy process of harmonisation of national legislation in promoting the internal market. However, once again, the main impact of this case was on the free movement of goods. There was therefore a need to review the commitment of the Member States to a common market covering all the policy areas of the Treaty. The focus of the 1992 deadline to complete the Internal Market provided the impetus needed to overcome the 'national' barriers to a common market.

Question 49

Discuss the importance of the Single European Act in achieving the single European market.

Answer plan

- the background to the Single European Act (SEA)
- the new policy areas added by the SEA
- the importance of new Articles, including Articles 8A and 100A on the internal market
- the impact of the SEA on Community institutions, notably the voting in the Council of Ministers and the powers of the European Parliament.

Answer

The Single European Act (SEA) came into force in 1987 following its ratification by the national Parliaments of all the Member States. The Act had been agreed at the Luxembourg meeting of the European Council in 1985. The European Council had assigned two objectives for the Inter-Governmental Conference given the task of drafting the SEA. These were the revision of the Rome Treaty and the drafting of a treaty in Political Co-operation allowing for the co-ordination of foreign policies and European security. As far as achieving the single European market is concerned it is the first of these objectives which is the most important. The SEA introduced new policy objectives and changes to the Community's decision-making process.

Five new policy objectives were added in the Single European Act. These were the Internal Market, Monetary Capacity, Social Policy, Economic and Social Cohesion and Research and Technological Development. Two important Articles were added to the Treaty of Rome to deal with the Internal Market. These are Article 8(a) EC introduced by Article 13 SEA and Article 100(a) EC derived from Article 18 SEA. Article 8(a) EC sets the aim of establishing the internal market by 31 December 1992. It also repeats the characteristics of such a market as an area without internal frontiers in which the free movement of goods, persons, services and capital is ensured in accordance with the provisions of the Treaty of Rome. The target date of 31 December 1992 is expressed as an aim and is not intended to be legally binding. In a declaration annexed to the Act, the signatory governments express their firm political will to take before the 1 January 1993 the decisions necessary to complete the internal market. However, a further declaration annexed to the Act also indicates that Member States can still derogate from their obligations under the Treaty in certain policy areas. It states that 'nothing in these provisions shall affect the right of a Member State to take such measures as they consider necessary for the purpose of controlling immigration from third countries, and to combat terrorism, crime, the traffic in drugs, and illicit trading in works of art and antiques. Some critics of the SEA believe that this annex extends the power of Member States to derogate from their obligations beyond that already found in the original Treaty.

As well as introducing Article 8A EC the SEA also introduces Articles 8B and 8C EC. Article 8(b) requires the Commission to report to the Council on progress made towards achieving the internal market by the end of 1992. Article 8(c) requires the Commission to take into account, when drawing up proposals to achieve the internal market, the fact that economies of some Member States vary in their development. This allows some derogation from the provisions of the internal market, although they must be temporary and cause the least possible disturbance to the functioning of the common market.

Another important provision is Article 18 SEA which adds Article 100A EC. This provides the means for enacting legislation to complete the internal market. Article 100 of the original Treaty facilitates, via the traditional consultative procedure, the issue of directives for the approximation of laws which directly affect the establishment or functioning of the common market. The new Article 100A EC is deigned to achieve the objectives set out in Article 8A EC by allowing the co-operation procedure to be used to adopt the measures for approximation. This co-operation procedure is discussed in more detail later but it is important to note here that measures in Article 100A are not restricted to directives. Although Article 100A is broader than the original Article 100 EC, Article 100A(1) specifically excludes fiscal provisions, those relating to the free movement of persons and those relating to the rights and interests of employed persons.

When formulating its proposals certain guidelines are given to the Commission. They are required to take as a base a high level of protection in their proposals concerning health, safety, environmental protection and consumer protection. This was included to deal with the concern of some Member States, notably those of northern Europe, that the process of approximation would lead to a lowering of standards. Obviously, by taking a high level of protection as a base line could cause some problems for certain Member States, especially those who were relatively new members of the Community. Article 100A(4) allows a Member State to derogate from an harmonisation measure on the grounds found in Article 36 EC or relating to the protection of the environment or the working environment. Any Member State wishing to do this must inform the Commission, which is required to ensure that the Member State is not using the derogation as a means of arbitrary discrimination or a disguised restriction on trade between Member States. If the Member State is thought to be acting improperly the Commission using Article 169 EC, or another Member State under Article 170 EC can bring the matter before the ECJ. In some instances the harmonisation measure itself can include a safeguard clause authorising the Member State to take provisional measures based on Article 36, subject to a Community control procedure.

The SEA contained two major changes in the Community's decision-making processes designed to speed up the voting procedure in the Council of Ministers and to give increased powers to the European Parliament. The Act extends the system of qualified voting in the Council. The system of qualified voting is described in Article 148 EC and is based upon each Member State having a certain number of votes, weighted to reflect its population. For example, France, Germany, Italy and the UK as the largest Member States have 10 votes each, whereas Luxembourg as the smallest has two. A majority is constituted by 54 votes out of a total of 76, requiring the agreement of both large and small Member States. This extension of qualified voting is for most of the new policy objectives introduced by the SEA. In the case of the internal market provision is made for qualified majority voting for the new Article 100A. There are certain sensitive areas concerning the internal market which still remain subject to the unanimity role.

A new version of Article 149 EC is introduced by Article 7 SEA, giving increased powers to the European Parliament in those situations where the Council acts by qualified majority voting. The effect of these changes is that the European Parliament now has the opportunity of pronouncing on the final decision of the Council instead of simply giving a consultative opinion on Community legislation. Once the Commission has formulated a proposal for the Council, the latter must reach a common position which is communicated to the European Parliament. The Parliament can then either approve the Council's decision, in which case the proposal is adopted, or else it can reject or amend it. Rejection or amendment must be carried by an absolute majority of the Parliament's members. In the case of rejection, the Council can only pass the proposal by unanimity. In the case of amendment the proposal must be re-examined by the Commission within one month, taking into account the European Parliament's changes. The proposal is then sent back to the Council which can adopt it by qualified majority voting, but can only amend it by unanimity. Those amendments from the Parliament which were not included by the Commission in the re-submitted proposal are forwarded to the Council where they may be adopted by unanimity. If the Council does not act within three months, or with an extension to four months, then the proposal falls.

The Single European Act is not without its critics. Some have pointed to Articles 2 and 3 of the original Treaty of Rome as indicating the foundations of the common market. The SEA they argue merely repeats these Articles but adds nothing to them. In fact, they argue, where it does add to the original Treaty it is in the ability of Member States to avoid their obligations by allowing derogations. The wide meaning of a common market is substituted by a more limited internal market, ignoring all the achievements of the Community. However, there are others who argue that as a result of enlargement and changing world circumstances the Treaty of Rome needed to have a new impetus and focus to bring it back to its original objectives. The Single European Act was a moral and political commitment on the part of all the Member States to make a reality of the internal market by 1993. The SEA reaffirmed the ideal of a common market in Article 8A EC and provided a mechanism by Article 100A EC and Article 149 EC to achieve it.

Question 50

The Maastricht Treaty was designed to meet the needs of a developing Community.

Discuss.

Answer plan

The Maastricht Treaty on European Union (TEU) was signed in 1992, although its implementation was delayed as a result of legal action in the UK and Germany. There is still some uncertainty about its impact on the operations of the Community and its citizens. This discussion question provides the opportunity to raise issues arising from the Inter-Governmental Conferences which were held to formulate proposals which are now embodied in the Treaty and the TEU in operation. It is important, for this type of question, to know what is happening in the Community, something which can be gleaned from good newspapers rather than textbooks. Your answer should cover the following points:

- the background to the Maastricht Treaty
- the meaning of European Economic and Monetary Union and European Political Union
- the need to deal with the democratic deficit in the Community and the measures implemented to achieve this
- changes to the institutional balance, especially the co-decision procedure
- the principle of subsidiarity
- citizenship of the European Community

Answer

On 11 December 1991 the leaders of the 12 Member States agreed the text of a Treaty on European Union, 17 associated protocols and 33 declarations. The protocols are additional agreements between some but not all the signatories. For example, the Protocol on Social Policy included all the Member States except the UK. The declarations do not have legal force but outline the ways in which the provisions of the Treaty should be interpreted or implemented. The agreement was the culmination of long and arduous negotiations following the reports of two Inter-Governmental Conferences (IGC's) between the 12 Member States. One was on Economic and Monetary Union and the other was on Political Union.

The anticipated completion of the Internal Market required the Community to review future developments. In addition there had been revolutionary changes in Eastern Europe, providing new opportunities and problems. Many of the old communist COMECON members had shown an interest in becoming future members of the Community, having achieved association status. Businesses within the EC were pressing for an end to fluctuating and uncertain exchange rates which imposed increasing problems for the movement of goods and services within the Community. The payment of commission and loses on the different buying and selling rates added to the problems of business. A possible solution was a move towards European Monetary Union, with a single currency based upon the European Currency Unit (ECU) that could be used freely throughout the Community. These factors provided the catalyst for the establishment of the Inter-Governmental Conferences.

However, any movement towards European Monetary Union would increase the powers of the Community. To off-set this there had to be a strengthening of the democratic accountability of the Community to balance this increased power. This increase in democratic accountability centred on the European Parliament and the concept of subsidiarity whereby decisions were to be taken as closely as possible to the citizens of Europe. The move towards European Union, a term which is given to the next stage in the process of integration between the 12 Member States, creates two inter-government bodies dealing with a common Foreign and Security policy and Home Affairs and Justice policy.

The institutional revisions are mostly designed to improve the efficiency and democratic nature of the Community's institutional structures and decision-making processes. The result has been an increase in the powers of the European Parliament and the complexity of the Community's decision-making procedures. Different procedures apply to different areas of legislation. For example, with a proposal for environmental legislation from the Commission there are four possible decision-making procedures: co-operation procedure, co-decision, consultation with unanimity and unanimous decision to vote by majority. The Treaty of Rome in 1957 provided for the consultation procedure with a single Parliamentary reading providing an opinion and unanimous or majority voting in the Council of Ministers. The Co-operation procedure was introduced by the Single European Act 1987 and gave greater involvement for the European Parliament when dealing with legislation on particular policies associated with the completion of the Internal Market.

The Maastricht or European Union Treaty introduced a new procedure called co-decision. For the first time Parliament can prevent legislation being adopted and in the Council of Ministers majority voting is required, with two exceptions where unanimity applies. Although this procedure is generally called the co-decision to differentiate it from the other procedures, the term does not appear in Article 189b of the Maastricht Treaty. Co-decision has some of the elements of the co-operation procedure but it goes further to give the Parliament the power to veto a legislative proposal. The veto can only be exercised after the convening of a Conciliation Committee, comprising members of the Council or their representatives and an equal number of representatives of the European Parliament. This Committee must approve a joint text within six weeks which is followed by a further period of six weeks during which the Council and the Parliament have to adopt the proposal or it fails. The time period can be extended by common agreement of both the Council and the Parliament for a further two weeks. If the Committee fails to agree the Council may confirm its common opinion within six weeks, which would require the Parliament to reject the text by an absolute majority of its members to stop the proposal being finally adopted. This is what is referred to as Parliament's veto. Article O of the European Union Treaty also provides the Parliament with the power of veto with regard to the accession of new members. The Council has to obtain the assent of the European Parliament before acting.

A new institution is added to the list of Community institutions. Previously there were four institutions, the European Parliament, the Council, the Commission and the Court of Justice. Now there is a fifth one, the Court of Auditors. Although the Court of Auditors has existed since 1977, its place in Article 4 indicates an upgrading of its status. This will increase the influence of the Court of Auditors at a time when the completion of the Internal Market will bring added pressure on combating fraud and financial accountability for Community funds. A new advisory body has also been added to the existing Economic and Social Committee. Under Article 198a to 198c a Committee of the Regions has been established to give opinions either in cases where they have been consulted by the Council or Commission or in cases where they consider it appropriate. Article 4a establishes a European System of Central Banks and a European Central Bank to add to the existing European Investment Bank.

Article 3b is added by the Maastricht Treaty to the EC Treaty and deals with the principle of subsidiarity. According to the words of the Article the Community may take action 'only if and in so far as the objectives of the proposed action cannot be sufficiently achieved by the Member States and can therefore, by reason of the scale or effects of the proposed action, be better achieved by the Community'. The principle is strengthened by the inclusion in the Preamble to the Treaty of the objective of a closer European union where decisions are taken as closely as possible to the citizen in accordance with the principle of subsidiarity. It would appear that it is for the Commission to justify its chosen action when presenting a proposal, ie why it is not leaving the action to be taken at another level such as a Member State. Thus, the validity of a proposed Community measure may be successfully challenged on the grounds that it offends against the principle of subsidiarity. As Article 173 EC continues to give the European Court the power to hear actions for annulment it will be necessary to wait until such an argument is brought before the judges.

The last major change introduced by the European Union Treaty concerns citizenship of the Union under Articles 8 to 8d EC. Citizenship of the Union is mandatory for nationals of the Member States since there is no provision for opting out. Thus, citizenship of the Union has been grafted onto the body of the EC Treaty. This will mean that as citizen's of the Union, nationals of the Member States will have, for example, the right to move and reside freely within the Community. They will also have the right to vote and stand as a candidate in local and European Parliament elections in whichever Member State they reside. In addition, the European Parliament is required to appoint an Ombudsman to receive complaints from any citizen of the Union concerning maladministration in the activities of the Community institutions, with the exception of the court's. In July 1994 the first legal attempt was made to identify the rights of a citizen of the Union when Gerry Adams challenged, in the High Court, the ban by the UK government which prevented him addressing a group of MPs at Westminster. Generally, the rights of a citizen of the Union are stated with regard to movement between Member States, but here the argument was about movement within the UK. The judge decided to make a reference under Article 177 EC to obtain the views of the European Court of Justice.

The European Union Treaty came into force on 1 November 1993, following referenda in Ireland, France and Denmark and legal action in both the UK and Germany where it was challenged in the constitutional court. Many provisions, such as those dealing with monetary union, will not be implemented until some date in the future when other objectives have been met. However, the Treaty is an attempt to deal with the challenges facing the Community. The 'democratic deficit' has been tackled by increasing the power of the Parliament and the addition of the Council of the Regions as an advisory body. At the same time the Community has widened its scope of activities. Many of the additions to the original treaty are not economic, representing the social and citizen dimension of the Community. It is for this reason that the 'economic' has been removed from the EC Treaty, so that it is now referred to as the EC or European Community Treaty. It would seem that the European Union Treaty is a natural extension to the Community, indicating its maturity and development towards the aims of its founders. With the possible increase in members in 1995, the Community is in a better shape than before the reforms started in the SEA and continued in the TEU. However, if the Community is to grow, more reforms involving its institutions are required.